The Dryden Press
Publications in Psychology

GENERAL EDITOR
THEODORE M. NEWCOMB
UNIVERSITY OF MICHIGAN

THE
SOCIAL
PSYCHOLOGY
OF
MUSIC

Paul R. Farnsworth

PROFESSOR OF PSYCHOLOGY
STANFORD UNIVERSITY

HOLT, RINEHART AND WINSTON · NEW YORK

Library of Congress Catalogue Card Number 57–11572

TO

Max F. Meyer

22746-0118

Printed in the United States of America

Preface

WHILE all the arts have, from time to time, been subjected to scientific scrutiny, music particularly has attracted the attention of scientists. Musical instruments and their tonal potentialities have traditionally been the concern of the physicists, but a number of psychologists share this interest. Physiologists and physiological psychologists have studied the auditory sense organs to learn the nature of the neurological processes by means of which tones are perceived. Laboratory psychologists have attempted to establish just what the musician does when he performs and to find what tonal sensitivities he possesses. Still other psychologists and a few sociologists have focused their interests on the affective and evaluative aspects of music.

All these interests are reflected to some extent in the textbooks that treat the area where music and psychology overlap. So far, however, there has been no complete agreement as to what are the boundaries of the psychology of music. One text may stress laboratory data and do a minimum of theorizing, another may present fewer "facts" but be far more philosophical in approach. One may treat of music and musicians as if the cultural milieu were of little importance, another may show more concern with the social determination of music activities.

Of course no book can include all that at one time or another has been said to be subsumed under the psychology of music. All that can properly be asked of an author is that he present what he regards as a coherent picture of the phenomena of the field, its major problems, and the solutions he deems most plausible. This, then, is what the present book attempts to do.

The psychology of music has been the subject of at least six text-books issued in the past two decades. The year 1937 saw the publication of Diserens and Fine's *A Psychology of Music* and Mursell's *The Psychology of Music*. The former book not only dealt with experimental literature but also devoted considerable space to the origin of music, animal auditors, mythology and folklore, and the relation of music to magic and sorcery and to religion, melancholy, and ecstasy. The Mursell book philosophized much more and interpreted research data rather narrowly in terms of Gestalt theory. Mursell's advice to music teachers was reserved for *Music and the Classroom Teacher* and other treatises.

Seashore's *Psychology of Music* was issued in 1938. With no interest in those aspects of music which are primarily social psychological, Seashore limited himself largely to a description of the excellent but apparatus-bound studies of his own laboratories. He attempted some years later to broaden his coverage of the field with *Why We Love Music* and *In Search of Beauty in Music*. Seashore prided himself on following no "school" of psychology. Yet he was one of the most ardent hereditarians psychology has produced, and his books quite clearly reflect this nativistic bias.

In 1940 one of Seashore's students, Max Schoen, published his *The Psychology of Music*. Built on his earlier work, *The Beautiful in Music*, Schoen's book presented a well-rounded picture of the experimental findings through the 1930's. A later, more philosophical work of Schoen's appeared as *The Understanding of Music*.

No new texts appeared after 1940 until 1953, when Révész's well-known *Einführung in die Musikpsychologie* was translated into English and published in Great Britain in somewhat revised form. A year later it was issued in the United States under the title *Introduction to the Psychology of Music*. Révész's book contained a good survey of the European findings in music psychology but touched only lightly on American research. The tone of the Révész volume was absolutistic and hereditarian.

Lundin's *An Objective Psychology of Music* was also published in 1953. As the only American text to appear in thirteen years, it had the important task of digesting the research materials of more than a decade. This book has a cultural and relativistic flavor and an inter-behavioristic orientation.

Two other American books have influenced music-psychology research, although they are not formal texts in the psychology of music. One was Pratt's *The Meaning of Music*, which was a series of essays rather than a textbook and hence made no attempt to cover the experimental literature. Showing a high degree of sophistication, Pratt's little book was written in large part as a defense of formalism.

The other work was given the rather frightening title *The Musician's Arithmetic*. Its author, Max Meyer, to whom the present book is dedicated, is one of the most brilliant theorists and experimenters in the field. Indeed, it was the manuscript of Meyer's treatise which first stirred the interest of this author in the psychology of music. Meyer's book offered exciting neurological speculations as well as important research data, but it is admittedly difficult to read and therefore has had an extremely limited audience. Although over the years the present writer has become increasingly disappointed at the slow growth of scientific neurology and has occupied himself less and less with theorizing along the lines suggested by Meyer, he still appreciates Meyer's refreshing approach and feels that the serious student will find *The Musician's Arithmetic*, Meyer's early articles, and his more recent *How We Hear* well worth careful attention.

During the three decades since the author first came upon Meyer's works, he has been occupied with a host of research problems and has finally adopted a relativistic, culturally oriented point of view. He would be one of the first to admit that scientists have hardly begun to answer the problems of music aesthetics. Many problems, of course, may never be resolved. Yet a good number already have at least tentative answers, the elaboration of which will be found in the chapters to follow. Since little experimental work has so far been done on non-European music and the less serious forms of Occidental music, this book will necessarily be concerned mainly with the serious music of the West.

To write for both psychological and musical audiences is a difficult task. Yet this book attempts to interest these two audiences. It is the author's belief that the reader will need no more psychological knowledge than that which any intelligent and reasonably well-educated adult usually possesses. But unless the reader has some sustained interest in music he probably will not look beyond the title of this book. His musical knowledge, however, need not be extensive. To help him with the psychological and musical terms with which he may be unfamiliar, a glossary is provided on pp. 280–287. For the reader who desires more detailed knowledge of the research material described in the articles listed in the footnotes, a key to the reference abbreviations is given on pp. 288–292.

The reader who wishes to keep abreast of the work being done in psychological aesthetics should consult the *Journal of Aesthetics and Art Criticism*, which once a year carries a list of articles that have appeared during the previous calendar year. After noting the articles which interest him and before reading the articles themselves, the reader would be advised to examine the abstracts printed six times a year in *Psychological Abstracts*. For a more comprehensive coverage of the older articles than is offered by this book, the reader is referred to *A Bibliography of Periodical Literature in Musicology and Allied Fields and a Record of Graduate Theses Accepted* (published as volumes 1 and 2 in 1940 and 1943 by the American Council of

Learned Societies). Attention should also be directed to A. R. Chandler, "A Bibliography of Experimental Aesthetics, 1865–1932" (*Ohio State University Studies*, 1 [1933]); to A. R. Chandler and E. N. Barnhart, *A Bibliography of Psychological and Experimental Aesthetics, 1864–1937* (Berkeley, University of California Press, 1938); and to W. A. Hammond, *A Bibliography of Aesthetics and of the Philosophy of the Fine Arts from 1900 to 1932* (New York, Longmans, Green, 1934).

The author is indebted to many people and publishing houses. Since in general they know of his appreciation he will not name them here. An exception must be made, however, in the case of the Stanford University Press, which kindly allowed him to take over for this book almost the entire manuscript of his earlier *Musical Taste*. This material now makes up much of Chapters 6 and 7.

P. R. F.

Stanford, California
July 1957

Contents

CONTENTS

THE SOCIAL PSYCHOLOGY
OF MUSIC

CHAPTER ONE

The Psychological Approach
to Music

LIKE most discussions which attempt to show that some particular area of study is a science, arguments about the scientific status of the psychology of music can settle little or nothing. Some definitions would allow science to include almost all systematic investigation, while others would restrict the term to the older and better-established disciplines of the natural sciences. Yet it can be truly said that the psychologists who have interested themselves in the aesthetics of music aim to be scientists. They try to employ the best tools available, to handle their experimental variables according to the accepted rules of science, and to treat their findings with a reasonable degree of statistical sophistication. Admittedly, there have been times when they have kept too close to their laboratories and have withdrawn somewhat from musical reality. Several decades ago, for example, a number of psychologists claimed to be able to test innate musical capacities. They also maintained that these tested capacities could not be improved by training, a dogma which was most irritating to those musicians who had devoted their lives to the improvement of tonal perception and control and knew that their labors had not been in vain. But, as more and more data have been collected, the psychologists have come to agree with the musicians that the "musical ear" can indeed be improved (p. 186). Nowadays, psychological aestheticians are more careful to work in a musical context.

I

The Psychology of Music and the Social Sciences

It is often said that psychology was born from a union of philosophy and the natural sciences. With the passage of time, however, the social sciences began to envelop psychology until, at present, many of the research problems and techniques of cultural anthropology, sociology, and psychology are surprisingly alike. This growth of psychology—its retention of its older affiliations with the natural sciences (if not with philosophy) and the addition of its newer interests in the social science area—is reflected in the development of the psychology of music. Past workers in the field, notably members of the Carl Seashore group at the State University of Iowa, rather limited themselves to experiments of the natural science sort (p. 8). Others, particularly researchers of the past few years, have tended to be at least equally interested in problems adapted to the techniques of the social sciences. It is natural that those who deal primarily with the biological aspects of music should feel that the more important antecedents of musical activity are to be found in the nature of the human organism, whereas those further removed from the natural science laboratory should look more to cultural forces for their explanations.

While the present treatise attempts to cover the major experiments of psychological aesthetics whatever the techniques employed, its orientation is admittedly a sociopsychological one. Believing as he does that the earlier workers tended to overstress the importance of the biological bases of musical behavior almost to the point of ignoring its cultural determinants, the author has here tried to bring the picture a little more to balance. No doubt the result will seem to some to be an overbalance on the cultural side. But whatever the effect, the choice has been deliberate. Its justification will perhaps become clearer as the book is read.

2

The Unreliability of Common Sense

The behavioral scientist tends to question the validity of much that he perceives. He is less likely than the layman to accept the obvious, what the dictionary terms "common sense," for he has found that he and others "know" many things that are simply not true. Let us take as an illustration the very widespread belief that marijuana heightens the auditory capacities. Even many musician-addicts are convinced that they are more sensitive to tonal stimuli when given this drug. Yet psychophysiological research gives no support to the idea.[1] In this area, alertness and the feeling of alertness are not closely related.

Or let us consider the almost universal belief that Negroes are more sensitive to tone and rhythm than are whites. Large numbers of these two American subgroups have been tested in tonal memory and in the discrimination of differences in pitch, loudness, time, rhythm, and timbre. No striking Negro (or white) superiority has ever been demonstrated. In the several studies in this area the racial differences that do emerge are so slight that one group or another will yield the higher average score because of factors local to the immediate testing situation (Chap. 8). But if the superiority of either one of these subgroups were at all impressive, it would transcend these local conditions and make itself unmistakably apparent.[2]

Common sense teaches that some humans are born monotones. These unfortunates cannot carry tunes and are doomed to go through life embarrassed by the fact that they cannot sing or perhaps even recognize our national anthem—a serious disability in these days of political witch-hunting. The follower of common sense typically accepts the fatalistic genetics of earlier decades and does nothing about the matter. To him the monotone appears to have an inherent anatomical defect. But luckily there are psychologists and music educators who check on common sense. They have shown that most,

3

if not all, monotones have psychological rather than biological disabilities and can be helped to overcome their tune weakness. Monotones are often people who have met with emotional difficulties in the early grades of school.[3] Possessed of more than average dislike of the schoolroom or of the music teacher, or of both, and quite frequently holding to the attitude that singing is an activity for sissies, monotones may become uncooperative during that early period when music fundamentals are usually most easily learned. Later in life they will find that with great effort they can master the concept of pitch but that they must have considerable aid from psychologists or music educators to do so (p. 186).

Although many other illustrations could be given of the occasional unreliability of common sense, let us content ourselves with just one more example. Capacities for handling two-four, three-four, four-four, six-four, and even eight-four beats per measure seem to be generally regarded as "instinctive." American music students handle such time signatures without formal training but flounder when asked to beat out the five-four or the seven-four. Man simply lacks the "instinct" for these latter, says common sense. Yet if this were so, the lack should be general and not limited to a few culture areas. The psychologist Max Meyer should not have found natives of North Africa dancing and swaying to these beats. But, according to his observations, certain of the natives were almost as skillful with the five- and seven-four as we are with the two- and three-four. Later, on his return to his American laboratory, he found it quite easy to train his students to tap out the five- and seven-four with great accuracy.[4] These young Americans soon forgot that they had no "instinct" for such activities.

The Search for Alternative Hypotheses

Another characteristic of the scientist is his willingness to search for rival hypotheses. While the layman may be content with one apparently reasonable "cause" for some phenomenon, the scientist investigates a variety of possible antecedents. It looks reasonable, for example, to assume that the true beat in music[5] has a rate which is determined by some organic rhythm like the heartbeat, and for many years the assumption of an intimate connection between body function and music response was treated as a fact. But Lund put the matter to test in an attempt to see whether there might not be some other determinants.[6] Although he did not find what these latter were, he did show that true beat and heartbeat have little association. During 1939 this psychologist took meticulous measurements of many performances of the Roth Quartet and of several symphony orchestras and found the true beat to vary all the way from 40 to 100 pulsations—a far cry from the 70–75 beats the heart gives each minute.

The search for alternative hypotheses makes the scientist loath to accept as finally valid all that gets into print. In the process of creating new theories and rechecking behavior he sometimes finds that what the books say about some phenomenon is no longer true— if it ever was. Thus, long ago the notion was written into at least a few textbooks that the great vocalists sang *pure, steady* tones. Happily, this invalid observation appears in print now but rarely. In fact, it is a wonder that anyone ever did hold to the purity idea, for one needs only to listen to a relatively pure tone, say that of a tuning fork, to realize that it is the *impure* and not the *pure* tone with which music deals. And there is a host of excellent psychological works on the vibrato which demonstrate beyond doubt the unsteadiness of the preferred vocal and violin tone (p. 8).

Other almost totally incorrect sets of musical rules can be found in some of the older books on baton movements. Typical diagrams show a preponderance of straight-line motions and periods of relative rest at the beat-instants. Bartholomew checked these diagrams against the baton performances of conductors.[7] He attached

5

a tiny lamp to the end of a baton which had been so wired that the light dimmed at the exact instant of the beat. By photographing the path of the light this experimenter found curvilinear rather than straight-line motions and points of rest closer to the "ands" after the respective beats. The fastest, not the slowest, speeds were often at the beat-instants!

On occasion, printed misinformation has been retained for practical reasons, the ethical aspects of which are not of a high order. As an illustration let us take one of the author's minor studies. Around 1930 considerable research was being undertaken with a certain make of player piano. Its manufacturer had long been advertising that it offered sixteen different intensities of hammer strokes, roughly twice the loudness possibilities of its two chief rivals. This statement was true enough from the standpoint of physics as there actually were twice as many intensity holes on the music roll being studied. But, as the author clearly proved, only *one half* of its loudness differences were discriminable by the typical layman whereas *all* of its rivals' were. Musically and practically speaking, then, the competing instruments were equally good in their handling of loudness differences. Yet the advertising went on unchanged.

Limitations of Psychomusical Investigations

The psychologist pieces together bits of information into an organized whole. But why does he choose to work on certain problems and not on others? His choice, it would seem, is to some extent forced by the availability and cooperation of his subjects and by the degree to which the complex phenomena of music can be subjected to scientific analysis.

The first of these conditioners is common to almost all the research choices of the psychologist. Unless he is working with sub-human animals which can be caged, or with the semicaged school child or college sophomore, who must cooperate willy-nilly, the psychologist often has great selection and motivation difficulties with his subjects. He commonly cannot get the cooperation of all those he might desire to test, and even those who do "cooperate" may answer his questions without sufficient care. His findings, then, are not always truly representative.

The second factor which limits psychomusical research operates throughout the social sciences and the humanities. Causal relations are rarely simple, and whenever analyses are to be made care must be taken that the dynamic interrelation of the phenomena in question is not disturbed. Otherwise, the data resulting from the analyses will be devoid of musical meaning. The practical effect of this limitation is that many fascinating musical problems cannot be studied by the aid of any of the analytic techniques currently used by the psychologist. In many areas he can only chew along the edges, so to speak. He cannot get his teeth into the meaty center of the problem.

The Possibilities of Research in Experimental Aesthetics

Psychological research in aesthetics can often throw much light on what is taking place in a particular music area, i.e., it has a *descriptive* function. Research may sometimes yield, in addition, pertinent information on the *reasons* for some particular bit of music behavior. It can also be of considerable aid in *forecasting*. But no science offers criteria by which artistic responses can be rated as "good," "proper for all time," "bad," or "improper for all time." In other words, the work of the psychological aesthetician leads to descriptions, explanations, and forecasts, but does not reveal aesthetic absolutes.

THE DESCRIPTIVE FUNCTION. To illustrate the first, or descriptive, function of psychological aesthetics we might well return to a consideration of vocal and violin vibrato.[8] Careful research in

7

this area has demonstrated that the cultivated singing voice of the adult shows periodic changes in pitch in approximately 95 per cent of its tones. Regular changes in intensity and timbre have also been found to occur. For both violin and voice the tone pulsates about 6·5 times a second. The extent of the pulsation of the violin tone (in the middle pitch range) is approximately a quarter of a tone. For the vocal tone the vibrato extent is twice this value although the listener can rarely believe this and interprets the range as somewhat smaller (a fifth of a tone). Both the musically trained and the relatively unmusical prefer the current vibrato rates to all others. Untrained individuals prefer a pitch range of approximately a quarter-tone, while the musically trained favor a pitch wobble of about a tenth of a whole tone.[9]

The typical vibratos of a number of virtuosos have been carefully measured. Hence, it is now possible for the aspiring young singer or violinist to compare his vibrato with that of his model by performing before some instrument which transmutes his own tonal efforts into visual stimuli.

VIBRATO OF SOME WELL-KNOWN SINGERS[*]

	Average Rate per Second	Average Extent in Whole Tones
Schumann-Heink	7·6	·38
Galli-Curci	7·3	·44
Caruso	7·1	·47
Rethberg	7·0	·49
Ponselle	6·9	·48
Chaliapin	6·8	·54
Jeritza	6·8	·53
Tetrazzini	6·8	·37
Talley	6·7	·54
Tibbett	6·6	·55
Gigli	6·5	·57
Hackett	5·9	·47
Homer	5·9	·51

[*] C. E. Seashore, *Psychology of Music*, N.Y., McGraw-Hill, 1938, p. 43 (with permission).

THE CAUSAL FUNCTION.[10]   While the second, or causal, function of psychological aesthetics can be illustrated from any one of a large number of studies, let us limit ourselves to a consideration of only two, the first to be concerned with the determiners of tempo preferences and the second with the reasons for the high regard in which the old Cremona-made violins are held.

Tempo preferences have been found to vary considerably from person to person. This large range is no doubt due to a number of factors, but at least one of these factors has been isolated and found to be what might be termed "occupational tempo." Thus Foley found that girls studying trades like dressmaking in which activity proceeds at a slow pace were prone to favor andante tempos; those working with power machines, a slow allegro. Typists, with their faster working speeds, tended to prefer a fast allegro bordering on presto. Their work speeds, it seems clear, so conditioned these girls that they came to prefer these rates even outside the shop and the office.[11]

And now for our second illustration of psychology's causal function. With the passage of time, the sales values of the violins built by the old masters of Cremona have grown enormously. The know-how of making great instruments has been lost and modern reproductions are weak imitations, it is commonly said.[12] But what makes a Stradivarius or some other old Cremona fiddle so magnificent? Is it its physical construction? Or may it not be, in part at least, a matter of attitude, of prestige long associated with this period of alleged violin-making supremacy?

The physical qualities of the old instruments and of their modern imitations have been carefully examined by Saunders.[13] His surprising finding is that on all but one of his tests any one of the old instruments differed from its modern copy less than it did from the other old violins. All the instruments, old and new, were much alike in the response curves they yielded. Saunders did find that the work required to make an old violin speak properly was, on the

9

average, a little less than that needed for the newer models. The Cremona violins with their older wood and drier varnish yield tones that are not quite so easily drowned out by the other instruments of the orchestra.[14] But aside from this energy variable no great differences emerged.

There is, then, the suggestion hypothesis. The awareness that a particular instrument was made by a great master makes the listener feel that the tone is superior and stimulates him to pay more for it than he would for a modern violin. All that is needed to prove that the suggestion hypothesis has some validity is to arrange a psychological experiment in which Strads and their well-built modern imitations are played behind a screen a number of times in random order. The results prove that the person has yet to be found who can consistently pick the Strad.[15] The old masters, it would seem, built marvelous violins. But along with the instruments they built reputations which were even more marvelous!

THE FORECASTING FUNCTION. To illustrate the third, or forecasting, function of psychological aesthetics let us look again to the psychology of suggestion and next to the forecasting of grades in conservatories of music. From what we know of the principles of suggestion we might forecast that musical preferences could be affected by an experimenter if he set himself the task of altering his subjects' likes and dislikes. That such effects can actually occur was shown by Rigg, when he offered the same music to three groups of college students.[16] The members of one group were led to regard what they were hearing in a romantic light. No special psychological "atmosphere" was suggested to the members of the second group. The last group of students was successfully led to associate the music with Hitler and the Nazi movement. The proof that the three different "atmospheres" elicited three different degrees of acceptance was shown in the three mean preference scores. When thought of as

Nazi music the compositions were least appreciated. When the romantic atmosphere was suggested the acceptance was greatest.

Knowing very well that to many laymen the word "classical" suggests high-brow, boring music, the arrangers of a Danish broadcast program of serious music changed the title of their series from "Classical Music" to "Popular Music" but kept unchanged the style of their musical offerings. The latter label, they felt, suggested pleasanter, easier-to-grasp music. That they had properly gauged the connotations of these terms was rather dramatically demonstrated in the fact that the number of listeners doubled after the changed titling.[17]

It can safely be predicted that certain compositions will be better liked if the listener is led to think they were composed by a man of some eminence. Thus, if Bach's *Concerto in D Minor* is played to lay audiences who believe the composer to be the relatively unknown Buxtehude, the acceptance will be far less than if the listeners are told that the composer is their revered J. S. Bach.[18] Similar suggestive effects have been demonstrated in the area of jazz preferences and in the pictorial arts.

And now let us look at the forecasting of conservatory grades. Many colleges nowadays have established what they call "critical levels" of college aptitude, minimum scores which an applicant must reach in order to matriculate. These critical levels have been empirically determined from the scores of past failures. They are, then, of considerable value for forecasting, since persons making scores below these critical points will almost certainly fail before the time of graduation. Stanton, working at the Eastman School of Music, found a critical level of this type for entering music students.[19] She based her level on a test of tonal imagery, a case history, a college aptitude test, and a battery of music aptitude tests (Chap. 9). After years of experimentation, Stanton found she could foretell with considerable accuracy which of the applicants would be the failures.

The Absence of Absolutes

Because there are certain biological periodicities close to the 6 or 6·5 pulsations per second that is the vibrato rate the contemporary musician prefers above all other rates, one theorist has assumed this periodicity to be the "proper vibrato rate for all time." To him the fact that the musically elite currently prefer a rate identical with one of the periodicities of "nature" proves that they like what it is biologically proper to like.

This type of reasoning is not acceptable to the social scientist, for he knows that what is deemed proper in one period of time may not be so considered in the next.[20] The position taken in this book, the belief that scientific research does not yield absolutes and final answers, is well expressed by Tiffin in an article in which he describes some of his vibrato researches:

> This work is intended to present objective unequivocal information about the vibrato used by this generation of artists and students of voice. It is not contended that this type of vibrato is ultimately beautiful. No esthetic value judgment is included in the results. It may be argued that the vibrato in use by present day artists is a fad and that their voices would be improved if it were made less prominent or even entirely eliminated. This may quite possibly be true. Perhaps if this study is repeated fifty years hence, the average extent of the vibrato then in use will be found to be quite different from the one now employed. This will simply mean that standards of artistry have changed, as all esthetic preferences change from time to time. . . . No attempt is made to prophesy future artistic taste nor to justify current preference in terms of ultimate esthetic principles.[21]

Absolutes are not revealed by psychological research for the simple reason that there are no musical absolutes to be found. There is, for example, no absolutely "good" music, music whose goodness transcends time and space. As the British psychologist Vernon phrases it: "That music is 'good' which happens to appeal especially to the subjective tastes of the musicians of the period, these tastes being to a large extent determined irrationally by temperamental and various environmental conditions, by suggestion, contra-suggestion, conservatism and iconoclasticism."[22]

A Preview of Later Chapters

Our first consideration will be the scale, the relative and socially agreed upon placements of all the notes the musician attempts to play or sing. The interval, i.e., any two simultaneously or successively played tones, and the melody, a succession of intervals felt to possess unity, furnish the basic underpinnings of musical structure and are for this reason considered in Chapters 3 and 4.

Since the first, and often the only, question many laymen ask about a piece of music is, "What story does the composition tell?" it seemed appropriate to present in the fifth chapter material on music as a possible medium of communication. And as a person's attitude toward the meaning of a composition clearly forms an important part of his taste, of his over-all attitude toward that composition and its composer, the language chapter is followed by two on musical taste—Chapter 6 on the nature of taste and Chapter 7 on the several ways of measuring it.

The discussion of the basic musical abilities and their measurement (Chaps. 8 and 9) might justifiably have appeared earlier in the book, for in a very real sense all perception, affection, and attitude presuppose abilities. There are other ways of viewing the problem, however. A person's abilities will mature only if the social climate is propitious. They can be expressed only in the context of a man's own and his culture's taste, and this taste may prove stimulating or inhibitory. In this limited sense, then, ability may be thought to depend on taste and so deserve treatment, as it has in this book, after taste has been considered.

The consideration of the applications to medicine and industry appears as the final chapter, for before one tries to apply any knowledge he should make certain that he has learned all he can about what he is to apply.

With this brief introduction to the social psychology of music, let us examine next the musical scale, the totality of those fixed (but relatively placed) pitch positions which the musician uses in his melodic and harmonic endeavors.

Notes

1] C. K. Aldrich, "The Effect of a Synthetic Marihuana-like Compound on Musical Talent as Measured by the Seashore Test," *Publ. Hlth Rep., Wash., 59* (1944): 431–433; M. Mezzrow and B. Wolfe, *Really the Blues*, N.Y., Random House, 1946.

2] One of the most extensive of the studies which compared Negroes and whites was that by G. B. Johnson reported in "Musical Talent of the Negro," *Mus. Superv. J., 15* (1928): 81, 83, 96. After testing 3350 Negroes of fifth grade, eighth grade, and college level on the Seashore Measures of Musical Talent he states: "It becomes evident that the only fair conclusion to be drawn from the data is that there are no significant differences between whites and Negroes on those basic musical sensibilities measured by the Seashore tests."

3] K. M. Ramm, "Personality Maladjustment among Monotones," *Smith Coll. Stud. Soc. Wk., 17* (1947): 264–284.

4] M. F. Meyer, *The Psychology of the Other-one*, Columbia, Mo., Missouri Book, 1922.

5] By true beat or takt is meant the pulsations which underlie phrase rhythms irrespective of time signatures or number of notes in the phrase.

6] M. W. Lund, "An Analysis of the 'True-beat' in Music," Doctoral Thesis, Stanford U., 1939. In a somewhat similar analysis of the true beat of phonograph recordings, Hodgson found that slightly less than half of the measures fell between 60 and 70 per minute. Although he had undertaken his researches in the belief that true beat may be causally related to heart beat, Hodgson now admits the impossibility of proving a causal relationship. Walter Hodgson, "Absolute Tempo," *Mus. Teach. Nat. Assoc. Proc. 1949, 43 Ser.,* 1951: 158–169.

7] W. T. Bartholomew, "Baton Movements," *Peabody Bull., 29,* No. 2 (1933): 37–39. Using a similar technique, F. Giese found that when 35 persons were asked to conduct for the same composition there were huge individual differences in the style of conducting. Giese's data show some similarity in the pattern of conducting (a) the different works of the same conductor and (b) compositions of the same musical school ("Individuum und Epoch in Taktierbewegungen bei verschiedenen Komponisten," *Arch. Ges. Psychol.*, *90* (1934): 380–426).

8] The most extensive work on the vibrato was done at the Seashore laboratories of the State University of Iowa. See the *U. of Ia. Stud. Psychol. Mus.*, vol. *1* (1932), which contains articles by E. Easeley, M. Hattwick, M. T. Hollinshead, F. E. Linder, J. Tiffin, M. Metfessel, R. S. Miller, S. N. Reger, D. A. Rothschild, H. G. Seashore, and A. H. Wagner; an earlier research from this same laboratory was that of M. Schoen, "An Experimental Study of the Pitch Factor in Artistic Singing," *Psychol. Monog.*, *31* (1922): 230–259. Excellent work has also been done by L. Cheslock, "Introductory Study on Violin Vibrato," *Peabody Cons. Mus. Res. Stud.*, No. 1 (1931). See also W. E. Kock, "On the Principle of Uncertainty in Sound," *J. Acoust. Soc. Amer.*, *7* (1935): 56–58; "Certain Subjective Phenomena Accompanying a Frequency Vibrato," *J. Acoust. Soc. Amer.*, *8* (1936): 23–25; A. M. Small, "An Objective Analysis of Artistic Violin Performance," *U. of Ia. Stud. Psychol. Mus.*, *4* (1936): 172–231; J. R. Tolmie, "An Analysis of the Vibrato from the Viewpoint of Frequency and Amplitude Modulation," *J. Acoust. Soc. Amer.*, *7* (1935): 29–36; L. Sjöström, "Experimentellphonetische Untersuchungen des Vibratophänomens der Singstimme," *Acta Oto-laryng.* (Stockholm), Suppl., *47* (1948): 123–130.

9] J. F. Corso and D. Lewis, "Preferred Rate and Extent of Frequency Vibrato," *J. Appl. Psychol.*, *34* (1950): 206–212.

10] "Explanation" as used in this book is, in a sense, merely an extension of the concept "description." A phenomenon to be explained is described in the context of the other variables to which it is related. Where these latter are antecedent in time they are popularly referred to as its "causes."

11] J. P. Foley, Jr., "The Occupational Conditioning of Preferential Auditory Tempo," *J. Soc. Psychol.*, *12* (1940): 121–129.

12] This "loss of know-how" has been greatly exaggerated in the popular mind.

13] F. A. Saunders, "The Mechanical Action of Violins," *J. Acoust. Soc. Amer.*, *9* (1937): 81–98. A. Small has shown that the "better" stringed instruments differ from the "poorer" largely in their emphasis on frequency bands below 2500 d.v. ("The Tone-color [Timbre] of Stringed Instruments," *Mus. Teach. Nat. Assoc.*, *1940* (1941): 354–360). See also E. G. Richardson, "Orchestral Acoustics," *Sci. Month.*, *80*, 1955: 211–224.

14] Even the "lost art" of making old Italian violin varnish is lost no longer. See J. Michelman, "Lost Art of Strad Varnish," *Sci. Month.*, *81*, 1955: 221–223.

15] Data from personal communications as well as from one unpublished study by the author. *The Oxford Companion to Music* (P. A. Scholes, ed., London, Oxford U. Press, 1943, p. 988) reports that in London and in several other places there have been similar failures to discriminate the tones of the older from those of the newer instruments.

16] M. G. Rigg, "Favorable versus Unfavorable Propaganda in the Enjoyment of Music," *J. Exp. Psychol.*, *38* (1948): 78–81.

17] T. Geiger, "A Radio Test of Musical Taste," *Publ. Opin. Quart.*, *14* (1950): 453–460. It is conceivable that the long-continued use of the Geiger procedure might increase the number of persons who habitually tune in on musical programs even when the music is titled "classical." Unfortunately, the reported data do not cover this possibility.

18] The organist-composer Buxtehude, although largely unknown to the present-day lay public, was well known in the late seventeenth and early eighteenth centuries. But now it is the name of J. S. Bach that is familiar to all laymen who have had any appreciable degree of formal education (p. 276).

19] H. M. Stanton, "Measurement of Musical Talent," *U. of Ia. Stud. Psychol. Mus.*, 2 (1935): 1–140.

20] Even in the short period that scientists have been observing musical behavior, a number of changes in basic activity have been noted. Thus, the manner of breath control of the great Schumann-Heink was quite acceptable in her day but causes much distress or even amusement to those of us who listen, on recordings, to what appear to be her periodic gasps.

21] J. Tiffin, "The Role of Pitch and Intensity in the Vocal Vibrato of Students and Artists," *U. of Ia. Stud. Psychol. Mus.*, 1 (1932): 134–165.

22] P. E. Vernon, "Method in Musical Psychology," *Amer. J. Psychol.*, 42 (1930): 127–134.

CHAPTER TWO

The Social Psychology of Musical Scales

M USIC is made of socially accepted patterns of sounds. These sounds are either noisy, with no perceptible pitch, or they are tonal, and can be located on a high–low continuum. The tones may differ in loudness, timbre, duration, volume, density, and quite possibly in still other characteristics.[1] While all pitches in the middle range are of potential musical use, only a few appear in any one composition. That is, convention limits the number and relative locations of the pitches. This chapter will consider the several attempts at pitch limitation, matters studied in music under the category of scales.

The Tone Elements of Music

Unlike the music of some other cultures in which the sounds slide up or down without discrete steps and the patterns are rarely twice alike, the music of the West has been built around fixed tones, so far back as there are records. These tones, the stepwise, ordered arrangement of which constitutes a scale, have been tied to a variety of frequencies with their exact pitch locations largely matters of local tradition or of convenience to the musical performer. It is, for example, of little theoretical importance whether violin A is tuned at 433·2 d.v. (Philharmonic pitch), at 435 d.v. (French pitch), or at some other agreed-upon frequency.[2] Of more importance to the

17

musical structure, to the melody and harmony, is the ratio formed by an interval's two tones. The absolute size of the spans is generally not of paramount importance since a large span covering 4000–8000 d.v. has much the same psychological effect as a small span spreading from 100 to 200 d.v. Both spans are termed octaves[3] and are characterized by the ratio of 1:2. It is out of ratios that melody and harmony are constructed, and so long as the ratios are unchanged, the notes can be raised or lowered without damage to the tune. Such an alteration of the pitch locations merely shifts the melody to another register. To understand the basic facts of the psychology of music, then, one must learn how ratios have been employed in scale construction.

The tones of the ratio 1:2, the octave, are easily produced on pipes, they sound well together, and they are so easily confused[4] that identical letter names have traditionally been given them.[5] For these and perhaps other psychological and biophysical reasons, the octave relationship was already recognized in the earliest documents history has provided. The ratio of 1:2 (also written 1/2) holds for lengths of pipe of constant bore, and pipes were much played upon by the ancients. This ratio and those of 2:3 (the musical fifth) and 3:4 (the musical fourth) were so well known by the time of Pythagoras (approximately 550 B.C.) that the diatonic (or seven white-note) scale of his day was conceived of as being built with the octave and the fifth (or the fourth) on the ratios 1:2 and 2:3 (or 3:4).

Scales of Ancient Times

PYTHAGOREAN SCALE. Pythagoras derived his scale by starting with a scale position, say F, and moving progressively up by musical fifths (2:3) or down by fourths (3:4).[6] Thus, if one begins with F and counts up a musical fifth, i.e., by seven semitones, one comes to C. Next G is reached, then D, A, E, and finally B. Proceeding further, the several black notes are successively located. Since each of these scale points is to its next higher fifth as $2:3$, the ratios given in row 1 of the table below obtain, i.e., F:C:G:D:A:E:B as $64:96:144:216:324:486:729$ (six contiguous $2:3$ ratios).

SCALE OF PYTHAGORAS

	C	C Sharp	D	D Sharp	E	F	F Sharp
1	96		216		486	64	
2	384		432		486	512	
3	256		288		324	341·3	
4	1/1		8/9		64/81	3/4	
5	3		27		243	1	
6	3^1	3^8	3^3	3^{10}	3^5	$3^0(3^{12})$	3^7

	G	G Sharp	A	A Sharp	B	C
1	144		324		729	192
2	576		648		729	768
3	384		432		486	512
4	2/3		16/27		128/243	1/2
5	9		81		729	3
6	3^2	3^9	3^4	3^{11}	3^6	3^1

Note: For the purposes of this book the sharps of this table have no significance as such. They could, in fact, have been replaced by the flats of D, E, G, A, and B. They are written in here merely to indicate that there are chromatic scale steps between C and D, D and E, F and G, G and A, and A and B.

In building his scale by adding together successive musical fifths (see row 1 and the paragraph above), Pythagoras covered almost four octaves, that is, $64:128$ is one octave, $128:256$ another, $256:512$ a third octave, and $512:729$ is a part of a fourth octave. If the largest value, 729, is taken as a reference point and the values of the lower pitch locations are successively doubled until their magnitudes fall between 729 and the next lower octave, $364·5$, the letter steps are now located within a single octave span (row 2). It is not customary, however, to locate C at 384. "Scientific pitch" places it at 256 cycles and the other letter locations are given in row 3. While the values of rows 2 and 3 differ in magnitude they denote identical ratios. Thus,

C:D can be expressed either as 256:288, 384:432 or as 8:9, the reduced ratio given in row 4. Similarly, C:E can be either 256:324, 384:486 or 64:81.

It should be noted that the removal of the powers of 2 from a series of ratios or frequencies disturbs the octave location but not the letter arrangements. Thus, if a certain C is given the value of 256, other C's will be 128, 64, 512, or other numbers found by dividing or multiplying 256 by a succession of 2's. Now the dividing through the ratios of row 2 by 2's until odd numbers are reached reveals more clearly the Pythagorean philosophy of scale construction and yields a series of skeleton values in row 5, which have been termed "tone symbols" by Max Meyer.[7] Pythagoras, it can now be seen from the values in row 6, formed his scale by the use of the prime numbers 1 and 3 exclusively.[8]

A SUGGESTION FROM ARISTOXENUS (CIRCA 350 B.C.). If the process of climbing by seven semitone steps, by fifths, is continued from B, the accidentals are located (from B to F sharp, then to C sharp, G sharp, D sharp and A sharp) and finally the starting point F is reached, this time as 3^{12}. This value, derived from the 2:3 ratio of the fifth, cannot coincide with any power of 2, which the octave 1:2 requires. Obviously, then, the Pythagorean cycle of fifths cannot lead to a perfect octave.

Having noticed the imperfection of the Pythagorean system, the Greek philosopher Aristoxenus suggested tempering the intervals to make each half-step equal in ratio to every other one. We shall see later that such a change would have made the fifth just small enough so that twelve fifths would have fitted precisely into an octave pattern, i.e., into seven octaves. Although nothing practical came of this suggestion at the time, over the years theorists (Galileo, for one) kept reviving the notion until it was finally put into practical use in J. S. Bach's day (p. 25).

A SUGGESTION FROM PTOLEMY (CIRCA 200 A.D.).   Ptolemy was one of several who felt that worthwhile scales might be constructed with prime numbers other than 1 and 3. Any relatively small number might be employed, thought Ptolemy, in the rationalization of the diatonic scale. It is clear that these conclusions were not reached as the result of psychological research. Their chief importance derives from the fact that other theoretically minded musicians of a later date held similar views. The scale next to be considered is a compromise between the Pythagorean conception and the Ptolemaic.

Scale of Just Intonation

What is generally given in textbooks on music, physics, and psychology as the diatonic scale of Western music is the scale of just intonation. In the construction of the scale of just intonation the Pythagorean scale was modified by the introduction of ratios based on the prime number 5. This modification can be understood through a comparison of the tone symbols of the two scales. The symbols for F, C, G, and D are identical. The tone symbol for the Pythagorean A, 81, was changed to 5, a multiple of which, 80, approximates the 81 of the older scale. As will be seen later (p. 27), this is a comparatively small change, but it affected the location of B and particularly that of E, the Pythagorean form of which had been creating some difficulties for the musicians.

Over the centuries, Western music had been giving increasing stress to harmony. While the simpler ratios of the Pythagorean scale fitted well this development, the 64:81 ratio of the third, from C to E, gave particular trouble. So, in the course of time, its ratio was changed to the simpler 4:5. This introduction of another prime number to rival the Pythagorean 3 caused the scientifically minded to look to the overtone, or harmonic, series for help in justifying this

21

departure in scale construction.9 For what could be more scientific, thought they, than to construct out of the lower harmonics a scale for harmonic usage. In fact, the early scientists, and some later ones, became so enamored of the overtone notion of scale rationalization that they attempted to preserve this just scale from all further change, to make it the "scale of nature." It was held that early man had consciously or unconsciously "recognized" the overtones and out of them he had derived his musical scale.10

It is unfortunate for the theorizing of these overtone enthusiasts that the "natural" or just-intoned scale has not been universally accepted. On the contrary, in a number of cultures the octave has been carved in quite "unnatural" ways (p. 25). Then, too, in deriving the scale from overtones our ancestors would have had to recognize partial tones as high as the forty-eighth. Yet, in spite of the evidence against the overtone theory it has served to raise the just scale to the status of the diatonic scale of science.

SCALE OF JUST INTONATION

	C	C Sharp	D	D Sharp	E	F	F Sharp
2	24		27		30	32	
3	256		288		320	341·3	
4	1/1		8/9		4/5	3/4	
5	3		27		15	1	
6	3^1		3^3		(5×3)	3^0	

	G	G Sharp	A	A Sharp	B	C
2	36		40		45	48
3	384		426·6		480	512
4	2/3		3/5		8/15	1/2
5	9		5		45	3
6	3^2		5^1		(15×3)	3^1

A Scale with the Prime Number 7

A scale composed of the prime numbers 1, 3, 5, and 7 has been attempted by several people,[11] but it has never been adopted by any large group of musicians.[12] A possible scale of this type is described in the table below.[13]

SCALE WITH THE PRIME 7

	C	C Sharp	D	D Sharp	E	F	F Sharp
2	16		18		20	21	
3	256		288		320	336	
4	1/1		8/9		4/5	16/21	
5	1		9		5	21	
6	3^0		3^2		5^1	(7×3)	

	G	G Sharp	A	A Sharp	B	C
2	24		27	(28)	30	32
3	384		432		480	512
4	2/3		16/27		8/15	1/2
5	3		27	(7)	15	1
6	3^1		3^3	(7^1)	(5×3)	3^0

This scale differs from the others shown so far not only in its use of the prime 7 but also in the fact that its tone symbols have been modulated up a fifth (or down a fourth). That is, the tone symbol 1 which fell on F in the other scales here falls on C.

The Need for Modulation

A glance at the scale tables will show that the Pythagorean scale had whole steps with ratios of 8:9 and smaller steps (not actual half-steps) of 243:256. The just-intoned scale had two whole steps—8:9 and 9:10—and smaller steps of 15:16. The scale with the prime number 7 had three whole steps—8:9, 9:10, and 7:8—and two smaller steps—20:21 and 15:16. All three of these scales, it is clear, made direct modulation virtually impossible. Yet the new

23

harmonic music of the West demanded modulation, and a *do* to *re* interval of 8:9 will not sound like one of 9:10.

If, in an era of modulation, any of these three scales were to be kept, either the listener would have to adjust to serious mistunings or the instrument builder would need so to alter his sound sources that many auxiliary tones sharper or flatter than those already available could be played.[14] Unfortunately the latter practice became common and was at least in part responsible for the cumbersome system of sharps, flats, and other signs with which Western music is still burdened. As an aftermath has come the apparently unending argument over the exact pitch location of the signs, i.e., whether sharps should be pitched higher than flats, or vice versa.

Mean-Tone Temperament[15]

We have noted that music theorists from the time of Aristoxenus on have advocated tempering the intervals. In line with such theorizing is mean-tone temperament, which came into use in western Europe in the seventeenth century and was almost universally accepted during the eighteenth until equal temperament won the day. It is a shaving or flatting of several of the fifths so that the Pythagorean hope of a scale of fifths could actually be fulfilled. With mean-tone temperament, modulations within a few of the most used keys were possible. It was unfortunate, however, that what today are similarly pitched sharps and flats, e.g., C sharp and D flat, were still given different pitch locations and were regarded as different notes.

SCALE OF MEAN-TONE TEMPERAMENT

	C	C Sharp	D	D Sharp	E	F	F Sharp
3	256		286·1		320	342·4	

	G	G Sharp	A	A Sharp	B	C	
3	382·8		428·0		478·6	512	

Equal Temperament

Equal temperament in Western music was accomplished by dividing the octave into twelve equal semitone steps, i.e., equal so far as ratios were concerned but not in terms of the span of frequencies.[16] This scale of equal temperament is the one for which J. S. Bach fought and to which the modern piano is tuned. The ratio of the semitone in the scale of equal temperament is 1 : 1.059.

According to musicological research, it appears that equally tempered scales also occur in the Orient. It is said that the Siamese at times divide their octave into seven equal steps and the Javanese divide theirs into five equal steps.

WESTERN SCALE OF EQUAL TEMPERAMENT

	C	C Sharp	D	D Sharp	E	F	F Sharp
3	256		287.3		322.5	341.6	

	G	G Sharp	A	A Sharp	B	C
3	383.5		430.3		483.2	512

UNITS OF RATIO MEASUREMENT. Either the octave or the semitone of the equally tempered scale could have served as a unit of ratio measurement if a relatively large unit had been desired. Yasser has urged the adoption of the decitone, the centitone and the milli-tone (tenth, hundredth, and thousandth of the tone of the scale of equal temperament) as feasible units.[17] As a small unit the thousandth part of the octave has been suggested. In most general use, however, is the cent, which is a hundredth part of the semitone of the equally tempered scale.[18] The octave in this system of measurement equals 1200 cents, the semitone 200.

Let us from now on attempt to think in terms of these cent units and examine the previously described scales to see how perceptually important the changes from one scale to the next really were. But first we must look at thresholds, at man's ability to discriminate between intervals of differing size.

The Stability of Intervals

Intervals may be distorted, made somewhat larger or smaller, without loss of identity. It is indeed fortunate that this is true, for otherwise the transition from the just-intoned scale to the mean-tone or the equally tempered might have been more difficult to accomplish. Just how much interval distortion can be tolerated it is difficult to say, since the researches in this area are not entirely in agreement. But it does appear that for most people the uniqueness of the fifth is disturbed more easily than that of the third or sixth. Happily enough, the historical changes were in line with this aspect of human psychophysiology. As will be noted in the following table, the fifth was kept at approximately 700 cents in all the Western scales. Even the Siamese and Javanese had scale points which might be thought of as approximating the fifth. The fourth was kept at approximately 500 cents. On the other hand, the third, sixth, and seventh varied more extensively from scale to scale.

Careful work by Pratt and his associates shows that the threshold for perceiving changes in interval quality is approximately 20 cents in the middle of the tonal range.[19] This value checks with the findings of the present author, whose student subjects hear no difference between the fifths of the several scales, between the several fourths (except perhaps where the "7" scale is concerned), or even between the seconds. The difference between the Pythagorean seventh and the mean-tone seventh, which is 27 cents (1110 — 1083), is occasionally perceived. But more subjects discriminate with better than chance accuracy a number of the other larger differences. The scales so far discussed are, then, perceptually as well as mathematically different to some contemporary laymen. However, the vibrato, when present, would tend to make most of these differences imperceptible.

VALUES IN CENTS OF SCALE INTERVALS

	C	D	E	F	G	A	B	C
Pyth.	0	204	408	498	702	906	1110	1200
Just	0	204	386	498†	702	884	1088	1200
M.T.T.	0	193	386	503	697	890	1083	1200
E.T.	0	200	400	500	700	900	1100	1200
Siam.	0 171		343	514	686 857		1029	1200
Javan.*	0	240		480		720	960	1200
"7"	0	204	386	471	702	906	1088	1200

* It has been found that the Ganda eight-string harp of Africa is so tuned that the intervals between the strings all equal 240 cents (K. P. Wachsmann, "An Equal-Stepped Tuning in a Ganda Harp," *Nature*, *165* (London, 1950): 40–41).

† T. E. Simonton, in "A New Integral Ratio Chromatic Scale," *J. Acoust. Soc. Amer.*, *25* (1953): 1167–1170, has devised a chromatic scale with a perfectly symmetrical arrangement of just fourths. He claims that it combines the advantages of the Pythagorean, the just-intoned, and the equally tempered scales.

It is possible that the musicians of several centuries past had even more difficulty than we in perceiving the differences, since their tone-producing sources were markedly cruder than the apparatus of today. But of course the theoreticians expected to find differences. Believing as they did in the perfection of the just-intoned scale, they undoubtedly imagined greater differences than they actually perceived.

PITCH DISCRIMINATION. Let us suppose that one is asked to compare single tones rather than intervals, for example, the Pythagorean and mean-tone D's. Then, of course, pitch discrimination comes into play, and this sensitivity is far keener than that needed to detect differences between intervals. But even though the two D's can be discriminated by many people, the two major seconds cannot. So, despite the fact that pitch discrimination and tolerance for interval change are related, they are not the same.

Equal Temperament, Our Frame of Reference

Western music is today tied rather closely to the piano, and pianos are tuned to equal temperament. Yet there still are theorists who maintain that keen-eared musicians "sense" equal temperament to be a mere compromise. These sensitive people will, they hold, employ just intonation whenever it is possible to do so.[20]

The author has not had the privilege of testing many musically sensitive people. His subjects have, in the main, been laymen, amateur musicians, and teachers of music, and to them he has presented a variety of scales. He has found that if he does not label the scales, the commonest response when the just scale is played is that it is odd, interesting, and not particularly displeasing. Rarely does anyone prefer it to the equally tempered. But if the just scale is presented and labeled, a few of the better-trained musicians, feeling perhaps that they should prefer it, may declare that they like its harmonic possibilities, that its thirds are so much better, etc. When the scales have not been identified, the typical listener appears to feel more comfortable with the scale of equal temperament, the scale of his present culture period. He does not "unconsciously" think in terms of just intonation.

It is true that the great Helmholtz quotes cases where violinists reverted to just intonation whenever their playing was unaccompanied.[21] These observations may or may not have been valid. But modern research paints a different picture. Greene studied the unaccompanied playing of six professional violinists.[22] As might have been anticipated, the accuracy of the intervals varied considerably. But the mean value of each interval was closer to what was advocated by Pythagoras than to that of just intonation. Later work by Nickerson on unaccompanied solo and ensemble performances of the same melody gave very similar results.[23]

Other Possible Scales

So far we have discussed only the Western diatonic scale of seven notes. While it is the basic scale of the West, several other scales have had a substantial degree of popularity. One of these is the pentatonic, where only the F, G, A, C, and D are employed, or, if one prefers, the black notes of the piano—F sharp, G sharp, A sharp, C sharp, and D sharp, i.e., spans of 2 semitones, 2, 3 and finally 2 semitone steps. A number of well-known Scottish tunes are based on this scale and many Chinese as well.

Even at a time when the diatonic scale was more rigidly adhered to than it is today, it was allowable to make occasional use of any one of five other notes not in the scale. These accidentals, as they were called, were thought to give variety or color. When added to the seven diatonic tones there was formed the twelve-semitone scale of the modern piano, i.e., the dodecuple. These twelve tones have been more and more freely used as a scale. The rise of atonal and polytonal music has greatly facilitated their acceptance.

The accidentals have also been employed by Debussy and others in whole-tone music, e.g., C, D, E, F sharp, G sharp, A sharp, C. It has been found that this scale seems strange to many people, who believe that since this is obviously not their accustomed major scale it must be minor—which of course it is not (p. 89).

Scriabin has used a scale whose steps are C, D, E, F sharp, A, B flat to give a distinctive character to his music. Perhaps others will follow him in devising still other scale steps as their personal idiom.

Scales made up of a variety of microtones have been suggested at one time or another. One of the most bizarre was that of the fifth-century Chinese, Chien Lohtze, who proposed a 360-note scale to match the 360 days he thought made up the year. It is quite clear that this theorist had done no research on the psychology of human perception.

The Hindus have a 22-note scale which can be sung with consider-able accuracy. The Moravian musician Haba, who has advocated splitting the semitone into a number of microtones, claims to be able to sing intervals as small as one-sixtieth of an octave. But even if he is able to do this, he would lack appreciative listeners.

Our interest is clearly not in freakish virtuosity but in those extensions to our present scale that could prove successful. A number of musicians and psychologists have seen the quarter-tone as the next logical development, partly because our music system now operates on a semitone base and the quarter-tone is half of the semitone. A number of quarter-tone pianos and organs have been built and a considerable body of quarter-tone music has been written.[24]

It will be recalled that the threshold for interval discrimination is approximately 20 cents. But this is the value at which Pratt's observers could detect the differences only half of the time. To be completely functional, however, an interval should be discriminated properly not half of the time but all the time. The value for the smallest interval that will be perceived as different 100 per cent of the time Pratt has found to be about 50 cents, the span of the quarter-tone in the equally tempered scale.[25] Quarter-tones, then, are psychologically feasible. But no interval much smaller than the quarter-tone would seem to be acceptable except to the person of extraordinary sensitivity.[26]

An interesting demonstration for the musically unsophisticated is to play one octave in quarter-tones and to ask what has been heard. A common answer is that the chromatic scale of two octaves has been played. Most persons will find at least a few of the quarter-tone intervals pleasing. Generally, the most pleasing quarter-tone span is the one that extends from a bass of C to a tone between the minor and major third, an interval which approximates one in Siamese music. In fact, this interval is typically rated as pleasanter than either of the seconds or sevenths.[27]

Summary

In this chapter we have seen that the basic scale of Western music has been for centuries the seven-note diatonic, whose precise ratios have varied from time to time. The Pythagoreans had held that a succession of twelve musical fifths of ratio 2 : 3 could be arranged to cover seven octaves, i.e., there would be a return to the starting letter some seven octaves higher. Hence the primes 1 and 3, which alone appear in the ratio of their musical fifth, were, according to the Pythagoreans, the only primes needed in the building of the diatonic scale.

It was early noted that the twelve Pythagorean fifths were a trifle too large to squeeze into seven octaves, and again and again there arose the hope that other primes might be used in the scale ratios. The first to be accepted was the 5, which appeared in what was termed just intonation. The addition of this prime was accomplished by flatting the third, the sixth, and the seventh. Since the new scale ratios facilitated work in harmony, there developed a school of thought which subscribed to the notion that the just-intoned scale steps had been borrowed from positions on the overtone or harmonic series. It was held that man had recognized, consciously or unconsciously, the tonal partials and had made use of them in creating his scale. Such a philosophy inspired theologians to call on the Deity for support of His scale and led early scientists to regard the just scale as "natural." The scale became so honored that all efforts to alter it met with tremendous opposition, even though the arguments for its "God-given quality" and its "naturalness" were invalid.

Although there were attempts to bring in primes other than 3 and 5, the more lasting changes to the scale came with mean-tone and equal temperament. The former made a limited modulation possible, while equal temperament allowed for free modulation ranging through all keys. In equal temperament, as the term implies, the octave is divided into twelve equal intervals.

31

Taking the cent, or hundredth part of the semitone of the equally tempered scale, as the unit of scale measurement, it was found that tolerance for interval change is approximately 20 cents. Since many of the scale changes had been less than 20 cents in magnitude they probably caused but little difficulty except to a few theorists and musically sensitive persons. Scale changes above threshold magnitude do exist, however, and most persons can tell that the several scales are not identical.

There is no evidence that we hesitantly accept equal temperament for practical reasons only, i.e., solely because it allows modulation, and really prefer to do our musical thinking in terms of just intonation. Psychological research discloses no outstanding preference for the "natural" scale and suggests that whenever unaccompanied violinists deviate in their playing from equal temperament their intervals are actually closer to those of Pythagorean intonation. On the other hand, there is no reason to suppose that the diatonic scale of equal temperament is Western music's final scale form. For as Mursell says, "Any scale is a construct of the social mind, a phenomenon of social agreement."[28] The diatonic has had many rivals— pentatonic, dodecuple, whole-tone, etc.—and in some circles is now being modified to include quarter-tones. Quarter-tone spans of 50 cents can be heard as intervals and therefore are perceptually reasonable scale units. Research indicates that microtones much smaller than 50 cents are more rarely perceived as qualitatively unique by the typical listener and hence are not functional for music.

A number of scale properties still remain to be described. But they can better be understood after more attention has been given to the interval, in particular to the role the interval plays in melody. The interval and its role, then, will concern us in the next chapter.

Notes

1] For an authoritative consideration of tonal characteristics see S. S. Stevens, ed., *Handbook of Experimental Psychology*, N.Y., Wiley, 1951.

2] The value 435 d.v. (double vibrations), or 435 cycles, indicates that the sound-giving body, be it a string, a fork, or a column of air, is vibrating 435 times a second.

3] For the sake of convenience, the names given the intervals in Western music will be employed here even though the terms have proved to be definitely misleading to the unsophisticated. The octave, so called because it makes use of eight white notes on the piano, is better described as a span of 12 semitones; the fifth, which involves five white notes, as seven semitones; the fourth, named for the four white notes used, as five semitones; etc.

4] C. Stumpf, a psychologist who was a pioneer in the area of musical aesthetics, was perhaps the first to show that naïve subjects confuse the two tones of an octave more than any other two tones. See his *Tonpsychologie*, Leipzig, Hirzel, 1883, 1890.

5] In A.D. 600 Pope Gregory the Great ordered a single name to be given all tones the frequency ratio of which is 1:2 (or to some power of 2).

6] The fourth is merely the octave minus the fifth, i.e., 12 semitones minus 7 equals 5 semitones.

7] M. F. Meyer, *The Musician's Arithmetic*, Boston, Ditson, 1929.

8] Since F is not only the starting point but also the fifth above A sharp, it can be either 3^0 or 3^{12}.

9] A vibrating body, be it a string or a column of air, vibrates not only as a whole but also in sections. Thus, one-half the body gives forth its unique tone (the octave), one-third gives its own pitch (octave plus a fifth), etc. These auxiliary tones are termed overtones and with the fundamental tone constitute the series of partials or harmonics. The ratios of the fundamental to these harmonics are as 1:2, 1:3, 1:4, 1:5, etc.

10] A somewhat similar concept occurred in the naïve geometry of architecture. Here, it was held, man was somehow psychobiologically in tune with the root squares, the golden sections, and the other "God-blessed" forms used so much by the Greeks of the classical period.

11] The experimental aesthetician M. F. Meyer has made use of the small primes 1, 3, 5, and 7 in a neurological interpretation of musical intervals (*The Musician's Arithmetic*).

12] It is of some sociopsychological interest that in the sixteenth century a taboo existed against the use in Western music of prime numbers not in the series 1 to 5. The reason offered was that since God in His Wisdom had arranged for only six directions—above, below, before, after, right, and left—the number 6 had metaphysical significance. To use a larger prime would be to go contrary to God's Will. The classical Chinese had a similar rationalization although they spoke of only five "proper" directions—up, down, before, after, and center.

33

13] A scale developed by H. W. Poole, an American organ builder (see Meyer reference, note 11).

14] That the listener will adjust to mistunings can be demonstrated. Several anthropologists have reported that their pitch discrimination is temporarily impaired after long contact with alien intervals, and one such claim has been checked. It has been noted that the inland Chinese, whose musical instruments tend to be carelessly tuned, make poorer scores on pitch discrimination tests than do the coastal and American-born Chinese, for whom exact tuning is more a part of the culture (P. R. Farnsworth, "An Historical, Critical, and Experimental Study of the Seashore–Kwalwasser Test Battery," *Genet. Psychol. Monogr., 9* (1931): 291–393.)

15] H. H. Dräger, "Zur mitteltönigen und gleichschwebenden Temperatur," *Bericht über die Wissenschaftliche Bachtagung der Gesellschaft für Musikforschung, Leipzig, 23. bis 26. Juli 1950*, pp. 389–404.

16] O. I. Jacobsen defends the idea that the tempered and the "natural" scale each has its place for contemporary performance. ("Harmonic Blending in the Natural versus the Tempered Scale," *J. Musicol., 2* (1941): 126–132.)

17] J. Yasser, *A Theory of Evolving Tonality*, N.Y., Amer. Lib. Musicol., 1932.

18] Another unit of ratio measurement is the *savart*, which has a span of approximately 4 cents.

19] C. C. Pratt, "Quarter-Tone Music," *J. genet. Psychol., 35* (1928): 286–293.

Thresholds for intervals made from pure tones are slightly different from those formed from musical, i.e., impure, tones. Pratt's data were elicited from psychologically trained observers. Hence, it is reasonable to suppose that the more typical listener would have a threshold somewhat above 20 cents. The reader should not confuse threshold and sensitivity, terms which are negatively related. Where the listener's threshold is *low*, i.e., where he perceives the interval quality as changed after very little expansion or contraction of the pitch span, he is said to be *highly* sensitive.

20] Other theorists worry because much highly rated music was composed with meantone intonation in mind but is now played with equal temperament.

21] H. L. F. Helmholtz, *On the Sensations of Tone*, N.Y., Longmans, Green, 1912, p. 486. See also A. C. Roncalio, "Just and Equal Temperament," *J. Musicol., 3* (1941): 120–122.

22] P. C. Greene, "Violin Intonation," *J. Acoust. Soc. Amer., 9* (1937), 43–44.

23] J. F. Nickerson, "Intonation of Solo and Ensemble Performance of the Same Melody," *J. Acoust. Soc. Amer., 21* (1949): 593–595.

24] Max Meyer (*The Musician's Arithmetic*) and others have long advocated the introduction of quarter-tones into our music system and have argued that a new staff which omits key signatures and the usual signs is in order. One such staff has been suggested with the staff lines arranged as are the piano's black keys. The only sign needed in this new staff would be for the quarter-tone. See also P. Moon, "A Proposed Musical Notation," *J. Franklin Inst., 253* (1952): 125–143.

25] C. C. Pratt, *op. cit.*

26] An organ with a 31-note scale to carry out the harmonic ideas of the seventeenth-century mathematician Christiaan Huygens has been built by the Dutch physicist, A. D. Fokker ("Equal Temperament and the Thirty-one-keyed Organ," *Sci. Month.*, *81* (1955): 161–166). The basic interval of approximately 39 cents would appear to be on the very border of practicality at best.

27] P. R. Farnsworth and C. F. Voegelin, "Dyad Preferences at Different Intensities," *J. Appl. Psychol.*, *12* (1928): 148–151.

28] J. L. Mursell, "Psychology and the Problem of the Scale," *Music. Quart.*, *32* (1946): 564–573.

CHAPTER THREE

The Interval

I N the preceding chapter it was shown that the building blocks of music are the tonal intervals. This chapter will continue the examination of these musical constituents and will pay special attention to a number of characteristics they have been said to possess.[1]

Distinctive Quale

It goes almost without saying that each interval has its own distinctive quale, the psychological characteristics by which it is recognized. We have already mentioned the fact that, physically speaking, the interval may be a number of things. The tones of the major sixth, for example, may have frequencies of 256 and 432, 256 and 426·6, 256 and 430·3, 384 and 648, or even 512 and 864 d.v., to mention only a few. But all these physically different stimulus configurations have a psychological quale in common, a major sixthness. The major sixth, like all other intervals, has stability within a margin of span tolerance (p. 26).

A number of researchers who are interested in phenomenological description have attempted to describe verbally the several interval characteristics. The results have not been strikingly successful. It is unlikely that an octave rendered by a flute will be described in the same terms as will the identical interval presented by a piano, a violin, or a tuba. However, the reader can check his own reactions to intervals played on a variety of instruments and see if the fifth always sounds dilute, hollow, and harsh; the fourth rich, harsh, and coarse; the second gritty and grating; the third mellow and sweet; the sixth luscious and juicy-mellow; the seventh astringent and sharp-rough; and the octave smooth, as the Edmunds and Smith observers found them.[2]

The reader will probably already know that by much practice he can improve his ability to recognize the intervals. He will possibly also know that descending intervals are more difficult to recognize than the ascending (p. 39). If he tests himself he will very likely find that he, like Ortmann's subjects,[3] is relatively poorer in his recognition of minor intervals and particularly of minor sixths, sevenths, and thirds, and, like Maltzew's observers,[4] poor also in the identification of tritones. Recognition, he will find, tends to be best in the middle register, the tonal range most used in music. But whether the greater use of the middle range has made recognition better or better recognition has forced greater usage is as yet unanswered.

Vibrato, Tremolo, and Trill

Vibrato concerns physical spans too small to be perceived as intervals. Although the violinist or vocalist produces a series of definite pitch spans whenever he employs his vibrato, the listener reacts as if he were hearing embellished single tones. He does not hear the two pitches as such but rather as one pitch midway between them, and he continues for a time to hear a single tone even though the performer oscillates his tone over a wider and wider pitch span.

Whenever the embellishment has become so marked as to be quite extreme, the effect is more likely to be termed a tremolo than a

37

vibrato, although no definite boundary line can be drawn to separate the two. If the extent of oscillation becomes greater still, somewhere between three-quarters of a tone and two whole tones, the listener ceases to hear a single wobbly tone and instead perceives an oscillation between two tones, a successive interval, or trill. The trill, then, emerges as qualitatively different from the tremolo and the vibrato. The two pitches are now heard as separate tones which may alternate even at vibrato rate. In making a trill the performer often over-reaches his interval. He does this to compensate for the fact that his listener tends to underestimate the size of the trill just as he does the extent of the vibrato.[5]

Apparent Pitch of Intervals

After stating that an interval has two boundary pitches, it may seem paradoxical to speak of interval pitch as if the interval were a single tone. Yet each interval is an entity and as such possesses a relative pitch which even naïve listeners can recognize.

Many years ago while at work on the pitch of intervals, Stumpf, a German psychologist, proposed a principle which he supposed had universal application.[6] He held that the pitch of the lower component of an interval is always dominant over that of the upper, that is, that the pitch of the lower is so much more obvious that it has the greater effect on the pitch of the interval configuration. In his experiments he presented two octave intervals to his listeners, one whose frequency span was approximately from 130 to 260 d.v. and the other from 260 to 520. His audience reported that it was the apparent pitch of the first interval which was more unlike the pitch of 260 d.v. (approximately middle C). They seemed, then, to be attending more to the pitches of the lower components.

Stumpf's generalization seems in line with the dictum of the harmonists who state that the normal orientation of a tonal pattern is from below upward. To quote Watt: "Rising makes the impression of tonal recession, falling, that of approach. We begin a scale involuntarily from below, not from above, and we end it below again."[7] Perhaps this tendency toward upward movement is responsible for the fact, mentioned above, that ascending intervals are easier to recognize than the descending.

Which is more unlike middle C in pitch?   Which is higher in pitch?

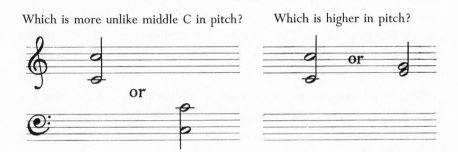

Unfortunately, the British psychologist Valentine was unable to verify this principle of Stumpf's, for his subjects regarded the pitch of the higher interval as more unlike that of 260 d.v.[8] When he further asked for a comparison of the pitch of a certain octave with that of a smaller interval which lay wholly within this octave, his subjects voted for the octave as the higher in pitch. Thus, it is quite apparent that his subjects were, in each instance, more impressed by the higher pitch.

Puzzled by these conflicting sets of data, the present writer performed two experiments along similar lines, one in the early 1920's and the other fifteen years later.[9] In his researches he attempted to learn whether these divergent findings might not somehow be related to the fact that Stumpf had used musically naïve men in his experiments while the majority of Valentine's subjects had been schoolchildren with some musical training. It was the author's theory that children, sopranos, and well-trained musicians generally have had so much experience in melody hunting, in looking at the upper lines of their music, that the higher pitches of a complex of tones now stand out for them.

To verify this idea that melody hunting is an important variable in establishing the pitch of intervals, the writer tested relatively unmusical persons, sopranos, contraltos and altos, and male singers. The resulting data showed that the relatively unmusical, and to some extent the male singers, voted in line with Stumpfian theory. The sopranos, on the other hand, and many of the other singers of both sexes behaved as had Valentine's schoolchildren. Clearly, then, Stumpf's rule must be modified to embrace the effects of training in melody hunting. Stumpf was correct in stating that the pitch of the lower component of an interval is dominant, but only for the musically untrained and for some basses. For other persons it is the higher component which more markedly affects the pitch of the interval.

The Major-Minor Effect

Misled by the terms "major" and "minor," many people assume that the major sixth, for example, calls forth a major or joyous affect and the minor sixth a minor or gloomy-feeling tone. It can easily be demonstrated, however, that intervals, as such, have no major or minor characteristics. Moreover, the major and minor chords, the musical structures which *do* possess such attributes (p. 88), are each composed of a major and a minor interval. It would have been far better, therefore, had more writers followed the lead of Alchin and the small number of bolder harmonists who have changed the interval labels from "major" and "minor" to "large" and "small."[10] To term a sixth a "large sixth" is to impute to it no special psychological characteristics.

Finality Effects

A simple demonstration of finality effect can be made by running over a succession of C's and F's on the keyboard and asking the listeners for an appropriate stopping point. Among listeners steeped in Western music there will be little argument. The stop will almost invariably be made on an F. Yet the vote would have been for one of the C's if the demonstration had been immediately preceded by several renditions of the C scale. The repeated playing of this scale with C as the first note will make C the tonic or keynote, which some have called a "magnet tone." Because of the emphasis on C, all melodies ending on this note, or intervals and chords with it as a bass, will seem more restful, more finished, more final. Even an ending that ordinarily is not regarded as at all restful will take on this characteristic of finality if it is listened to as an ending many times.[11] We see here, then, a principle of return, a desire to come back to an emphasized note.

But, the reader may well ask, why was so much emphasis on C needed to make it the more appropriate ending? Why was a stop on F otherwise the more final? The answer would appear to depend on the way Western scales are constructed. In the key of F, C is a perfect fifth above F; and the fifth, or dominant, is without much doubt the second most important note of the scale. C is the upper boundary note of both the major and minor chords (F, A, C; F, A flat, C). On the other hand, F is only the subdominant (a perfect fourth above C) in the key of C and is heard in that capacity far less often than C is heard as the dominant in the key of F. Hence, experience leads us to structure C's and F's with F as the tonic, with the notes in the key of F.

If the listener had heard a succession of unemphasized C's and G's, his inclination would have been to vote for a C as the more appropriate ending. This time it is C which is the subdominant in the

41

key of G and G the dominant in the key of C. Therefore C is the more likely keynote and gives the better ending.

A second principle which operates in inducing finality effects is that of falling inflection.[12] Just as in many languages the voice rises with an unresolved question and falls with an assertion, so in Western music there is a feeling of resolution in the lower tone of a successively played interval or the lowest point of a descending melodic line. This phenomenon has appeared in the data of a host of researchers and is quite possibly linked to the fact, mentioned earlier, that a scale is normally begun from below and is ended as a descent. The effect of falling inflection is enhanced by a slowing of the tempo.

It also appears that size of interval is related to restfulness and finality. Thus, Zener has shown that increasing the size of successive intervals from one to eleven semitones rather steadily decreases the finality effect.[13] But with chords the effect of size of span is quite different, for the larger chords may be as restful as or even more restful than the smaller.

Striking finality effects can be obtained by playing a successive interval (or broken chord or melody) where the ratio of the frequency of one of the tones is to that of the other as 2 or some multiple of 2 is to some other number. For example, in the interval of the perfect fifth, whose ratio is 2:3, the 2 is the point of more rest. This power-of-2 effect is often termed the Lipps-Meyer law after the eminent psychologists Lipps[14] and Meyer,[15] who first worked in the area and postulated similar theories to explain the phenomenon.

Much of the factual side of the Lipps-Meyer law is unquestioned, but considerable controversy has arisen over the explanation of what it describes. Is there some neurological reason for the phenomenon which makes it universally applicable, or should it be subsumed under the co-principles of emphasis and return and applied only to certain cultures? Thirty years or more ago, the present author was inclined to accept a neurological position similar to that of the earlier theorists. In fact, in researches undertaken in the 1920's, he thought he had found lesser but still measurable finality effects associated with the ratio symbol 3, smaller effects with 5, and still smaller effects with 7.[16] In these experiments he had employed stimuli tuned in equal temperament which he hoped would approximate the symbols 3, 5 and 7. A decade later he was able to use tones pitched to just intonation, i.e., with quite exact tuning.[17] But this time these lesser finality effects did not appear.[18] His inability to validate the earlier work strengthened his belief that the neurological factor, as reflected in these primes, was not of major importance in finality effects.

Among those who have attempted to show that the Lipps-Meyer effect is the resultant of cultural conditioning rather than biophysical structure is Updegraff, whose research was arranged to determine whether the conventional resolution of a suggested harmony or the "power of 2" was the more influential in determining finalty.[19] The former, she found, appeared to be somewhat stronger. More important, perhaps, was her discovery that Chinese students regarded Chinese melodies as more finished and restful while Americans voted for their own melodies. In other words, the decisive element for Updegraff's subjects was familiarity, not the pitch relationships of the endings.

Others have found that American-reared Chinese give responses much like those of Caucasian Americans. Orientals recently from the coast of China feel the finality effects of our Western music less keenly than American Chinese, while those from the Chinese interior, where our style of music is not so well known, do not share out notions of finality. Because of these racial-national differences in response, it would appear that cultural conditioning is the more likely explanation for the Lipps-Meyer power-of-2 effect. It is conceivable, however, that in addition to the "pulling power" which practice would give the tone symbol 2, there may also be some less important neurological or other biophysical causation.[20]

Interval Resolutions

Harmony textbooks teach that the successively played intervals that make up the diatonic scale can be divided into those that are "restless" or unresolved and others that have repose and finality. The table below shows the traditional resolutions in the tonic sol-fa system. Any other intervals, such as *do–re* or *do–ti*, yield a "restless" or unresolved effect.

RESOLUTIONS

Tonic Sol-Fa System	Scale Letter in Key of C
re to *do*	D to C
re to *mi*	D to E
fa to *mi*	F to E
sol to *do*	G to C
la to *sol*	A to G
ti to *do*	B to C

Half of the resolutions listed in the table are quite obviously examples of the principle of return. Wherever C has been sufficiently emphasized to achieve keynote status, all successive intervals ending on C, that is, on *do*, will display the finality effect. Thus, the descending major second *re–do*, the descending fifth or ascending fourth *sol–do*, and the ascending minor second *ti–do* all return to the keynote. If scaled in just intonation the intervals are seen to end on a symbol 2 tone (9 to 2, 3 to 2, and 15 to 2) as does the *la–sol* interval (27 to 3, or 9 to 2).[21] These resolutions, then, can be described in terms of the Lipps-Meyer effect. It is interesting to note that performers often sharp the *ti* a little, anticipating, as it were, the resolution. (It will be recalled that the ratios of equally tempered scales do not employ such small numbers. However, they approximate the values given here for just intonation and can presumably be described similarly.)

The chief chord in the key of C major is C, E, G, which occurs not only with C as the bass but in two other positions as well. In the first inversion, E, G, C, the E (or *mi*) is the bass, and in the second inversion, G, C, E, the chord is based on G (or *sol*). Hence, *mi* and *sol* become magnet tones, weaker than *do*, but effective nontheless. *Mi* "pulls" *re* and *fa* to it and *sol* "pulls" *la*. Of the two, *mi* makes a stronger ending than the *sol*, since the first inversion with *mi* as its bass is more used in music than the second inversion. It is apparently for this reason that *mi* needs little or no resolution.

It would be interesting to speculate about the reactions of people who had heard only music in minor keys. The expectation would be that since *me* (E♭) would now replace *mi* as the much-heard bass of the chief chord, the ascending major second (*re–mi*) and the descending minor second (*fa–mi*) would no longer display marked finality. But there is little probability that people will ever be so tonally confined.

Tonality

At this point it is reasonable to ask how any music can escape having a marked tonic. We note the modernist's interest in atonality and we meet much enthusiasm for polytonality, which the layman may erroneously regard as another form of atonality. We are also aware that the Oriental, although perceiving finality in his own music, fails to sense the tonalities of our Western music. If the tonalities are really there, why does he not perceive them?

The Oriental's lack of sensitivity for our tonics simply underscores the point that tonality is, in the last analysis, what one puts into the music. It is a subjective matter. The Oriental, unfamiliar as he is with the Western music system, needs to hear our resolutions over a considerable period of time before he is equipped to appreciate our expectancies. But after a time he can learn to share experiences with us even as we, in time, can learn to react "properly" to the nuances of some of the Eastern systems. Musical sensitivities are culturally (but not racially) bound.

In creating his earlier atonal, or keyless, music Schönberg tried to insure that no tone would be emphasized above its neighbors and so acquire keynote status. His method for achieving this atonality barred the repetition of any one of the chromatic scale's twelve tones until the other eleven had all been played. As Schönberg had hoped, this self-imposed rule yielded music which seemed, at least on the first few hearings, to possess no tonality; it led to no feelings of finality. Yet many persons have saturated themselves with Schönberg's music to the point where they have begun to read a modicum of tonality into his music. Atonality, regardless of what Schönberg thought, is a relative matter after all.

Milhaud and others have for some time been composing polytonal music. Although to many it sounds keyless, from two to six keys are functioning at once in the several melodies of the musical fabric.[22] Attention to any one melodic line will disclose an obvious tonic. Yet the lay listener normally focuses his attention on the complex, not on a single strand, so that to him the music is virtually atonal.

Although we speak somewhat carelessly of the evolution of music, it is more accurate to talk simply in terms of cultural changes. We know that "primitives" the world over tend to have weakly structured music systems and that they probably have somewhat less feeling than we for Western tonality.[23] Of our own early music we know little or nothing. By the time the records of the Western world were such that its music system could be described with reasonable accuracy, polymodality was already in vogue. But over the years the modes gradually disappeared until only the major and minor remained. Late in the sixteenth century the stage was set for strong tonality as we now know it. Tonality is still with us in spite of the endeavors of the atonalists, but whether it will be with us several centuries hence in its present strength is anyone's guess.

46

Consonance and Dissonance

Textbooks on harmony state flatly that the octave, the fourth, the fifth, the thirds, and the sixths are concordant or consonant, while the seconds, sevenths, and all diminished and augmented intervals are discordant or dissonant. These books, however, have little or nothing to offer the student who quite properly asks what makes the minor seventh dissonant or the minor third consonant. The student may know that he prefers the dissonance of the minor seventh to the concordance of the minor third.[24] He may also realize that a musical detective can generally find some musical context in which almost any dissonance will seem highly agreeable. It is clear that the traditional conceptions of consonance and dissonance do not so readily apply to the present, and that there can, in fact, be no unchanging definition of either.

Among the rationalizations offered for the consonance-dissonance classification, the most accepted, perhaps because of the prestige of the theorist, has been that proposed by Helmholtz.[25] According to this scientist, the consonant intervals are those whose fundamentals and/or overtones are free from the roughness caused by beats.[26] Smoothness, then, is the Helmholtzian criterion of consonance. Krueger has offered a similar theory of beating difference-tones.[27] It is remarkable how these theories have persisted in the face of numerous refutations. One need only arrange for one of the two tones of the interval to be piped to the left ear and the other to the right to see that all psychological effects are largely unchanged even when the possibility of air-borne beats has been eliminated. Moreover, no beats can be created by the sounding of successively played intervals. Yet even Helmholtz classified these latter just as he did the simultaneously sounded ones. Here is an example of name magic, for an interval without beats is branded as dissonant simply because the same interval with beats is dissonant.

Stumpf's theory of fusion can be objected to on similar grounds.[28] For when he says that the consonant interval tends to fuse into a unitary impression which defies analysis, he is quite obviously speaking solely of the simultaneously sounded interval. Successively played intervals can be easily separated into their component tones by the musically untrained as well as the trained, and the listener is always certain that he is hearing two tones. But with the simulta- neously sounded interval, with the well-fused octave particularly, there may be moments of doubt for many persons.

A theory stressing the internal structure of the interval was pro- posed by Lipps.[29] According to his view, the consonant intervals are those with simple ratios, and the dissonances those with the more complex ratios. Thus, the consonant fifth has the simple ratio of $2:3$ and the dissonant seventh the more complex $8:15$.

There are many difficulties with Lipps's theory. One of the most serious, perhaps, is its failure to cover the fact that the consonant interval can, within limits, be stretched or squeezed, the ratio made more complex, without an apparent change in the interval quale.[30] If the interval is still recognizable as, say, the perfect fifth, it will be rated as consonant no matter how much larger or smaller it has been made or how complex its ratio has become.

The hypothesis of adaptation, that consonance depends on the number of times an individual, or his ancestors, has heard a given interval, has been supported both by Ogden[31] and by Moore.[32] Although the two men differ in the details of their theories, they agree in employing in an explanatory sense the once popular but now discarded biological doctrine of the inheritance of acquired charac- teristics.[33] Hence, we shall not consider their ideas further except to note that they have both suggested the possibility that consonance is not absolute, fixed once and for all. If such a suggestion were followed, the theorists might then go a step forward, drop the

consonance-dissonance dichotomy, and replace it with a continuum. This would indeed be a gain for musical theory.

So far we have considered theories which have identified consonance with smoothness, with fusion, with simplicity of interval ratio, and with stage of cultural and individual adaptation. These four criteria appear to be so dissimilar that one wonders whether their proponents had the same phenomenon in mind. That they probably did not has been quite well demonstrated by several studies in which persons have been asked to judge intervals first in terms of smoothness, then for blending, and later on for fusion.[34] Three quite different sets of judgments emerge. They are so different, in fact, that the early Seashore *Sense of Consonance Test,* whose directions asked for judgments on all three criteria at once, proved quite unworkable and was abandoned.[35] The test subjects became hopelessly confused and ended by rating the intervals in terms of their agreeableness.

In their studies of consonance, the theorists of the past largely ignored the fact that the human organism is capable of learning. Inherent in their theories was the assumption that a given interval should call forth identical responses in all people regardless of the extent of their musical training. But as Cazden says: "The difficulties in the study of consonance and dissonance dissolve as soon as we realize that these qualities are not inherent in perception as such but are learned responses, adaptations to an existing pattern of the social group."[36]

A successively sounded major third is perceptually different from a simultaneously played third. A major third in a Bach work is quite different from a major third in a whole-tone composition. A major third has a different effect on a Hottentot and a European theatregoer. A major third is not an abstraction. It is composed of two tones which may be played together or one after the other, which may be played as a part of this composition or that, and which may be heard by a person of our own or some other culture.[37] But to speak of the

major third (or of any other interval) as a consonance is to do no more than parrot a dogma. Musical science would be the better were this concept dropped from the scholarly literature.

Summary

The music student knows that all but the tone-deaf can readily learn to recognize the several intervals of the diatonic and chromatic scales. But what he may not know is that each interval span can, within certain limits, be stretched or squeezed without harm to its distinctive interval quality. He will find that interval uniqueness is only one facet in the composite of psychological effects on the listener. The register of the interval, the rate and loudness of its playing, the timbre of the instrument on which it is played, and the melodic and harmonic contours it helps to form all have their part in creating what each listener has learned to want. Hence, the interval as an abstraction or in isolation has only slight musical significance. What is of real importance is the interval in some specific musical context.

The simultaneous playing of two tones forms, by definition, a simultaneous interval, and the sounding of first one tone and then another a successive interval. When the two tones are rapidly alternated yet are still perceived as two tones, a trill is produced. The trill differs from the vibrato and the tremolo in that the latter are heard as single pitches. The trill, then, is a successive interval, while the vibrato and the tremolo are but ornamented single tones. Although composed of two easily localized tones, each interval is felt to possess a definite pitch level. If the listener has been trained to "melody hunt" among the higher voices, the top boundary tone is more likely to give the interval its pitch location. But if the listener has been attending to lower registers it will be the lower boundary tone which provides the pitch.

Intervals possess a number of perceptual characteristics, but although certain intervals are traditionally labeled "major" or "minor," no one of them displays major or minor effects. Such effects appear only as phenomena of chords and modes.

In Western music a number of intervals are regarded as restful, as yielding the effect of finality, whereas others are looked upon as unresolved. Certain theorists tend to be impressed by the fact that, other things being equal, it is the interval of simple ratio that calls forth the greatest feeling of finality and rest in persons steeped in Western music. These men regard finality effects as physiologically engendered even though members of other cultures often fail to find the well-resolved intervals of the West to be restful. Other, more sociopsychologically minded theorists have offered habituation as their main explanatory principle. At the moment, however, the issue is still unclear. The formalists[38] and those given to biological explanations may be correct in their belief that the human organism is natively geared to feel the simple-ratio intervals as the more restful. But it is a fact that continued experience with a so-called unresolved interval will lead to a growing feeling of rest and finality. Even atonal music becomes familiar in time.

Most theorists and composers are beginning to see that an interval can be evaluated only in terms of its context and that labeling certain intervals consonant or dissonant is a stumbling block to musical creativity and appreciation. No interval is, per se, unmusical even when it cannot be formed from diatonic or chromatic notes. But since the listener of any culture is to some degree a traditionalist, he must be taught to like the rarely used and the unfamiliar, and these must be presented with caution. Indeed, music history is in large part the story of the handling of innovations, of the gradual acceptance of what was once musically unacceptable.

Notes

1] A number of the phenomena we shall be describing concern chords and melodies as well as intervals and could quite logically have been treated in other chapters. The reader must forgive the rather arbitrary decision to consider them here.

2] E. M. Edmunds and M. E. Smith, "The Phenomenological Description of Musical Intervals," *Amer. J. Psychol.*, *34* (1923):287–291.

3] O. Ortmann, "On the Melodic Relativity of Tones," *Psychol. Monog.*, *35*, No. 1 (1926): 1–47.

4] C. v. Maltzew, "Das Erkennen sukzessiv gegebener musikalischer Intervalle in den äussern Tonregionen," *Zsch. f. Psychol.*, *64* (1913): 161–257.

5] C. E. Seashore, "The Vocal Trill," *Mus. Ed. J.*, *29*, No. 3 (1943): 40.

6] C. Stumpf, *Tonpsychologie*, Leipzig, Hirzel, 1883, 1890.

7] H. J. Watt, *The Psychology of Sound*, Cambridge, Cambridge U. Press, 1917.

8] C. W. Valentine, "The Aesthetic Appreciation of Musical Intervals among School Children and Adults," *Brit. J. Psychol.*, *6* (1913): 190–216.

9] P. R. Farnsworth, "Notes on the Pitch of a Combination of Tones," *Brit. J. Psychol.*, *15* (1924): 82–85; "The Pitch of a Combination of Tones," *Amer. J. Psychol.*, *51*, No. 3 (1938): 536–539.

10] C. A. Alchin, *Applied Harmony*, Los Angeles, published by the author, 1921.

11] P. R. Farnsworth, "The Effect of Repetition on Ending Preferences in Melodies," *Amer. J. Psychol.*, *37* (1926): 116–122.

12] A study which demonstrates the finality effects of falling inflection is that by L. Kaiser, "Contribution to the Psychologic and Linguistic Value of Melody," *Acta Psychol.*, *9* (1953): 288–293.

13] K. E. Zener, "The Perception of Finality in Simple Tonal Sequences as Determined by Pitch," Doctoral Thesis, Harvard U., 1926.

14] A good English language account of the T. Lipps views can be found in volume 2 of *Psychology Classics*, K. Dunlap, ed., Baltimore, Williams and Wilkins, 1926.

15] M. Meyer, "Elements of a Psychological Theory of Melody," *Psychol. Rev.*, *7* (1900): 241–273; "Experimental Studies in the Psychology of Music," *Amer. J. Psychol.*, *14* (1903): 456–478.

16] P. R. Farnsworth, "Atonic Endings in Melodies," *Amer. J. Psychol.*, *36* (1925): 394–400.

17] P. R. Farnsworth, "Further Data Concerning the Lipps-Meyer Law" in "Studies in the Psychology of Tone and Music," *Genet. Psychol. Monog.*, *15*, No. 1 (1934): 40–44.

18] J. Handschin, in *Der Toncharakter: eine Einführung in die Tonpsychologie*, Zürich, Atlantis Verlag, 1948, asserts that if the tones of the scale are arranged in an order corresponding to the number of fifths they are removed from F, then the smaller the order number the more masculine will be the character of the tone. Handschin has apparently identified stability and restfulness with masculinity.

19] R. Updegraff, "A Preliminary Study of the Nature of Finality in Melody," *Proc. Ia. Acad. Sci.*, 23 (1926): 279–282.

20] A Gestalt explanation of the power of the symbol 2 comes from J. L. Mursell who suggests the well-known Law of Prägnanz, which holds that persons tend to perceive objects in the simplest arrangement possible. Since the 2 is the smallest symbol to appear among the scale symbols, it furnishes the simplest possible arrangement and so provides the most satisfying of endings. See J. Mursell's "Psychology and the Problem of the Scale," *Music. Quart.*, 32 (1946): 564–573. A biological explanation of tonality, this time keyed to characteristics of the basilar membrane of the inner ear, has been offered by H. Wunderlich in "Theory of Tonality," *J. Gen. Psychol.*, 37 (1947): 169–176. For the views of a biologically minded musician who believes that the Lipps-Meyer effect is more than a matter of mores, see A. I. Elkus, "Tonal Centers and Central Modalities," *Mus. Teach. Nat. Assoc. Proc. 1949, 43 Ser.* (1951): 203–206. E. Franklin has recently suggested that the principles so far suggested to explain finality effects can be subsumed under one rule. His notion is that the Lipps-Meyer law functions only when "applied to melody formation as subordinate to the movement of the bass or the implied bass." (*Tonality as a Basis for the Study of Musical Talent*, Göteborg, Sweden, Gumperts Förlag, 1956, p. 48.)

21] Actually 9 to 1. The essential nature, however, is not altered by multiplication or division by 2.

22] See Milhaud's *Third Symphony* for an example of six-key polytonality.

23] Most American Indian music, however, shows considerable tonality. See D. P. McAllester, *Enemy Way Music*, Cambridge, Mass., Peabody Museum, 1954.

24] P. R. Farnsworth and C. F. Voegelin, "Dyad Preferences at Different Intensities," *J. Appl. Psychol.*, 12 (1928), 148–151.

25] H. L. F. Helmholtz, *On the Sensations of Tone*, Ellis, trans., N.Y., Longmans, Green, 1912.

26] When two tones which are very close to each other in pitch are sounded together, the amplitude of the resulting sound is periodically augmented and decreased, thus eliciting a throbbing or beating effect. For example, the sounding of two tones whose frequencies are 1000 and 1001 d.v. will yield one beat per second. If the number of beats is over 20, the individual beats are not heard; the effect is merely one of roughness. When, under certain conditions, two tones with, say, frequencies of 8000 and 8700 d.v. are sounded, a difference tone of 700 cycles may be distinctly heard. Before the development of instruments which give visual pictures of sound waves, piano-tuners made use of beat counts in adjusting piano strings. Until recently it was assumed that musicians, too, were relying on beat phenomena to help them tune their instruments. But it now appears that they depend rather on apparent pitch. See J. F. Corso, "Unison Tuning of Musical Instruments," *J. Acoust. Soc. Amer.*, 26 (1954): 746–750.

27] F. Krueger, "Differenztone und Konsonanz," *Arch. Ges. Psychol.*, 1 (1903): 205–275.

28] C. Stumpf, *Tonpsychologie*, Leipzig, Hirzel, 1883, 1890.

29] T. Lipps, *Psychological Classics*, vol. 2, K. Dunlap, ed., Baltimore, Williams and Wilkins, 1926. What might be regarded as a variant of the Lippsian theory is that proposed by D. B. Irvine, "Toward a theory of intervals," *J. Acoust. Soc. Amer.*, 17 (1946): 350–355. Irvine would classify intervals by families on the basis of the length of the composite wave form. By this scheme, the fourth (3:4) and the major sixth (3:5) would belong to one family, the major third (4:5) and the ninth (4:9) to another, etc. In other words, all intervals whose ratios are as 3 to something would be grouped into one classification, 4 to something into another, and 5 to something into still another.

30] J. Peterson and F. W. Smith, "The Range and Modifiability of Consonance in Certain Musical Intervals," *Amer. J. Psychol.*, 42 (1930): 561–572; J. Peterson, "A Functional View of Consonance," *Psychol. Rev.*, 32 (1925): 17–33.

31] R. M. Ogden, *Hearing*, N.Y., Harcourt, Brace, 1924.

32] H. T. Moore, "The Genetic Aspect of Consonance and Dissonance," *Psychol. Monog.*, 17, No. 2 (1914): 1–68.

33] For an excellent refutation of genetic theories of consonance see "An Experimental Test of the Genetic Theory of Consonance" by E. G. Bugg and A. S. Thompson, *J. Gen. Psychol.*, 47 (1952): 71–90.

34] E. G. Bugg, "An Experimental Study of Factors Influencing Consonance Judgments," *Psychol. Monog.*, 45, No. 2 (1933); C. P. Heinlein, "An Experimental Study of the Seashore Consonance Test," *J. Exp. Psychol.*, 8 (1925): 408–433; C. P. Heinlein, "Critique of the Seashore Consonance Test," *Psychol. Rev.*, 36 (1929): 524–543.

35] C. E. Seashore, *Manual of Instructions and Interpretations for Measures of Musical Talent*, N.Y., Columbia Graphophone, 1919.

36] N. Cazden, "Musical Consonance and Dissonance: A Cultural Criterion," *J. Aesth.*, 4 (1945): 3–11.

37] R. W. Lundin, "Toward a Cultural Theory of Consonance," *J. Psychol.*, 28 (1947): 45–49.

38] C. C. Pratt, known through his earlier publications as a formalist who plays down the role of learning in the arts, now espouses what might be called contextual relativism. Although Pratt backs away from cultural relativism and approaches his problems with a physical science rather than a social science bias, his theoretical position would not appear to be in complete opposition to that taken in this book ("The Stability of Aesthetic Judgments," *J. Aesth.*, 15 [1956]: 1–11).

CHAPTER FOUR

Melody

ALTHOUGH intervals have great musical significance, one must usually present a somewhat larger configuration of tones before the layman will feel that music as such really exists. At least for the musically unsophisticated the basic element of music is a series of tones he terms a tune or an air. It is what he can recall and name. He tends to regard most other musical phenomena as the tune's embellishments. This chapter will consider in some detail the tune, what musicians call the melody.

Melody, like so many other concepts in music, is very difficult to define. The best general definition is that a melody is made up of successively sounded intervals and must have some sort of organization. But the nature of that organization has puzzled both the musical theorists and the experimentalists. In the literature is the frequent statement that a melody is a tonal sequence displaying optimum variety within unity. Such a description may have some validity; yet it tells us too little. We still need to know how optimum unity and variety can be identified.[1]

The formalists attempt to state their definitions entirely in terms of tonal stimuli. Certain tonal sequences, they say, are by their very nature properly unified and show optimum variety. There are more than a few formalists who feel that intuition tells them what is proper and optimum. But the majority fall back on the practices of their favorite composers. Only what a Bach, a Beethoven, or perhaps a Brahms regarded as properly melodic can be accepted. These formalists would freeze music at one of its periods. When they are reminded that musical practices are in the process of continual change, they either hold firmly to the rules followed by the earlier elite and frown upon the modernists, or shift models with the thought that absolute principles are only gradually revealed. True, absolutes are implicit in the tonal stimuli and so are fixed and eternal. But man must search them out with the reward of only partial success.

The relativistic position, the one accepted by most social scientists, favors a definition in terms of human learning.[2] It holds that a listener comes to regard a sequence as forming a unity only through hearing it over and over again. Not every sequence, of course, will have the chance of repetition. For all of us live in a social organization which brings to our attention certain sequences and ignores, if it does not actively frown upon, others. But culture is never static. As it changes, its sanctions change. Hence, what was once regarded as properly unified and optimally varied may later be thought of as hackneyed, and what once had too much variety may eventually take on unity.

Many years ago Emerson, employing intervals smaller than our semitones, constructed what might be called microscopic melodies.[3] The sequences seemed to possess little tonality as the musician of the West knows the term. Yet Emerson's subjects learned to regard these unusual patterns as unified and to develop certain expectancies concerning them. Emerson had in effect established a tiny musical subculture.[4]

A melody, then, seems best defined in terms of learning. It is a personal thing, a matter of expectancy. Theoretically speaking, any sequence of tones could conceivably constitute a melody for some culture group. But at any one time and place only a fraction of the many possible will receive official approval. In spite of this, the nonconformist will persist in experimenting with unapproved patterns until, for him at least, these become melodies. The extent to which the radical can convince others that they should accept these sequences is a mark of his greatness.

Principles of Attention and Learning

Ortmann has shown that the laws of primacy, recency, and emphasis, which educational psychologists have found so helpful, also hold for melodies.[5] First and last notes he found to stand out prominently. They often become focal centers for the melody and aid the listener in his quest for unity and coherence. The highest and lowest notes were also seen as attention-getting. Moreover, any one of the remaining notes of the melody could, he found, be made equally or even more prominent by giving it more loudness or emphasizing it in some other way.

Ortmann's observations can easily be verified by analyzing responses to Seashore's *Measure of Tonal Memory*.[6] In this test three- to five-note sequences are played twice, with one of the notes changed on the second rendition. The task is to recognize the change. Now it might be guessed that the three-note melodies would always be the easiest to remember and the five-note the most difficult. But the problem is not so simple. For the difficulty in recall is in part a function of the prominence of the note which has been altered. Altering the first or the last tone, or the highest or the lowest, may produce a radical change in the tonal configuration, regardless of the number of tones in the sequence.[7]

The law of frequency is one of the most important principles in melody formation. The themes of the radical who is composing in some new and unfamiliar idiom seem tuneless, i.e., unmelodic, until they are heard a number of times. The layman who is forced to listen

57

to such material may lament the good old-fashioned melodic music of the past, without realizing that some of what he now calls melodic music his great-grandfather, on first hearing, described as tuneless. Repeated hearing over the years has led to acceptance and, with it, the feeling that this kind of melody now possesses adequate unity and coherence.

Many American laymen and psychologists are hard put at times to understand why musical theorists seem so blind to the importance to their art of the law of frequency, ignoring so completely the function of learning. The explanation appears to be that music theory stems pretty largely from European philosophy, which was long dominated by the great formalist Kant. This or that is so, said the formalists, because *inherent* in the *stimulus configuration* are the qualities that make it this way. The formalists ignore the possibility that reasons may lie in frequency of association, in cultural inheritance.

The present author does not hold to the formalistic position. He feels that many, if not the majority, of explanations necessary for understanding the phenomena of music must be looked for in the habits of the listener, in what he has learned from his personal and culture history.

Melody and Pitch Level

Now and again one may hear of a small child who, after hearing his customary evening lullaby, will complain that "Mama didn't sing my song tonight." Mama, of course, will insist that the song was the same as on previous nights. And so it was, except that it was sung at a pitch level slightly higher or lower than the usual one. For this child and for a tiny fraction of the population, pitch level is an important part of melody. A melody whose *do* is pitched at, say, 440 d.v. will for this extremely small number of persons be psychologically different if *do* is perceptibly raised or lowered.

There was a time when most of the authorities considered the ability to identify pitch level, termed "absolute" or "positive" pitch, the resultant of some Mendelian principle of inheritance and an infallible index of musical precocity. But the facts of the case are not quite as the early theorists described them.[8] We now know that no person can identify accurately by letter every tone given him or can sing or play correctly any demanded pitch. Varying with a number of circumstances, his accuracy will most probably be better for tones whose timbre he knows best. It will, for example, be good for piano tones and poorer for the purer tones from a tuning fork or some laboratory instrument.[9] It will be better for tones in the middle range, in the registers most used in music. It will be poorer for black than for white keys.

A small boy of five studied in the Stanford Psychological Laboratory began, while still in kindergarten, to notice the pitch level of his mother's songs and to "correct" her when her do's were as much as a semitone away from their accustomed pitch level. At this age, however, he could not make such fine discriminations with piano tones, even with those of his home instrument. But in about two years he showed great skill when tested on his own piano, and in another year's time he could do as well on the very different laboratory piano. Still later, his skill became phenomenal with violin and clarinet tones. Here we see a growth in pitch-level skills paralleling growing experience with a variety of timbres.

Persons claiming absolute pitch generally display more skill in recognizing pitch level than do other musically minded persons who make no such claims. Yet the overlap in ability between those willing to claim the ability and the more modest is large.[10] Without practice the high scorers often decrease in skill. Those lower in ability can vastly improve their status with assiduous practice.[11]

After hearing a pitch of 256 d.v. frequency, most of us could play or sing a 512 d.v. pitch with reasonable accuracy. Or if given some kinesthetic cue, if allowed to probe for the lowest or highest note we can sing, some of us could figure, so to speak, where 512 should be. But we definitely would need some sort of reference point. We would be reacting in terms of relative, not absolute, pitch, or so said the early writers. In absolute pitch, on the other hand, there is no need for auditory or kinesthetic reference points, for the reactions are allegedly "intuitive"; the faster they are, the more accurate they will be.

The reader may still be convinced that absolute pitch is a matter of biological inheritance.[12] However, the evidence can even more readily be interpreted as showing either that absolute pitch is but extreme relative pitch, one end of the relative-pitch continuum, or that the two abilities, while perhaps not completely identical, are highly correlated and are both dependent on musical experience.[13] It is a fact familiar to all psychologists that in learning a motor skill an individual at first makes use of a variety of cues or crutches.[14] As the skill improves, less and less attention will be paid these cues. By the time the person has achieved real mastery over his task, he can and does forget his earlier aids. In fact, if he tries to use them, he will be likely not only to slow his performance but seriously to harm its quality. He does his best if he behaves in an unthinking, "intuitive" fashion. Thus it is with the learning of absolute pitch.

Some years ago the author developed his own accuracy in recognizing violin A (440 d.v.) to the point of less than an eighth-tone error. At first he found it necessary to hum the lowest note he could manage, taking this note as a point of reference to "figure" the A position. After many weeks of effort, the need for the audible humming disappeared, but for a time he still needed to imagine the humming. Later, this need also vanished and the A could be sung immediately or the A string of the violin could be tuned without outside reference.

It has been said that many "primitives" possess absolute pitch. While this claim has not been verified, it is reasonable to suppose that a person whose tonal experiences were confined to a *do* of constant pitch would rather quickly develop a relatively good feel for pitch level. Certainly better pitch-level responses should be more expected in an area where all persons used only French pitch (p. 17) than in another area where a variety of standard pitches was used. Many German schools do not teach the movable-*do* system so common in America. They follow the "tone-word" method which, by assigning a singable name to each tone of the chromatic scale, gives a more nearly absolute frame of reference.[15] It is not surprising that children so taught make fewer errors in pitch level.

So far we have not delimited the term absolute pitch. Seashore would reserve it for abilities with errors of a tenth of a semitone (10 cents) or less.[16] Bachem's criterion is almost as stringent.[17] But other contemporary researchers allow a far larger margin of error. No census of the general population has ever been made to find the percentage enjoying absolute pitch. If one is ever undertaken it is obvious that the figures can be made large or small depending on the narrowness of the criterion adopted for absolute pitch.

It is safe to conclude that only a person extremely interested in pitch level or who has been indoctrinated with the notion that each melody has its "proper" key (p. 86) will be greatly upset by melody modulations of small magnitude. The great majority of us think musically in terms of intervals, not single tones of fixed pitch. Therefore, unless a melody is raised or lowered to a relatively unmusical register, its basic characteristics will not be greatly affected by changes in pitch level.

Melody and Loudness

Melodies with unconventional skips and harmonies are noticeably less bizarre when played at low intensities. No doubt loudness calls attention to what otherwise would tend to slip by unnoticed. The table below shows a typical set of preferences obtained from college students for intervals based on middle C.[18] Note that, by and large, the softest renditions are the most preferred.

RELATION OF LOUDNESS TO INTERVAL PREFERENCE

1	4th soft	13	minor 3rd soft	25·5	4th loud
2	major 3rd soft	14	major 6th loud	25·5	minor 6th loud
3	octave soft	15·5	major 6th medium	27·5	tritone loud
4	tritone soft	15·5	octave medium	27·5	minor 7th loud
5	minor 6th soft	17	4th medium	29	minor 3rd loud
6	minor 7th soft	18·5	major 7th soft	30	major 2nd loud
7·5	major 6th soft	18·5	minor 6th medium	31·5	major 7th medium
7·5	major 3rd medium	20	5th medium	31·5	minor 7th medium
9	5th soft	21·5	major 2nd soft	33	minor 2nd loud
10	tritone medium	21·5	octave loud	34·5	major 2nd medium
11	major 3rd loud	23·5	5th loud	34·5	minor 2nd medium
12	minor 3rd medium	23·5	minor 2nd soft	36	major 7th loud

If made sufficiently loud, a pitch in the middle register may appreciably change in apparent pitch. While estimates differ, one good experimentalist claims to have observed a change as large as a minor third.[19] Ordinarily an increase in the loudness of a low or middle-register vocal tone tends to increase its pitch, of a very high tone to decrease the pitch. Soft tones are, in general, flatted.[20] The blaring discordance then, may, because of its extreme loudness, have pitch relationships slightly different from those the composer intended. Indeed, it is conceivable that on very rare occasions the shift in pitch might lead to less discordance.

Much that is invalid has been written about the control of loudness in playing the various musical instruments. There is, for instance, the assumption on the part of many piano teachers that an almost infinite number of tone qualities can be elicited simply by varying the way in which the fingers strike the piano keys. But Ortmann[21] and others have shown that the mechanics of piano action allow for very little tone variation. The few effects that do obtain are made possible

through hammer velocity, impact and hammer noises, and pedal—
nothing else. Most of the effects allegedly brought about by
striking the keys in various ways are illusory.

As anyone with only a passing acquaintance with the modern piano
knows, there are at least two, and sometimes three, foot pedals.
These are the sustaining or loud pedal, the soft, and, particularly in
American-made instruments, the sostenuto. Scores for pedal effects
like those for intensity generally are in rather a primitive state. Even
so it is surprising that professional pianists are in so little agreement
as to the "proper" use of the pedals. Heinlein, who did extensive
research in this area, found marked disagreements among the
performances he examined.[22] As a matter of fact, no performer he
studied was able even to duplicate the pedal performance he himself
had made ten minutes earlier. Heinlein found music teachers to
have little precise knowledge of just what the pedals can and cannot do.

It should be noted that performers do not follow their pitch scores
exactly. They intentionally sharp and flat slightly, and employ a
variety of melodic ornaments. Yet these deviations from the pitch
scores are relatively slight. "Inaccuracies" in intensity control, on the
other hand, are far more extensive. With intensity-score indicators
so crude and knowledge of finger and pedal possibilities so meagre,
it is no wonder that the control of loudness often mirrors the
idiosyncrasies of the performer more than it does those of the
composer.

Because of terminological inadequacies, it is difficult for the
musician to designate a particular loudness. There is available, however, a unit of loudness, the phon, which appears to be enjoying some
use. (The number of phons is equal to the number of decibels a tone
of 1000 cycles is above the reference intensity when judged equal in
loudness to the tone in question.) The phon is approximately the
smallest increment of loudness that can be noticed under ordinary

circumstances. The table below gives some idea of the average loudness of various noises.

Type of Noise	Phons
Airplane engine 10 feet from propeller	120–130
Riveting machine 35 feet away	102
Pneumatic drill a few feet away	90–100
Conversation	60
Quiet suburban street	40
Quiet whisper	20

The contemporary conductor Leopold Stokowski is said to interpret his scores as follows:

ppp= 20 phons	*p*= 55 phons	*ff*= 85 phons
pp= 40 phons	*mf*= 65 phons	*fff*= 95 phons
	f= 75 phons	

Melody and Timbre

It is unfortunate that authorities write at times as though a perfect fifth, a minor chord, or a melody will have identical characteristics whether played on a marimba, a harmonica, a tuba, or an old Cremona violin. What they are neglecting are the differences in timbre, the constellations of partial tones each instrument adds to the fundamental tones.[23] The tuning fork and certain organ pipes will yield the purest, simplest tones one can meet outside an acoustics laboratory, for their tones are relatively free of overtones. The air columns around them vibrate largely at only one frequency for each pitch. But orchestral instruments, by and large, give very impure tones. In some, certain of the overtones even match the fundamentals in loudness.[24]

Flute tones and soprano voices are relatively pure; tones from soft horns, soft male voices, pianos and strings are richer, more complex; tones from wood-winds (except the flute), loud male voices, and loud brass (in this order) are still more complex and may be described as brilliant, cutting, blaring, or even strident. The tones of the clarinet emphasize the uneven-numbered partials and are usually regarded as hollow and nasal.[25] (See also Chap. 5, p. 92.) Melodies in a low register have richer quality than those of high pitch.

Many of us associate melodies of bagpipe timbre with things Scottish, the fife or drum with the military, the oboe family with the oriental world, and the pipe organ with church. Because we often associate the male falsetto with buffoonery, a serious melody sung in falsetto may lose much of its serious quality. Yet for the Cantonese, whose stage employs no female voices, the male falsetto replaces the female voice and so warrants serious listening.

There are those who feel that music should always be played precisely as its composer played it. To these people it is a sin to play Bach on a modern organ or to arrange his music for the present-day orchestra. One can only wonder how many of these conservatives really prefer Bach on the baroque organ and how many are victims of their own intellectualizing. However, there is no question but that the psychological effects of Bach's polyphony depend in some degree on the type of organ employed.

It is a bit disheartening to find that as one grows older the timbre of what one hears progressively changes. The human ear becomes gradually deafer, especially for tones in the highest registers and the higher overtones cease to exist. The average thirty-year-old hears almost as well as he did a decade earlier. But the man fifty years of age is likely to be appreciably deafer, particularly for tones of 2048 d.v. and above. By seventy years the deafness may extend as low as the 1024 d.v. level.[26]

Another way of looking at this age-decrement is to compare the hearing of the several age-groups at one pitch level, say at 8192 d.v. In the decade from the early twenties to the early thirties there is little change. But by age forty there is often a ten-decibel loss. The testable loss tends to grow to approximately 25 decibels by age fifty and to more than 40 decibels by age sixty.[27] These loudness losses have little relevance to the hearing of the melody's fundamentals, but they bar the older person from hearing the full richness of the overtone matrix.

Many instruments have important resonance areas in the higher pitch reaches. The partials in these areas are lost to the older listeners. In consideration of these hearing losses we should, perhaps, be more considerate toward crotchety old music critics. When one such critic maintains that the tones of a certain orchestra or virtuoso performer are not so full and rich as they once were he is quite correct; for to his aging ears the tonal mass truly is less rich. What he fails to realize is that the time has come for him to leave to his younger colleagues the evaluation of tonal effects.

We saw earlier (p. 9) that the timbre effects elicited from the playing of old Cremona violins are in part illusory. There are other situations where the alleged timbre effects are better attributed to some other sense than the auditory. An instance of this sort concerns what is said to be the coldness of Heifetz's violin performances.[28] In one study it was first demonstrated that Heifetz is indeed regarded as one of the coldest of concert performers. But whenever his recorded performance of a particular composition was compared with another's recording of the same piece it was usually the latter's playing that was rated as the colder. Morini and Elman were thought to be quite definitely colder, and Totenberg and Milstein at least as cold. Only Szigeti seemed occasionally less cold. It would appear, then, that the Heifetz coldness is probably due to the visual effects of his stiffer posture or lack of facial expression. Since Heifetz's manner of playing looks colder, we imagine that it also sounds colder.

Melody and Sonance

Tone quality and timbre appear as synonymous terms in most musical treatises. But, as Metfessel points out, timbre refers only to *instantaneous* pictures of the sound complex.[29] Under the broader caption of tone quality must also be considered the *progression* of the complex for which Metfessel has coined the word "sonance." Sonance, as the term is now used, refers to the progressive changes and fusions which take place within the tone from moment to moment. Like timbre, sonance furnishes a setting for melody and can greatly affect its psychological characteristics.

The most worked-over area of sonance is that of the vibrato, a melodic ornament described elsewhere (Chap. 1). It will be recalled that in employing the vibrato the singer or instrumentalist varies his tones periodically from those of the score. Sonance also appears in nonperiodic and in erratic tone fluctuations.[30]

Seashore has been much impressed by the fact that a melody is never sung or played precisely as scored. The introduction of the vibrato and of glides, and the intentional sharping or flatting of tones illustrate how the performer can stamp his individuality on the music. Seashore has generalized from these data to the point of formulating an aesthetic rule: beauty, he thinks, lies in artistic deviation from the rigid and regular. He has offered the analogy of the photograph, which, with its too faithful copying of an object, is not so highly rated as the less representational painting (p. 142). But whether or not the deviation principle should be elevated to the position of an artistic law, we must agree that the "horizontal" impurities of the vibrato and of the erratic and the nonperiodic fluctuations of tone are, musically speaking, extremely important. Sonance, then, must be considered along with those "vertical" impurities we term timbre.

Melody and Noise

We have seen that a melody shows different psychological characteristics when it is played on instruments of dissimilar timbre. Noise, too, attaches itself to melody and aids in the creation of most

67

musical experiences. Noise has been defined as "a sound either so complex, or so irregular, or both, that it seems to have no tone when heard by itself."[31] There is no definite boundary between noise and tone, for experts can sometimes detect a pitch which to the layman seems only a conglomerate of unpitched sounds.

The rubbing of the bow, the tapping of the fingers on the piano keys[32] or on the fingerboard of a violin, the hissing of the breath in playing the flute, and the plucking sounds necessary to harp-playing all serve as excellent examples of noise in music. Contrary to the belief of some, noise is not unpleasant per se, nor is it to be avoided at all costs. On the contrary, it is often deliberately sought to give pleasure.

That beating effects add to the fullness of tonal experience can be observed by listening to the pipe organ. This versatile instrument assigns more than one pipe to each pitch but does not achieve for them precisely the same pitch. The beats so created help to give the pipe organ its characteristic quality, an effect which is much missed in the thinner sounding and more exactly tuned electric organ. There are organs which achieve the effect of massiveness and awe by possessing pipes whose frequencies are below the human threshold of audition. While these slow periodicities cannot be heard as tones, they can be felt as building vibrations and sometimes heard as faint rattlings.

The modern orchestral composer often feels the need for more noise effects than the traditional instruments can provide. He may excite and shock his audience with his use of apparatus which yields rhythmic grunts, siren wails, noises usually associated with the factory, and even more unusual sounds. Henry Cowell, a contemporary American composer, has put noise to work in his piano compositions. Plucking sounds arise from a harplike picking of the piano strings. An eerie, wailing effect comes from a light stroking or massage of the strings. And, following Dandrieu, who in the early

1700's expressed the cannon's roar by striking the lower harpsichord notes with his fist, Cowell has long been playing "tone-clusters" where the fist, the flat of the hand, or even the entire forearm simultaneously depresses all the keys it can encompass. Cowell's techniques are especially effective for program music.

Melody and Tempo

It is a matter of common observation that the tempo or speed with which a melody is played is often an index of its function. A composition set to walking speed may well be a march, another at very slow speed a dirge, and still another at some intermediate speed a waltz. As we shall see in the next chapter, the tempo of a melody is an important determinant of its activeness, of whether it is reacted to as major or as minor.

Some years ago a Duo-Art player-piano, made by the Aeolian Corporation, was used in an attempt to learn if college students had one specific tempo well fixed in mind for waltz time.[33] The subjects were blindfolded and told to move back and forth a large speed lever until the playing of the composition they were hearing was at the rate they deemed proper. The lever settings given by this group were generally in the neighbourhood of 116 quarter-notes to the minute, just what the Aeolian Corporation regarded at that time as proper. The fox-trots were usually set at a considerably faster tempo, at approximately 143.

Further research on dance tempo was carried on six years later by Lund with a similar sample of college students.[34] Lund found that faster speeds were by this time considered proper, 139 for the waltz and 155 for the fox-trot. Lund noted that many dance-orchestra leaders recognize two waltz times, a slower one that approximates the value uncovered in the earlier study, and the so-called concert or faster style whose tempo is about the figure his subjects considered

69

proper. The fox-trot also has several tempo variants, of which two, the Charleston and the Black Bottom, had considerable popularity for a time.

Conductors and performers often alter the tempo in order to develop some particular effect. In one movement of the *Eroica Symphony* (*The Funeral March*), Beethoven's own marking was set at 80. Koussevitzky cut the speed to 74 for his conducting, Beecham to 62, and Toscanini to 52. Wagner once complained that the *Tannhäuser Overture* took twelve minutes under his own baton but as long as twenty under certain other conductors.

Music seems to have more than its share of nomenclature difficulties. Confusion abounds in this tempo area where terms such as time, tempo, periodicity, takt, true beat,[35] and rhythm are variously defined. In the next section we shall discuss the relation of melody to rhythm. The reader should be warned that other authors might have included portions of the discussion on rhythm in this section on tempo. But although tempo and rhythm are obviously very closely related, they are by no means identical.[36]

Melody and Rhythm

Rhythm is more than the periodicity resulting from the continuous repetition of a simple sequence such as *do, re, mi, fa*. To elicit rhythm, one element from among the four symbols must be emphasized in some way to make it stand out from its fellows. If the *do* alone were made more intense, if it were held longer than any one of the others, or of it were somehow made qualitatively unique, say given a very different timbre, then the sequence would possess what has been termed objective rhythm.

All three of these modes of emphasis are used in music, often simultaneously. The pianist, in striking more strongly the first note of a rhythmic pattern, not only makes the tone louder but automatically alters its timbre in slight degree as well. Unwittingly, he also breaks the regularity of his timing and tarries longer than he thinks he does on the stressed tone.[37] In trying, then, to use intensity as a means of emphasis the pianist has also employed both timbre and timing to create his rhythms. The organist, of course, cannot so easily control his intensity relationships and must depend more on timing in his attempts to bring about emphasis.

Rhythms serve the listener by increasing his perceptual span, dividing up patterns of melodic material so that larger units can be more readily grasped. When the rhythmic emphasis is on the important positions of the scale, e.g., on the tonic, dominant, etc., the tonality structure is made more obvious and the listener's anticipations are whetted. By shifting the accent to a tone which is normally not accented in a given rhythmic pattern, that is, by syncopation, the listener's anticipations are strengthened even more and the intensity of the adjacent time-keeping beat is intensified.[38]

The most obvious gift rhythm brings to music is its invitation to motor activity. This activity may reach only the covert stage with movements too slight to be casually observed, or the rhythms may induce overt nodding, foot tapping, and still other activities, such as often occur while jazz music is played.[39] The early church, with its stress on contemplation rather than on action, looked askance at rhythm and endeavored to eliminate it as far as possible.[40] The earthy, activity-inducing quality of rhythm is well demonstrated in work music. Simple labor, such as that of unskilled workmen passing heavy loads down a line, is made easier because of the highly rhythmic chanties they sing. And although many lay dancers pay little or no attention to the rhythm of the music to which they are dancing, the more skillful do dance in time with the music and are guided by it.

Combing through the work of the past, Mursell has tentatively concluded that there are only seven unit groups among the musical rhythms.[41] In the table below, the dash designates the emphasized element in each case. The reader can readily find illustrations of the iamb, trochee, dactyl, and probably the amphibrach, although the latter is much the least frequent. Handel's *Dead March* from *Saul* illustrates the single beat, and Chopin's *Opus 53* the tremolo. Lundin offers the rumba as an example of the anapest.[42]

UNIT GROUPS IN MUSICAL RHYTHMS
— *accented*, ◡ *unaccented*

◡ —	Iamb	◡ ◡ —	Anapest
— ◡	Trochee	◡ — ◡	Amphibrach
— ◡ ◡	Dactyl	◡ ◡ ◡	Tremolo
	| — | — |	Single Beat	

According to the experimentalist Dunlap, music with short rhythmic units tends to possess a joyous quality and that with longer units seems more somber.[43] It would appear, however, that Dunlap is referring less to rhythm than to tempo, and we have already noted that faster music seems more active or major, while slower tunes appear more somber or minor. The available evidence indicates that the affects given melody by rhythm depend very much on either cultural conditioning or personal experience. In our culture we do not rush a corpse to its grave, but carry it slowly and with measured tread. Hence, rhythms with single beat may seem funereal. Infantrymen usually favor one or the other foot, so the trochee may well take on a march flavor. Other illustrations of our associations could be gathered, but they would be somewhat different from those of a people of an alien culture.

We have already commented on the fact that Western music has specialized, so to speak, on the rather simple rhythmic patterns— the 2-beat, 3-beat, 4-beat, and, to a lesser extent, the 6 and 8. The 5 and 7 occur so rarely that laymen are usually ignorant of their existence and fail to appreciate them. These rarer rhythms do occur in the Orient and could enjoy more use in the West if dances or drills were devised which forced movements in these patterns (p. 4).

It is fortunate that the ability learned by one set of muscles "crosses over" in some degree to other sets. A rhythmic pattern, say a 5-beat one, learned through drill with the right hand, is in actuality learned by the entire organism. The left hand, either foot, or, in fact, any mobile part of the body, can beat out the rhythm. After the pattern has been thoroughly mastered it can be superimposed, as it were, upon a sequence of events which physically has only periodicity. Such a superimposition is termed "subjective rhythm." A person asked to hear a metronome beat first in 2-beat rhythm, then in 3- and later in 4-beat can readily do as requested even when he knows that there is no rhythmic pattern in the physical stimuli. But he could not hear a 5-beat rhythm unless, of course, he had had considerable contact with 5-beat music or had been subjected to laboratory drill with this rhythm. If a melody possesses a strong and familiar objective rhythm, the listening is in terms of that rhythm. But if the objective rhythm is very weak, the listener may supply his own subjective rhythm.

A number of the early missionaries to Africa brought back the surprising tale that the natives seemed poor in rhythms and often beat randomly on their drums. Since drumming was a sort of telegraphy as well as musical behavior and so was a highly skilled activity, such a report did not seem very reasonable. More careful observations proved the missionaries to have been quite mistaken. These later studies showed the rhythmic patterns to be extremely precise but too complicated for Western-trained laymen to follow. The African drummers, it was found, were simultaneously tapping in several patterns, i.e., 2 against 3, 3 against 4, 2 against 3 against 5, etc.

Western music has not entirely neglected polyrhythms. They can be observed, for instance, in MacDowell's *Tragic Sonata* or in Chopin's *Nocturne in D Flat*. Certain modern composers, notably Henry Cowell, have employed cross- or polyrhythms rather extensively, and composers of "hot" jazz have traditionally superimposed

73

rhythmic cycles of three beats on the fundamental rhythm of two or four beats.[44] But the majority of conservatories and schools of music offer no special training for their mastery. It is assumed that somehow the student will be able to play these polyrhythms on the occasions he finds the need.[45]

The schools that do teach the handling of polyrhythms employ one of two procedures or some combination of these. The most obvious procedure is the kinesthetic method, by which the hands (or feet) are separately trained in two or more rhythms. This is supposedly the scheme featured by Jaques-Dalcroze in his dance system of eurhythmics.[46] The method is also used by the pianist Arthur Hardcastle, who on being tested by the author some years ago was found to be very skillful. Hardcastle could tap 2 against 3, 3 against 4, 3 against 5, 3 against 7, and 4 against 7 with less than a 10 per cent error.

A second approach to the mastery of polyrhythms is by counting to oneself the least common multiple (or fraction of this) of the rhythms to be played. For example, in learning to play 2 against 3, one counts from 1 through 6 and taps with one hand on the 1, 3 and 5, and with the other on the 1 and 4.

One Hand		Other Hand
×	1	×
	2	
×	3	
	4	×
×	5	
	6	
×	1	×

Where the multiple becomes large, it can be split into parts. When playing 3 against 5, one hand taps on the first and fourth counts of the first group of five, on the second and fifth counts of the second group, and on the third count of the third group. The other hand taps on the first count of each group of five.

ONE HAND		OTHER HAND
×	*1*	×
	2	
	3	
×	*4*	
	5	
	1	×
×	*2*	
	3	
	4	
×	*5*	
	1	×
	2	
×	*3*	
	4	
	5	
×	*1*	×

At Stanford University there has been devised a third, or Gestalt, procedure which appears to have an advantage over the other methods in that complicated patterns can be learned almost as readily as the simpler. The scheme necessitates cutting a player-piano roll or pressing a phonograph record. In presenting the polyrhythms, say the 2 against 3, the roll or record is made to offer a succession of middle C's in 2-beat rhythm and a series of G's in 3-beat. The learner merely listens and attempts to duplicate the C's and G's at some higher or lower piano register. If the piano roll is employed, the beginner has additional cues from watching the keys as they are automatically depressed.

Harmony

Singing in unison is undoubtedly as old as music. But when boys and men, or women and men join in singing the same melody, the natural differences in the lengths of the vocal folds make it easier for the men to sing an octave below the others. The octave span was probably adopted for perceptual reasons as well. Its two tones fuse so completely that the musically untutored often imagine the singing to be all in unison. This confusion is less likely to occur with any of the other intervals.

Another early breakaway from unison singing came with the drone bass. Here, one tone is continuously sung or played for the duration of the melody. In effect, the drone becomes a keynote which adds greatly to the stability, i.e., to the tonality, of the musical structure. At times the *sol*, or dominant, is additionally employed as a drone. Nowadays the drone bass is most readily heard in bagpipe music, and the pipe organ has a place for it in the pedal, so called because the foot sustains the drone.

Many of the world's music systems went no farther along the road to harmony. Their major innovations were often in rhythmic development, an area in which Western music has done relatively little. But the West, perhaps during the ninth century, took a logical next step in developing the organum in which there were now added, in addition to the octave, voices a fourth below and a fifth above, both moving parallel to the theme. Here, then, is a type of harmonizing, although one with little variety.

After several centuries the monotony of parallel octaves, fifths, and fourths finally drove composers to the scheme of opposing motions, where two melodies moved in opposite directions. At first the only intervals officially recognized were the same three "perfect" ones. But since the very mechanics of opposing motion necessarily created other intervals, thirds and sixths gradually came into vogue. With these innovations, simple parallel motion gradually dropped in favor to the point where later harmonists proscribed its use. It was, in fact, not until the contemporary period that composers once again dared employ it to any considerable extent.

It is a fact of music that the composing habits of any era tend to become rigidly codified. The rules take on the character of taboos which keep all but the braver composers from experimentation. Yet each great composer establishes his own school by breaking at least a few of the rules which have fettered music up to his time. By this process of breaking old rules and making new ones, simple opposing motion gradually broadened into polyphony, in which several melodic strands are simultaneously sung or played. Although polyphony's great rival, homophony, appeared during the Renaissance and gradually won a dominant position in Western music, it never entirely replaced polyphony. In fact, a good proportion of modern music is quite polyphonic in character.

During the heyday of polyphony, any simultaneously sounded interval or chord was more or less a fleeting, fortuitous affair which happened with certain juxtapositions of the several melodic lines. In homophonic writing, however, a single line became the focus of attention and the other parts took on a decidedly secondary aspect. These latter became the clothes, the ornaments, for the melody. The effect was music as the present-day layman hears it. Chords and intervals became important in their own right, and arguments about which ones were allowable were heard. But gradually the harmonic rules changed until, as the reader well knows, almost every chord has by now had its day of glory.

Summary

Although in the past it was taught that, to be a proper melody, a tonal pattern must have inherent unity and coherence, it now appears that the unity is not in the tonal line at all but is literally read in by the listener. It is naturally difficult to feel unity in patterns which are virtually impossible to sing or play. Yet even such tonal contours, if heard sufficiently often, become increasingly familiar so that the hearing of any one of the tones arouses the feeling that this should be followed by the next tone in the sequence. It is this expectancy, then, that characterizes our conception of melody.[47] Melodies are perceptual phenomena which obey the principles of learning.

Melodies are far more than familiar sequences of tones. To the few persons with "absolute pitch," a melody may appear to change its characteristics if the pitch register is altered ever so little. But for the great majority of the musical public, melodies can be modulated freely without much change in psychological effect. Relative and absolute intensities, on the other hand, are important to almost all listeners. Since this is so, it is unfortunate that the staff signs for loudness variations are extremely crude and that the control of loudness changes by vocalists and instrumentalists is incredibly poor. For loudness nuances may make just the difference between the acceptance of a melody or its rejection. But perhaps in the years to come, musicians will develop symbols which will permit more exact notation. It should be noted that finer units of measurement, e.g., phons, already are available to the musician.

Pure tones have no place in music. Indeed, each musical culture features a variety of tonal impurities—timbres, sonances (e.g., vibrato), and noises—and trains its public in their appreciation. New timbre effects are accepted slowly and grudgingly. For centuries this conservatism in Western music could be readily excused. But now that the innovator can draw on the almost inexhaustible resources of modern electronics there is less justification for timidity. The job is largely a propaganda one of convincing the public that all worthwhile timbres were not discovered by the old masters.

The older person often imagines that if he turns up the volume of his radio or phonograph he will hear his favorite melodies just as he heard them when he was younger. But deafness tends to be selective, with the higher registers affected earlier than the lower. Hence, the elderly miss much of the tonal complex and perceive their melodies as having a less rich timbre. Deafness, then, is more than a weakness in loudness sensitivity.

Tempo and rhythm often cue the listener to the melody's function. With one temporal arrangement a waltz is indicated, with another a dirge. The proper use of syncopation can whet the auditor's anticipations. Although certain other cultures have made great use of rhythmic complications, the West has not. A few courageous contemporaries have attempted to free their music from the tyranny of the quarter-note by the use of polyrhythms; but music teachers have made little effort to train their students in the execution and appreciation of such "novelties." They fail to realize that they are bypassing a rich source of aesthetic enjoyment.

Slow though the Occident has been in experimenting with rhythmic materials, it has led the world in melodic improvisation. From the stage of unison singing, the West slowly moved to the use of drone basses, the organum, opposed motion, polyphony and finally to homophony with its chordal structures. It should be noted that music systems do not necessarily evolve. The music of a people may remain relatively static, it may proceed along one line or another, or it may turn back toward an earlier set of forms. The composer's task is to keep his public from satiation, a goal which can be achieved in countless fashions.

In the present chapter we have concerned ourselves largely with the anatomical side of music, with its flesh and bones. We shall continue in the next chapter with our discussions of melody, but there we shall emphasize its more dynamic aspects. Several facets of the language problem will interest us.

Notes

1] G. D. Birkhoff, in *Aesthetic Measure*, Cambridge, Mass., Harvard U. Press, 1933, has presented a mathematical formula for assessing unity and variety which at first glance seems delightfully straightforward. But even Birkhoff has been unable to apply it to any except the simplest materials, as the present author found when, in the middle 1930's, he sent him several melodies to assess. Apparently Birkhoff derived his formula from the practices of composers as described in the harmony manuals.

J. G. Beebe-Center and C. C. Pratt, in "A Test of Birkhoff's Aesthetic Measure," *J. Gen. Psychol.*, 17 (1937): 339–353, have been brave enough to try out the formula with simple musical materials. Although they expressed themselves as hopeful of the ultimate utility of the Birkhoff scheme they have not published further in this area.

Another formalistic measure of beauty has been proposed by Cyril Burt in "The Psychology of Art" chapter of *How the Mind Works,* London, Allen and Unwin, 1933. Burt's *aesthetic index* is $\left(\exp \dfrac{D+I}{S}\right)^{-1}$, where D is the number of items into which the work is differentiated, I is the number of relations integrating the items, and S is the scope of apprehension under the usual conditions.

2] L. L. Thurstone, "The Problem of Melody," *Music. Quart.*, 6 (1920): 426–429.

3] L. E. Emerson, "The Feeling-Value of Unmusical Tone-Intervals," *Harvard Psychol. Stud.*, 2 (1906): 269–274. The work of Emerson and the studies by Max Meyer, "Elements of a Psychological Theory of Melody," *Psychol. Rev.*, 7 (1900): 241–273, and by W. V. D. Bingham, "Studies in Melody," *Psychol. Monog.*, 12 (1910): 1–88, are examples of the excellent early American researches on melody.

4] H. Werner, in "Musical 'Micro-scales' and 'Micro-melodies'," *J. Psychol.*, 10 (1940): 149–156, has shown that after a sequence has once been accepted as a melody it can be drastically changed without much loss of identity. His procedure was to reduce all intervals proportionately until they were of microtone size.

5] O. Ortmann, "On the Melodic Relativity of Tones," *Psychol. Monog.*, 35, No. 1 (1926): 1–47. See also J. P. Guilford and R. A. Hilton, "Some Configurational Properties of Short Musical Melodies," *J. Exp. Psychol.*, 16 (1933): 32–54; J. P. Guilford and H. M. Nelson, "Changes in the Pitch of Tones when Melodies Are Repeated," *J. Exp. Psychol.*, 19 (1936): 193–202; "The Pitch of Tones in Melodies as Compared with Single Tones," *J. Exp. Psychol.*, 20 (1937): 309–335.

6] C. E. Seashore, D. Lewis, and J. G. Saetveit, Manual, *Seashore Measures of Musical Talents*, N.Y., Psychol. Corp., 1956.

7] With an arrangement similar to that found in the Seashore Tonal Memory test, H. Wunderlich ("The Recognition Value of the Steps of the Diatonic Scale," *Amer. J. Psychol.*, 53 (1940): 579–582) studied the ease of identifying the scale steps. The *fa* and *ti* were quite difficult to identify as having been altered while the *do*, *re*, and *la* were readily identified. See also C. P. Heinlein's "A Brief Discussion of the Nature and Function of Melodic Configuration in Tonal Memory with Critical Reference to the Seashore Tonal Memory Test," *J. Genet. Psychol.*, 35 (1928), 45–61 and R. Francès' "Recherches Expérimentales sur la Perception de la Mélodie," *J. Psychol. Norm. Path.*, 47–51 (1954): 439–457.

8] For a review of the literature on absolute pitch see D. M. Neu's "A Critical Review of the Literature on 'Absolute Pitch'," *Psychol. Bull.*, 44 (1947): 249–266.

9] B. L. Riker, "The Ability to Judge Pitch," *J. Exp. Psychol.*, 36 (1946), 331–346.

10] L. A. Petran, "An Experimental Study of Pitch Recognition," *Psychol. Monog.*, 42, No. 193 (1932).

11] Building on the early work of M. F. Meyer, "Is the Memory of Absolute Pitch Capable of Development by Training?" *Psychol. Rev., 6* (1899), 514–516, others have found as he did that by dint of careful training, errors can be reduced to as small a figure as 33 cents. See Helen K. Mull's "The Acquisition of Absolute Pitch," *Amer. J. Psychol., 36* (1925): 469–493, and C. H. Wedell's "A Study of Absolute Pitch," *Psychol. Bull., 38* (1941): 547–548.

12] A. Bachem is one of the research men of this area who is still convinced that absolute pitch is an inherent type of behavior. ("The Genesis of Absolute Pitch," *J. Acoust. Soc. Amer., 11* (1940): 434–439; "Time Factors in Relative and Absolute Pitch Determination," *J. Acoust. Soc. Amer., 26* (1954), 751–753.)

13] W. F. Oakes, "An Experimental Study of Pitch Naming and Pitch Discrimination Reactions," *J. Genet. Psychol., 86* (1955), 237–259.

14] Even when the cues do not directly benefit the performance their presence may give the person confidence. Thus, L. M. Brammer found that the pitch-level scores of several violinists were no better when they were given the opportunity to tune their own violins than when the experimenter tuned the instruments for them under their orders. Yet the added kinesthetic cues the manipulation of their own fiddles gave them increased their confidence in their scores. ("Sensory Cues in Pitch Judgment," *J. Exp. Psychol., 41* (1951): 336–340.)

15] Karl Eitz, *Das Tonwort*, Leipzig, Breitkopf u. Haertel, 1928.

16] C. E. Seashore, "Acquired or Absolute Pitch," *Mus. Ed. J., 26* (1940): 18.

17] A. Bachem, *op. cit.*

18] The tonal intervals were played on a Duo-Art reproducing piano. When the intensity levers were set at "soft" the intervals termed "soft" were elicited. Other combinations of the levers yielded the "medium" and "loud" intensities. See P. R. Farnsworth and C. F. Voegelin, "Dyad Preferences at Different Intensities," *J. Appl. Psychol., 12* (1928): 148–151.

19] H. Fletcher, *Newer Concepts of the Pitch, Loudness and Timbre of Musical Tones*, N.Y., Bell Telephone, 1935; W. Köhler, "Tonpsychologie," *Handbuch der Neurologie des Ohres*, Berlin, Alexander u. Marburg, 1923, 419–464.

20] J. S. Hurley, "A Study of Pitch Tendencies in Certain Phases of Singing as Measured by the Conn Chromatic Stroboscope," Thesis, Syracuse U., 1940. The picture with bowed tones is somewhat different. Here professionals tend to flat with increases in bow pressure but to sharp with each rise in bow velocity. See R. J. Harrington, "The Influence of Pressure and Velocity of the Bow on Violin Intonation: A Stroboscopic Study," Master's Thesis, Syracuse U., 1952.

21] O. Ortmann, *The Physical Basis of Piano Touch and Tone*, N.Y., Dutton, 1925; H. C. Hart, M. W. Fuller, and W. S. Lusby, "Precision Study of Piano Touch and Tone," *J. Acoust. Soc. Amer., 6* (1934): 80–94.

22] C. P. Heinlein, "The Functional Role of Finger Touch and Damper-Pedalling in the Appreciation of Pianoforte Music," *J. Gen. Psychol., 2* (1929): 462–469; "A Discussion of the Nature of Pianoforte Damper-Pedalling together with an Experimental Study of Some

Individual Differences in Pedal Performance," *J. Gen. Psychol.*, 2 (1929): 489–508; "Pianoforte Damper-Pedalling under Ten Different Experimental Conditions," *J. Gen. Psychol.*, 3 (1930): 511–528.

23] One researcher believes he has demonstrated the existence of undertones, which he conceives as the inverse of overtones. But so far, few others accept their reality. See C. Révész's *Introduction to the Psychology of Music*, Norman, U. of Oklahoma Press, 1954, pp. 13–14.

24] For an excellent account of the timbre of band and orchestral instruments see Chapter 17 of C. E. Seashore's *Psychology of Music*, N.Y., McGraw-Hill, 1938.

25] The mounting of the mute on the bridge of a violin dampens certain of the higher overtones and makes the "shade" of the tone "darker." A "dark" vocal tone can be produced by holding the mouth "long," and a "light" tone by a "short" mouth. See D. Preston, "Pitch Variations in the Singing of Specific Vowels on Specific Frequencies Using Bright and Dark Tones," Master's Thesis, Syracuse U., 1945.

26] Variability, a general fact of life, is well illustrated in the area of auditory sensitivity. Many men deafen early while others keep their sensitivity relatively intact until quite late in life. But the average changes in hearing ability are as described above.

27] C. C. Bunch, "Age Variations in Auditory Acuity," *Arch. Otolaryngol.*, Chicago, 9 (1929): 625–636; H. C. Montgomery, "Do Our Ears Grow Old?" *Bell Lab. Rec.*, 10 (1932): 311–313; N. H. Kelley, "A Study in Presbycusis: Auditory Loss with Increasing Age and Its Effect upon the Perception of Music and Speech," *Arch. Otolaryngol.*, Chicago, 29 (1939), 506–513. Montgomery pictures the hearing losses of the aging as being somewhat slighter than does Bunch. Kelley presents them as still slighter, particularly for the frequencies below 1024 d.v.

28] P. R. Farnsworth, "Notes on 'Coldness' in Violin Playing," *J. Psychol.*, 33 (1952): 41–45.

29] M. Metfessel, "Sonance as a Form of Tonal Fusion," *Psychol. Rev.*, 33 (1926): 459–466. See also O. Ortmann's "The Psychology of Tone Quality," *1939 Int. Congr. Musicol.*, 1944, pp. 227–232.

30] Research men of the Seashore laboratories at the University of Iowa have made excellent studies of certain of these phenomena. The interested student can refer to C. E. Seashore's *Psychology of Music*, Chap. 9, or to the following monographs by Seashore's student associates for detailed pictures of the portamento and of typical attacks and releases of vocal tones: D. Lewis, M. Cowan, and G. Fairbanks, "Pitch Variations Arising from Certain Types of Frequency Modulation," *J. Acoust. Soc. Amer.*, 9 (1937): 79; R. E. Miller, "The Pitch of the Attack in Singing," *Ia. Stud. Mus.*, 4 (1936): 158–171; H. G. Seashore, "An Objective Analysis of Artistic Singing," *Ia. Stud. Mus.*, 4 (1936): 12–157; A. Small, "An Objective Analysis of Artistic Violin Performance," *Ia. Stud. Mus.*, 4 (1936): 172–231.

31] W. T. Bartholomew, *Acoustics of Music*, N.Y., Prentice-Hall, 1942, p. 159.

32] W. G. Hill, "Noise in Piano Tone, a Qualitative Element," *Music. Quart.*, 26 (1940): 244–259.

33] P. R. Farnsworth, H. A. Block, and W. C. Waterman, "Absolute Tempo," *J. Gen. Psychol.*, 10 (1934): 230–233.

34] M. Lund, "An Analysis of the 'True Beat' in Music," Doctoral Thesis, Stanford U., 1939.

35] For a definition of takt and true beat see Glossary.

36] G. Brelet, *Le Temps Musical*, Paris, Press. U. de France, 1949.

37] M. T. Henderson, "Rhythmic Organization in Artistic Piano Performance," *U. of Ia. Stud. Psychol. Mus.*, 4 (1936): 281–305. The work of Henderson and the other Iowa psychologists who have studied piano performance was made possible by a specially designed camera. For more detail on its use see L. Skinner and C. E. Seashore, "A Musical Pattern Score of the First Movement of the Beethoven *Sonata, Opus 27, No. 2*," *U. of Ia. Stud. Psychol. Music*, 4 (1936): 263–280.

38] H. E. Weaver, "Syncopation: A Study of Musical Rhythms," *J. Gen. Psychol.*, 20 (1939): 409–429. It should be noted that the jazz musician syncopates not only with rhythmic beats but with melodic contours as well. See also P. Fraisse and S. Ehrlich, "Note sur la Possibilité de Syncoper en Fonction du Tempo d'une Cadence," *Année Psychol.*, 55 (1955): 61–65.

39] J. B. Eggen, "A Behavioristic Interpretation of Jazz," *Psychol. Rev.*, 33 (1926): 407–409.

40] Kate Gordon, *Esthetics*, N.Y., Holt, 1913.

41] J. L. Mursell, *The Psychology of Music*, N.Y., Norton, 1937, p. 177. Mursell's table is reproduced here with the permission of the W. W. Norton Co.

42] R. W. Lundin, *An Objective Psychology of Music*, N.Y., Ronald Press, 1953, p. 95.

43] K. Dunlap, *A System of Psychology*, N.Y., Scribner, 1912, pp. 309–313.

44] See *Kitten on the Keys* or *I Can't Give You Anything But Love, Baby*.

45] P. R. Farnsworth, "Concerning Cross-Rhythms," *Sch. Mus.*, 33 (1933): 11–12.

46] E. Jaques-Dalcroze, *Rhythm, Music and Education*, N.Y., Putnam, 1921.

47] This is not to imply that expectancy is the only basic principle of learning. Unfortunately, there is no brief treatise on learning which can be read with profit by the psychologically unsophisticated musician. Those who wish more acquaintance with learning principles would do well to devote the time necessary to reading the learning sections of one of the elementary textbooks in psychology.

CHAPTER FIVE

Language Aspects of Music

WE have already seen that sometimes to some people a melody presents at least a small message. It may "talk about" an eerie feeling, a restlessness, an oriental atmosphere, a march time, or communicate still other impressions. But, granting all this, can it be said that music is a language in any strict sense of the word? To answer this question we must first agree on what we are going to mean by language and then examine the research material of the area.

Desire for Communication

Before the language process can be said to exist, there must be persons who desire to communicate their thoughts and emotions. If this were the only earmark of a language, music would qualify, for many composers, convinced that the world needs their favored religious, economic, or political ideologies, feel that they must share their beliefs through the medium of their musical creations. An occasional performer can be found who believes that he, too, has a share in the communication process through his unique way of handling musical materials. His thoughts, he insists, add to or modify what the composer has to say. It should be noted, however, that the confidence of composers and performers in what they think they can do is no proof that they can successfully employ musical elements as linguistic signs, that they can tell the stories they are so anxious to tell. The matter of success constitutes a somewhat different problem, which will be discussed later in this chapter.

Grammar

A second major earmark of language has to do with the formal relations among signs. Every language has its grammar. So does music, with its detailed rules governing the use of its melodic and harmonic signs. But no grammar is fixed once and for all. The use of "none are" would have been banned without question by any editor a few years ago. Now this phrase occasionally gets by on the rationale that usage seems to be giving it support. Thus it is with the rules of music. What was not allowed some time ago may now be viewed as acceptable. And some of the presently accepted usages may be frowned on in a later period. It is clear, then, that the rules of grammar change. But, even so, there has been a grammar for every school of musical composition.

Meaning

Few but professional musicologists take much interest in the grammar of music. It is a highly specialized area to be studied by the historically minded. More attention is likely to be given the desire for communication. What motivates a composer to create or a professional performer to reproduce music arouses a deep-seated curiosity on the part of many of us. Yet even motivation and creativity do not, as a rule, excite as much interest as does the problem of musical meaning, the story that music tells.

It has been suggested that the existence of a desire for communication does not of itself guarantee the presence of meaning. A hungry monkey may wail and screech in his attempts to communicate with his mate in a nearby food-filled cage. While the first monkey may interest the second with his antics, his vocalizations will not tell her to give him food. So far as she is concerned his vocal behaviors are not meaningful although he is obviously striving to make them so.

The problem now before us is to see to what extent musicians are communicating and in what degree they, like the hungry monkey, are deluding themselves into believing that others must somehow understand them. The remainder of this chapter will be concerned with this meaning aspect of music.

Alleged Key Effects

In Grecian times, long before the day of free modulation and tempered scales, a melody was supposed to reflect the unique psychological character of the mode in which it was written. If it was in the Dorian mode with its arrangement of a half-tone, three whole tones, a half-tone, and two whole tones (as in E, F, G, A, B, C, D, E), dignity, manliness, courage, and self-dependence were the qualities thought to be expressed. But if the Lydian mode was used, the melodic message was considered one of softness and self-indulgence. Because he believed that hearing the Lydian mode could be harmful to man's character, Plato banned it from his "Ideal Republic."[1] It is of interest that the internal arrangement of the Lydian mode is that of our current major scale.

There is no doubt that there were ancient scholars who imagined they heard these psychological, i.e., "meaning," effects. But it is also clear that no person of the present day is apt to be so affected unless he is told what effects he "should" hear.[2] Man is highly suggestible in this area as in many another, and it is not much of a trick to make him "hear" what he should hear.

It is of considerable interest that this notion concerning modal effects persisted even after the modes had been shaken down to two—

the present-day major and minor. In fact, the idea was further extended to the several keys of the major mode. Thus, the key of F major was said to be the key of the pastoral idyll (for example Beethoven's *Pastoral Symphony*); keys with five, six, seven, eight, or nine sharps made men think of heavenly matters; while the keys of F minor and F sharp minor were the tragic ones.

It is not difficult to speculate on how, before the advent of temperament, one key was associated with Heaven, another with the farm, and still another with tragedy. For, as was shown in Chapter 2, a melody whose *do* is to *re* as 8:9 will not sound precisely like one whose *do–re* ratio is 9:10. It would have been a simple matter to attach psychological qualities to these differences. But whatever they attached would have been pretty much pure whimsey. Of course, there would come in time a codification of the rules of this school of thought. Pastoral music *must* be written in the key of F major, the rules would read, and tragic music in F minor or F sharp minor. And all "sensitive" people would begin to "hear" pastoral effects whenever they knew that the key of F major was employed.

It may strike the reader as odd that even today there are composers who try to find the "proper" key for their melodic message. But with equal temperament, where *do*: *re* has the same ratio in every key, there is little possibility that key differences of a psychological character can exist. It is true that the listener with absolute pitch (p. 58) may know whether a melody is being played in E or F, and if he is versed in these traditional expectancies he may feel that the keys are vastly different. The only other possible differences arise from the fact that equal temperament is almost never quite secured, and from differential fingering. Weak fingers may be given too great a task in certain multi-blacknote keys. But such slight stimulus differences can hardly be expected to yield psychological effects such as those described above. It seems safe to conclude, therefore, that no key (as distinguished from modal) effects of any importance exist for the modern listener.

Major and Minor Modes

We have already seen that intervals, as such, are neither major nor minor. Centuries ago these modal labels were erroneously attached to intervals of the major and minor chords, where they remained as curiosities of nomenclature. But with chords and melodies there is more reason to apply these terms.

There are three positions of the major chord—in the key of C they are C, E, G; E, G, C; and G, C, E—and all were thought by the early theorists to have something in their structure which aroused in the listener a happy mood. The three positions of the minor chord— C, E flat, G; E flat, G, C; and G, C, E flat—with their different structure were thought automatically to elicit somber moods. But what in the structures allegedly causes these opposing feelings has never been satisfactorily stated. One of the few helpful suggestions has come from Meyer,[3] who points out that in the just-intoned scale the major (C, E, G) is well balanced with its symbol structure of 1–5–3, while the minor (C, E flat, G, or A, C, E) with its 5–3–15 has more ambiguity in that the 15 "points" both to the 5 (15 to 5 or 3 to 1) and to the 3 (15 to 3 or 5 to 1).

There is much of worth in Meyer's suggestion. But two sets of facts have been uncovered during this century which lead to a somewhat broader view than that of the earlier theorists: (1) The ability to distinguish major from minor is not nearly so common as the older statements would have us believe. (2) The structural difference between major and minor chords is not the only variable which suggests "majorness" or "minorness" to the listener. Let us, then, examine further the findings which cast doubt on the invariance of the correspondence between chordal structure and modal affect.

Shortly before World War I, Valentine, an English psychologist, began to question the idea that a particular chordal or melody structure automatically called forth a particular modal name.[4] His subjects, he found, made many errors in their attempts to separate the major from the minor. About fifteen years later, Heinlein made a similar observation.[5] Heinlein's much more extensive research showed that even his musically trained subjects labeled as minor more than a third of the major chords he presented to them, and labeled major approximately 12 per cent of the minor chords. Furthermore, Heinlein located a number of compositions in a major key which sounded minor to his subjects, and others in minor mode which were reacted to as major. Thus, a Sousa performance of Handel's *Largo* from *Xerxes* and the first theme of the largo movement from Dvořák's *Fifth Symphony*, both in major keys, seemed minor; and *Anitra's Dance* from Grieg's *Peer Gynt Suite*, written in minor mode, was described as bright and happy. A Kreisler rendition of his own *Caprice Viennois* was labeled melancholy by many and cheery by many others. Hevner, however, found that her musically trained group and even her relatively untrained subjects usually did rather well in separating the major from the minor melodies (as distinguished from simple chords).[6]

It has been noted that both the whole-tone chord, C, E, G sharp, and the chief Siamese chord (which is about halfway between our major and minor) tend to be classified incorrectly as minor.[7] There seems to be a fairly widespread misconception that whatever is not major must be minor. So much, then, for the invariance of the structure-mood relationship.

Modern research has brought to light three other variables which can affect the success with which people distinguish major from minor. These are loudness, pitch, and tempo. Thus, Heinlein noted that the louder and/or higher-pitched chords seemed more major and the softer and/or lower-pitched ones minor.[8] Flatting and wobbling the thirds and sevenths are tricks employed in the blues and later popular music to induce minor effects. Characteristic of much American Negro music is the alternation of ordinary major thirds and sevenths with "blues" (slightly flatted) thirds and sevenths. Other techniques to create a sad atmosphere are found in some jazz compositions—*Beale Street Mamma*, for instance—where there is an avoidance of the leading tone. The tonic is approached at a cadence through a blue third, the sixth from below, or, more rarely, the blues third and the second.[9]

That tempo is an important variable can easily be demonstrated if the reader will simply drag the timing of some otherwise major-sounding melody, or play rapidly some typical dirge. His classification of what had been a happy-sounding tune will now more likely be minor, and of the erstwhile dirge, major.[10]

We conclude that the problem of identifying the major chord or major melody is far more complicated than was once thought. It is admitted that major chords and melodies are typically employed, in Western culture at least, on joyful occasions. But the relationship is by no means invariant. Moreover, the effect can be nullified by deliberate changes in loudness, pitch, or tempo.

Color-Tone Linkage

Music has chromatic (i.e., color) notes and a chromatic scale. It also has timbre, which in German is *Klangfarbe*, that is, sound-color. Music has color, then, in a figurative sense. But is there a further, literal sense in which color and tone are joined? Is there a necessary connection between any particular frequency, interval, chord, timbre, key, or melodic sequence on the one hand and some given color? Many musicians and poets of the past and even an occasional scientist have thought so. The great Newton saw such a connection in the "fact" that both the diatonic scale and his own classification of colors had seven names. But since the days of Helmholtz it has been known that there is no finite number of colors. Newton might just as well have named eight or only four colors. Nevertheless, the idea that there is some inherent connection between color and tone has persisted and has led to the construction of a number of instruments which "play" colors (e.g., the clavilux), and sometimes tones as well.

In the table below are contrasted the key-color associations of two eminent Russian composers.[11] It should be noted that they agree but slightly.

KEY	RIMSKY-KORSAKOV	SCRIABIN
C major	White	Red
G major	Brownish-gold, bright	Orange-rose
D major	Yellow, sunny	Yellow, brilliant
A major	Rosy, clear	Green
E major	Blue, sapphire, sparkling	Bluish-white
B major	Somber, dark blue shot with steel	Bluish-white
F sharp major	Greyish-green	Bright blue
D flat major	Dusky, warm	Violet
A flat major	Greyish-violet	Purple-violet
E flat major	Dark, gloomy, bluish-gray	Steel-color with a metallic luster
B flat major	——	Steel-color with a metallic luster
F major	Green	Red

It is the general lack of agreement among those having tone-color associations which attests the absence of inherent connection between the two senses. There is often some similarity among the associations of the members of a family, but this much agreement can be expected because of common family experiences.

That color-tone associations are very common has been shown by many investigations. In one of Omwake's surveys of college students, 60 per cent reported that they had color-tone associations.[12] Less than 1 per cent of the general population has color imagery of hallucinatory intensity when stimulated by particular tonal signals.[13] The behavior of this tiny fraction of our population has been termed "colored hearing," or chromesthesia, one of several possible types of synesthesia.

If one can trust the introspective reports of chromesthetics, it would appear that some see a colored haze whenever they are stimulated by a particular auditory stimulus. Thus, when the nineteenth-century musician Joseph Raff heard a cornet, he viewed the world through a greenish haze; the flute produced in him an experience of azure blueness, and the hautboy, yellowness. The trumpet called up scarlet, the French horn purple, and the flageolet grey.

Chromesthetic behavior tends to run in families, but this does not necessarily imply biological inheritance. Chromesthesia is induced most frequently in persons with vivid imagery, and is facilitated by fatigue, shock, and the presence of certain drugs, e.g., mescaline.[14] The reaction is one-way, i.e., with color never calling up a tonal hallucination. In chromesthesia, higher tones are usually tied to brighter colors.[15] As a rule, chromesthetics cannot recall the date of the peculiarity's first appearance. Hence, they tend to regard colored hearing as inborn and universal and to look upon those who claim not to have it as insensitive individuals who are not realizing their potentialities.

So far as the writer knows, no one has ever been able to induce a chromesthesia under controlled scientific conditions. Kelly did what he could along this line, even going to the extent of giving his subjects peyote and physical shocks in the hope that these added stimuli might help elicit the effect.[16] But no one of his subjects even after 2000 associations of tone and color (even 3000 for one subject) became a chromesthetic.

In an ingenious experiment by Howells, subjects were given either a high or a low tone along with a green or a red light.[17] Most of the time the high tone and green light were given together and the low tone and the red. But occasionally the experimenter reversed the pairings. The subjects were told that their jobs depended on doing well and so were strongly motivated. They kept their eyes closed until the tones were heard. Then they examined the lights and quickly named them. Of considerable theoretical interest is the fact that there was a gradual increase in the number of naming errors made at the times of the unusual, i.e., high-tone/red and low-tone/green pairings. But whether this rise in the error curve indicates the creation of a chromesthesia or of only a pseudochromesthesia is problematical.

The reason for the presence of chromesthetic behavior in a few persons and its absence in most others is still not known.[18] Anatomical, physiological, and psychological theories have been suggested, but no one theory seems entirely satisfactory. Of course, there is the possibility that the correct answer may involve more than one theory. For example, it is conceivable that the chromesthetic is one whose brain structures and/or physiological functions are such that he makes tone-color conditioned responses more readily than do most of us. But he would also need to be a person for whom some accident of environment had allowed the tonal and color stimuli to occur together so that the conditioning could take place and a given tonal configuration could come to "mean" a certain color. Here, then, is one hypothesis. But whether it is correct or incorrect, the fact remains that no aspect of tone has, per se, a universal color-meaning.

"The Language of the Emotions"

Perhaps it is time to consider a warning sounded on several occasions by C. C. Pratt,[19] an aesthetician who sees a fundamental ambiguity in the idea that "music is the language of the emotions." Pratt notes that to many writers this expression appears to mean that the emotional character of music is a subjective commotion within the listener. To others, including Pratt, the emotional character is an objective property of the music itself. The confusion arises, thinks Pratt, in that the same words have quite properly been employed to describe the objective as well as the subjective events. Both John Doe and a certain musical composition may seem agitated, or calm, or passionate, or sentimental. But in Doe's case the affair is one of moods and emotions, of *kinesthetic-organic* forms, while with the music it is a matter of *tonal* form.

The attempts of the formalists to keep these two sets of phenomena separate should not deny the possibility that on occasion agitated music may stimulate agitation in the listener. The formalist may take a somewhat superior attitude and imply that the sophisticate does not allow his moods and emotions to intrude while he is listening to the "best" in music. But the rank and file of us are not functioning at such an "elevated" level and know of many occasions when joyous-sounding music has improved our mood or when a sad-seeming composition has elicited a sad effect.

A danger greater than that of denying the possible influence of music on mood and musical character lies in the assumption that tonal forms invariably arouse the moods and emotions whose names they share. Psychiatrists and clinical psychologists would no doubt rejoice if all they needed to cure the depressed or the maniacal were access to a variety of compositions whose "moods" had previously been carefully catalogued. Therapy under such circumstances could be administered in truly engineering fashion—composition X for one disturbance and Y for another. But music's effects are not so invariant, and the listener is, after all, no automaton. He has a personal, as well as a cultural, history which makes his reactions to any piece of music, to some degree at least, unique and therefore difficult to forecast.

Years ago the great Thomas Edison was so concerned at what he considered the whimsicalness with which composers titled their compositions that he hired a panel of experts to catalogue his 589 available recordings according to "mood." Out of these, the panel labeled 112 "true mood music."[20] Fifteen were guaranteed to stimulate and enrich imagination, 14 to bring peace of mind, 10 to make one joyous, and 8 to elicit moods of wistfulness. Ten were kept in the list for jolly moods and good fellowship, 9 for more energy, 11 for love, 10 for moods of dignity and grandeur, 12 for the mood of tender memory, 13 for the mood of devotion, 9 for stirring the spirit, and 16 to "catch the childish fancy and make it merry with glee."

No doubt hearing the Edison recordings worked wonders on the more suggestible. Yet Anna Case's singing of *Home, Sweet Home,* supposed by Edison's panel to bring peace of mind, might well have made the homesick person more distraught. And while some of the more religious-minded no doubt found Schubert's *Ave Maria* conducive to the peace of mind Edison had guaranteed, it is doubtful if all so benefited. In fact one could be almost certain that the forced hearing of this composition would make the confirmed communist more irascible.[21]

The mood elicited by the music will depend not only on the tonal configuration the listener hears but also on a variety of factors external to the music itself. Among the more important of these variables are the listener's personality structure,[22] the mood held just preceding the listening period, the word-meanings of the libretto if there is one, and the attitudes built up in the listener toward music in general and toward the piece in question. Although musical compositions can quite properly be placed into mood categories, they will not invariably arouse the moods in terms of which they have been described. We are thus forced to conclude that music can be regarded as a language of moods and emotions in a very limited sense only.

Adjective Lists for Classifying Music

Research by Schoen, Gatewood, Mull, and others has demonstrated beyond the possibility of doubt that synonymous words will be employed to describe the character of most music whenever the listeners are drawn from roughly the same subculture.[23] The degree of agreement is little affected by differences in listener intelligence, tested musical aptitude, musical training, or age level (if above the sixth grade).[24] As might be suspected, listener agreement is greater where the concern is with program music.[25] It is relatively poor for passages which are characterized in terms of "yearning," "tenderness," and "calm."[26] "Defiance" is more easily identified than "rage" or "fear."

A more systematically constructed adjective check list than any used in the past has been developed by Hevner.[27] It contains 67 words arranged in eight clusters. The mood quale expressed by the adjectives within any one cluster has been assumed to be almost identical. Hence, the characterization of any bit of music is typically made in terms of a profile of the eight clusters and not of the 67 adjectives, although the listener is urged to check every word he regards as appropriate. The clusters are arranged like the dial of a clock on the supposition that as one proceeds from any given cluster around the dial, the mood-similarity steadily decreases until the opposite cluster is reached; from there back to the starting cluster the resemblance increases.

The utility of the check list for the aesthetician can be illustrated by data from the files of the Stanford Laboratory. In one experiment, 200 college students were asked to listen to a number of brief tonal patterns. It will suffice for our purposes to show the responses to two of these musical passages. Only the adjectives checked by one-half or more of the listeners will be listed. For the first 12 measures of the First Movement of Franck's *Symphony in D Minor* (allegro non troppo) all but one of the adjectives were from cluster 2—heavy, gloomy, dark, solemn, and mournful. For the first 26 measures of Debussy's *Clair de Lune*, on the other hand, the adjectives checked were quite different. Here, two were from cluster 5, one was from 3, and two were from 4—delicate, graceful, dreamy, soothing, and serene. These checkings were quite reliably and consistently made. It is to be expected, of course, that the responses would have varied

HEVNER ADJECTIVE CHECK LIST

6
bright
cheerful
gay
happy
joyous
merry

7
agitated
dramatic
exciting
exhilarated
impetuous
passionate
restless
sensational
soaring
triumphant

5
delicate
fanciful
graceful
humorous
light
playful
quaint
sprightly
whimsical

8
emphatic
exalting
majestic
martial
ponderous
robust
vigorous

4
calm
leisurely
lyrical
quiet
satisfying
serene
soothing
tranquil

1
awe-inspiring
dignified
lofty
sacred
serious
sober
solemn
spiritual

3
dreamy
longing
plaintive
pleading
sentimental
tender
yearning
yielding

2
dark
depressing
doleful
frustrated
gloomy
heavy
melancholy
mournful
pathetic
sad
tragic

97

somewhat had there been changes in the manner in which the passages were played. All in all, the technique is a fairly sensitive one which allows a reasonably clear picture to be drawn of the mood character of the musical fragments.

Modified Adjective Check List

A	B	C	D	E
cheerful	fanciful	delicate	dreamy	longing
gay	light	graceful	leisurely	pathetic
happy	quaint	lyrical	sentimental	plaintive
joyous	whimsical		serene	pleading
bright			soothing	yearning
merry			tender	
playful			tranquil	
sprightly			quiet	

F	G	H	I	J
dark	sacred	dramatic	agitated	frustrated
depressing	spiritual	emphatic	exalting	
doleful		majestic	exciting	
gloomy		triumphant	exhilarated	
melancholic			impetuous	
mournful			vigorous	
pathetic				
sad				
serious				
sober				
solemn				
tragic				

Hevner's check list has been recently revised with a rearrangement of the adjectives so that the new clusters have considerably more mood consistency than the older clusters had.[28] In the course of the research it was found that one of the adjectives, "pathetic," fitted almost equally well two of the revised clusters. The adjective "frustrated" did not fit any of the clusters and so stood alone. It was found that neither the original Hevner nor the revised clusters could be placed in exact clock-face arrangement although the new clusters came closer than the old to satisfying such a scheme.[29] No doubt as time goes on this much-used Hevner list will be added to and further improved.

Variables Which Give Meaning to Music

Of the variables which give meaning to music, tempo plays the largest role. According to Hevner, who has carried on numerous experiments in this area, modality is probably second in importance.[30] Pitch seemingly ranks third. Harmony and rhythm are of far less importance, and whether the melody is ascending or descending carries relatively little meaning to the listener. In other words, the listener is most likely to change the affective terms with which he describes what he hears whenever its tempo is appreciably slowed or hastened. Other alterations of the musical matrix change less strikingly what he feels the music is saying to him.

The relative importance of these variables can be seen in Hevner's table, reproduced below. There is no need to consider here the statistics by which she derived her weights; for our purposes it is enough to say that they indicate the relative importance of the variables. The following example indicates how to interpret the table: For music described as dignified and solemn the most important variables appear to be firm rhythm, slow tempo and low pitch. Major mode, ascending melody, and simple harmony are of little importance.

Gundlach has made a somewhat different analysis of the variables which give meaning to music.[31] He factor analyzed data obtained from asking listeners to characterize a considerable number of melodies.[32] Out of this process emerged a factor which dealt with tempo, smoothness of rhythms, and loudness. A second factor had to do with orchestral range and the use of certain intervals, particularly firsts and seconds. A third factor was related to the use of large intervals. Gundlach found music carried by woodwinds to be characterized by terms such as "mournful," "awkward," and "uneasy;" by brasses as "triumphant," and "grotesque;" by the piano as "delicate," "tranquil," "sentimental," and "brilliant;" by strings as "glad."

RELATIVE IMPORTANCE OF SIX VARIABLES

Musical Factor	Dignified Solemn		Sad Heavy		Dreamy Sentimental		Serene Gentle	
Mode	Major	4	Minor	20	Minor	12	Major	3
Tempo	Slow	14	Slow	12	Slow	16	Slow	20
Pitch	Low	10	Low	19	High	6	High	8
Rhythm	Firm	18	Firm	3	Flowing	9	Flowing	9
Harmony	Simple	3	Complex	7	Simple	4	Simple	10
Melody	Ascending	4	—		—		Ascending	3

Musical Factor	Graceful Sparkling		Happy Bright		Exciting Elated		Vigorous Majestic	
Mode	Major	21	Major	24	—		—	
Tempo	Fast	6	Fast	20	Fast	21	Fast	6
Pitch	High	16	High	6	Low	9	Low	13
Rhythm	Flowing	8	Flowing	10	Firm	2	Firm	10
Harmony	Simple	12	Simple	16	Complex	14	Complex	8
Melody	Descending	3	—		Descending	7	Descending	8

PITCH, RANGE, AND TEMPO

High Pitch	European	sentimental, whimsical, animated, glad
	Indian	happy love, recitative
Low Pitch	European	mournful, somber, tranquil, dignified, grotesque
	Indian	general war, organization of war party
Wide Range	European	uneasy, animated, grotesque, brilliant, glad
	Indian	general war, organization of war party
Narrow Range	European	tranquil, dignified, delicate, mournful, awkward, somber
	Indian	healing, scout, warpath
Fast	European	brilliant, animated, uneasy, glad, whimsical, flippant, grotesque
	Indian	general war, organization for war
Slow	European	dignified, somber, tranquil, melancholy, mournful, delicate, sentimental
	Indian	in battle, sad love

Two tables constructed by Gundlach seem worthy of reproduction here. They contrast the connotation of certain variables in European-style music with those in the music of a number of American Indian tribes.

RHYTHMS AND INTERVALS

Factors	Characterization of Musical Phrases	Appropriate Situations for	
		Indian Songs	European Folk songs
Many Rough Rhythms	grotesque uneasy	after killing warrior scout song, victory	victory war march
Many Uneven Rhythms	delicate sentimental dignified exalted somber	disappointment in love parting happy love	death of lover description of, or song to, love
Few Uneven Rhythms	flippant animated grotesque brilliant	after killing warrior recitatives victory	victory
Many Smooth Rhythms	brilliant animated flippant glad	war medicine parting death of lover healing, happy love	lonesome or sad gay or playful
Many 1sts and 2nds	uneasy mournful awkward	war medicine death of lover healing, recitatives warpath	sentimental or serious love lonesome or sad absence or parting
Many 3rds	triumphant	absence of lover after killing warrior war organization	victory
Many Large Intervals	glad, exalted delicate	disappointment in love lonesome, scout	gay or playful lonesome or sad death of lover, war dirge

From the Harvard Laboratory of Social Relations comes an interesting study in semantics.[33] Metaphorical terms employed to describe voice qualities were taken from the writings of George Bernard Shaw and three contemporary music critics. These were offered to musically naïve subjects for use in describing nine operatic voices. There appeared to be far better than chance agreement among the judges and a tendency to lump the descriptive terms into three categories—one having to do with evaluation, another with potency, and a third with activity. The baritone voice was often termed "dull," "coarse," "closed," "dark," "heavy," "rough," "hard," and "thick;" the tenor as "bright," "thin," and "light;" and the soprano as "coarse," "soft," "light," and "thin."

Another attempted use of factor analysis for studying the meaningful elements of music can be seen in the researches of Henkin.[34] The items to be intercorrelated were the preferences of college students who had listened to ten pieces representative of (a) Baroque, pre-classic, and classic, (b) romantic, and (c) modern styles. Two independent, meaningful factors emerged, which Henkin designated as a melodic and a rhythmic factor. There was also the possibility of a third factor, orchestral color. When Henkin was deciding on his ten compositions, he searched for recorded music written in a "purely harmonic idiom" but was unable to find a single example. It was this lack of records with strong emphasis on harmony, he feels, that kept a harmonic factor from appearing in his final data.

The data of a slightly later study led Henkin to believe that the melodic and rhythmic factors are independent both mathematically and psychologically. These factors appeared to be relevant variables in eliciting the galvanic skin response. Musical style, dynamics, orchestration, timbre, and other compositional variables seemed to have no significant relationship with this physiological measure of affective response.

The Expression of Tensions

A number of researchers have felt that to characterize the meanings of music solely in terms of the Hevner mood-adjectives is to oversimplify. These theorists prefer to describe what music signifies in the framework of conflict, of the arousal, growth, change, and resolution of tensions. While granting that unfamiliar music designates no concrete goals and no specific, universally agreed-upon imagery, they hold that it can carry a message of goal-seeking, goal-blocking, and goal-finding. We have already seen an illustration of the resolution of tensions in the discussion of the keynote (p. 41).[35] But these theorists are more concerned with larger segments of behavior and feel that music can depict, though but vaguely, fairly extensive experiential episodes.

Rogge is one who has become impatient with the earlier, highly analytic studies of music's linguistic potentialities. To test the possibility that music can communicate in terms of human tensions, she developed a clever experimental design. Bloch's *Schelomo*, Ravel's *Daphnis and Chloe*, and Stravinsky's *L'Histoire du Soldat* were chosen for study. She first played these pieces to a group of eighteen college students who differed somewhat in musical training and for whom the compositions were unfamiliar. After these students were carefully queried about their reactions to the music, the interview material was analyzed to extract similarities in content. Out of the content similarities, two different paragraphs were constructed for each of the three pieces. These six descriptions were arbitrarily termed the "correct" descriptions.

Other students were then called in to read these six paragraphs and to decide which of Hevner's adjectives most adequately characterized the three mood patterns.[36] When agreement was reached, two new paragraphs were composed for each piece. These differed from the "correct" descriptions as to narrative, i.e., in concrete imagery, but could be characterized by the same Hevner adjectives. Hence, they were termed "correct in mood only." This meant that Rogge now had four paragraphs for each piece, two "correct" ones made up from interview material, and two "correct in mood only." To make the procedure clearer the four for *Schelomo* are given below.[37]

Correct

He wants to see her open her eyes, to see her looking at him. He wants to see that she remembers too. Remembers the years they had been apart, searching, following one another from border to border. He wants to see her remembering now the last few years they've been together. If he could whisper just once more how much he loves her, how the memory of her love for him is deep inside him. Her forehead is cold. Her eyes glass over. He cries out, begging her to return. Once again he is alone. He can't believe it. Then holding her hand, he begins to feel the strength of their love. He knows it will be strong enough to help him go on alone.

Correct

As he watches the shore fade away he wants to sit on the deck and sob. He can never return to that land he loves. He is exiled. Forever. Why hadn't they believed him when he had pleaded? Had there been one voice to defend his act? No, not one. Now, as the shoreline lies dim on the water he grips the rail. Had they all been blinded to his love by their own hate? Persecuted, suffering in loneliness, can he condemn them? Can he fear his future now, regret his love for his country? No, for so long as he knows that what he has done was right, will benefit his people, then he can somehow endure the coming years.

Correct in mood only

The pigeon flies back through the cold gray sky. The storm has passed, and she is anxious to return to the safety of her nest. When she is over a village she hears a bell tolling. She wants to stop, to descend and rest, but more than anything else she wants to reach home. She passes over another town searching for the building where she knows her nest lies strong and secure, and as she sees the chimney, she circles and begins to settle. As she alights on the ledge, and folds her wings, she sees that the storm has dislodged her nest and the three eggs.

Correct in Mood Only

As he approached her house he wondered if she had forgotten that night on the lake. He straightened his well-clad shoulders. How would she react to his success? Oh, he wished she might open the door and be as she was before, as she was that night on the lake. Going up the steps he remembered. Twenty years. Oh, if she still had that strong, direct warmth. She would probably shout his name when she'd see him. He heard footsteps inside. He held his breath. The door opened. As he saw the stooped old woman he closed his eyes. It can't be true. This wasn't her. He wanted to open his eyes, telling himself he'd been mistaken. But his eyes refused to open.

The table below indicates how a third group of some ninety students reacted to the descriptions while listening to the three compositions.[38] They had been asked to select the three descriptive paragraphs which best matched the three pieces of music. If chance

ROGGE DATA

Description	Bloch	Ravel	Stravinsky
1	★★16	1	1
2	0	1	★4
3	0	0	★3
4	6	★★28	0
5	2	★1	0
6	★11	0	1
7	2	★3	0
8	1	3	★★49
9	★★25	0	0
10	15	★★48	3
11	1	1	★★27
12	★11	4	2
Total	90	90	90

alone had operated, seven and one-half votes would have been cast for each of the twelve descriptions. But that the voting was not a chance affair is suggested by the concentrations at the double-starred positions, which indicate the "correct" descriptions. The single stars show descriptions which were "correct in mood only." These descriptions received relatively few votes.

Naturally, the Rogge study, like all pioneering experiments, can be criticized. One wonders, for instance, how the votes would have fallen had three pieces more alike in mood been selected. A good guess would be that Rogge maximized her effects by her choice of compositions. It is also quite possible that the votes for the "correct-in-mood-only" paragraphs might have been more numerous had the mood been judged directly from the music instead of from reading the "correct" descriptions.

In spite of certain inadequacies in the Rogge experiments, it is probably safe to conclude that unknown compositions may be described not only in terms of the Hevner adjectives but sometimes also in the language of goal-striving, goal-blocking, and the resolution of tensions.[39] Of course, a descriptive narrative with its specific imagery may not be the same for any two persons. But any narrative with patterns of stress parallel to the tension episodes of the music will be appropriate to describe the musical action.

Music as a Universal Language

We have seen that the major chord communicates its "proper" message only under rather limited circumstances, and that while our major scale may have symbolized decadence to Plato, it does not affect us in such a fashion. Although the Siegfried motive may be perceived by the devotee of the *Ring* cycle in the approved Wagnerian manner, it will have quite different meanings to those who have not been taught Wagnerian symbolism. Are there, then, no musical configurations which have similar meanings to people of widely dissimilar culture?

After considering the data of his tables, presented in the preceding section, Gundlach concluded that there is at least some slight similarity in the meanings the cultured European and the American Indian attach to the musical variables he had studied. But whether the similarities are extensive enough to raise them significantly from chance is a question. Morey played Schubert's *Doppelgänger* and the love duet from *Tristan* to members of the Loma culture in Liberia and found these "emotionally charged" compositions to have little emotional effect on the African natives.[40] Yet the argument has been made that had he played other sorts of European music he might have stirred their emotions.

When Dartmouth psychologists asked laymen to draw forms suggested by hearing a series of twelve short, simple, clarinet selections, there was more than chance similarity among the forms produced under the stimulation of any one of the selections.[41] Cowles likewise found some agreement among subjects who had been asked to select a particular picture to match a given musical selection.[42] And, reversing the experimental procedure, Willmann found a degree of correspondence among musical themes composed under the stimulation of four designs, e.g., a saw-toothed form.[43]

The commonality of response which appears in these experiments can be explained, in part at least, on purely practical grounds. It would hardly seem reasonable to expect a mother to scream a lullaby to her baby, regardless of the culture to which she might belong. She would be likely to employ soft tones, monotony, and anything else she and other mothers the world over had learned was sleep inducing. Similarly, a piece of extremely fast tempo could scarcely mean "march" to any human. In line with Pratt's argument (p. 93), one might hazard a small wager that were a Chinese, a Loma Negro, and an Italian forced to listen to a series of tones all of the same pitch and then told to draw whatever seemed appropriate, they would be more likely to draw horizontal lines than vertical or wavy ones.

Psychoanalytic Symbolism

The early psychoanalysts claimed to have discovered a symbolism which is universal in its sweep but unknown to the individual until made manifest through psychoanalysis. The force of the claim for universality was somewhat tempered, to be sure, by the inability of the analysts to agree among themselves on what symbolizes what. Yet this lack of agreement did not deter the bolder of them from extending their dogmas to embrace most if not all human activities. For illustrative purposes, only a few of the claims pertaining to music need be given here, since very little has been done by way of scientific check. Thus, Montani holds that minor modes containing the diminished third express feelings of the suffering, chastisement, and pain which characterize reactions to the castration complex.[44] According to Mosonyi primitive and noninstrumental music signifies narcissism, and "good" harmonies "mass ecstasy."[45] On occasion, the symbols reflect obvious associations, e.g., rhythm and sexual intercourse, and in other instances, only an analyst will see a logical connection.

Altshuler[46] and Tilly[47] have also suggested that music possesses sexual symbolism. However, these theorists feel that the symbols are, to some degree at least, recognized even by laymen. Their interest in such symbolism stems from the belief that music can be employed therapeutically. According to them, a "manly" patient who has emotional difficulties should be approached with music different from what must be employed with a man of more "feminine" personality. In other words, some music is "masculine" in character and other music is "feminine."[48]

A number of psychologists have attempted to set up experiments with the aim of indicating to what extent music can be described in terms of a masculine-feminine continuum.[49] As a result of these studies it seems clear that, *if forced to it*, laymen and musicians will agree in selecting certain composers as the creators of predominantly masculine music and others as the originators of rather feminine compositions. Thus, Wagner, Beethoven, Shostakovich, Bach, and Rimsky-Korsakov are regarded by many as having created music most of which was masculine in character; R. Strauss, Chopin, Debussy, Brahms, and Schubert are classified as writers of more feminine music. By and large, the march, loud music, and the music of the drums, bass viols, trombones, and trumpets are thought of as the more masculine; "decorative" music, soft music, and that rendered by the harp are classified as feminine.

These findings should not be taken to mean that certain musical phenomena necessarily function as sexual symbols.[50] Rather, the data appear to show that, in the American subcultures polled, individuals are sometimes willing to use "masculine" and "feminine" as category headings if these names are suggested to them and that there is considerable consistency in the way they employ them. But the making of such forced choices should not be interpreted as proving that Beethoven's music is inherently and universally masculine in any true sense of the term. The raters presumably have associated loud and low-pitched tones with men, marching rhythms with male soldiers, soft music with women, etc. When queried, the raters generally maintain that they would have much preferred to use other categories than those of "masculinity" and "femininity."[51]

Summary

Music has a grammar, a syntax. And its composers, the orators and authors of music, often have much to say. To this extent, then, music behaves as a language. But does music convey detailed messages which are understood similarly by large groups of listeners? This is a question that has aroused extended argument.

Key effects, at least for the modern listener, do not exist in any objective fashion. Nor is there a natural tone-color linkage although many persons associate a particular color with some pitch or timbre and a few have associations of hallucinatory intensity. However, major and minor effects are real, at least in certain cultures. Chordal structure, loudness, pitch, and tempo each plays its part in eliciting the words "happy" and "sad." Moreover, there are a number of other affective and tension responses which music can convey to the relatively unsophisticated listener. Some music can even be described as masculine or feminine, although this sort of categorization seems to have little significance and certainly none that would excite any but the Freudians. All told, then, it is clear that the "messages" of music are in the affective rather than the cognitive realm. Music stimulates no detailed imagery of a sort that is widely shared. To call music a language, then, is to distort out of all proportion the meaning of the term.

The paragraph given below illustrates rather well the fallacy in the thinking of those who would make music a language in the sense that English or French is a language. These notes, taken from a program of the Boston Symphony Orchestra, describe some of the varied reactions to Beethoven's *Seventh Symphony*.

Mark what commentators have found in the Seventh symphony: One finds a new *Pastoral* symphony; another a new *Eroica*. Alberti is sure that it is a description of the joy of Germany delivered from the French yoke. Dr. Iken of Bremen saw in it a political revolution. Nohl shakes his head and swears it is a knightly festival. Marx is inclined to think that the music describes a Southern race, brave and warlike, such as the ancient Moors of Spain. An old edition of the symphony gave this programme: "Arrival of the Villagers; Nuptial Benediction; The Wedding Feast." Did not Schumann discover in the second movement the marriage ceremony of a village couple? D'Ortigue found that the Andante pictured a procession in an old cathedral or in the catacombs; while Duerenberg, a more cheerful person, prefers to call it the love-dream of a sumptuous odalisque. The Finale has many meanings: a battle of giants or warriors of the North returning to their country after the fight; a feast of Bacchus or an orgy of the villagers after a wedding. Ulibichev goes so far as to say that Beethoven portrayed in this Finale a drunken revel to express the disgust excited in him by such popular recreations. Even Wagner writes hysterically about this symphony as "the apotheosis of the dance," and he reminds a friend of the "Stroemkarl" of Sweden, who knows eleven variations, and mortals should dance to only ten of them: the eleventh belongs to the Night spirit and his crew, and if any one plays it, tables and benches, cans and cups, the grand-mother, the blind and lame, yea, the children in the cradle, fall to dancing. "The last movement of the Seventh symphony," says Wagner, "is this eleventh variation."[52]

We are forced to conclude that, ordinarily, the images music arouses are specific to the experiences of the listener.[53] If several listeners have had similar experiences, are trained in the same school of imagery (e.g., the motive-hunting Wagnerians), their images will, quite naturally, be more alike. On the affective side there is more commonality of response, at least partly from the fact that, as Pratt phrases it, music sounds the way the emotions feel. Music can be used to indicate the build-up and release of tensions. It can, of course, be given almost any desired meaning if time is taken to stamp in the proper associations. Such specificity of designation, however, is not generally encouraged, for to most people the real essence of music lies in the fact that it gives each person an oppor-tunity to project his private experiences through his own personal images or even to listen without trying to elicit images of any sort.[54] Everyone can appreciate the grammar, the melodic and harmonic rules of the school to which the music of his immediate interest belongs. But he is not listening to a language in the fullest sense of that term.

Notes

1] One is reminded of the legislative threats against rock 'n' roll during the summer of 1956.

2] For an exception to this statement, see the next section of this chapter.

3] M. F. Meyer, *The Musician's Arithmetic*, Boston, Ditson, 1929.

4] C. W. Valentine, "The Aesthetic Appreciation of Musical Intervals among School Children and Adults," *Brit. J. Psychol., 6* (1913): 190–216.

5] C. P. Heinlein, "The Affective Characters of the Major and Minor Modes in Music," *J. Comp. Psychol., 8* (1928): 101–142.

6] K. Hevner, "The Affective Character of Major and Minor Modes in Music," *Amer. J. Psychol., 47* (1935): 103–118.

7] P. R. Farnsworth, "The Discrimination of Major, Minor, and Certain Mistuned Chords," *J. Gen. Psychol., 1* (1928): 377–379.

8] C. P. Heinlein, "The Affective Characters of the Major and Minor Modes in Music," *J. Comp. Psychol., 8* (1928): 101–142. L. Kaiser, in "Contribution to the Psychologic and Linguistic Value of Melody," *Acta Psychol., 9* (1953): 288–293, argues that falling intervals lead to sad affects while rising intervals the size of the fifth are exhilarative.

9] Note that it is not the blues third per se which yields a minor effect but rather the over-all melody in which the third is embedded. Intervals as such have no modal characteristics (p. 40).

10] For detailed material on the effect of tempo see M. G. Rigg's "Speed as a Determiner of Musical Mood," *J. Exp. Psychol., 27* (1940): 566–571. Rigg has verified Heinlein's work on the effect of pitch in "The Effect of Register and Tonality upon Musical Mood," *J. Musicol., 2* (1940), 49–61. See also K. B. Watson's extensive work on "happy" and "sad" music in "The Nature and Measurement of Musical Meanings," *Psychol. Monog., 54*, No. 2 (1942).

11] Taken from P. A. Scholes, *The Oxford Companion to Music*, second edition, London, Oxford U. Press, 1943. Reproduced by permission of the publisher.

12] L. Omwake, "Visual Responses to Auditory Stimuli," *J. Appl. Psychol., 24* (1940): 468–481. It has also been demonstrated that there is a slight tendency for persons who are more interested in color than in form to prefer tone to form. See W. A. McElroy, "Colour Form Attitudes, an Analogue from Music," *Austral. J. Psychol., 5* (1953): 10–16.

13] C. E. Seashore, "Color Music," *Mus. Ed. J., 25*, No. 2 (1938): 26.

14] J. Delay, *et al.*, "Les Synesthésies dans l'Intoxication Mescalinique," *Encéphale, 40* (1951): 1–10.

15] The fact that synesthesias are not entirely chance associations between two sense modalities is emphasized by D. I. Masson in "Synesthesia and Sound Spectra," *Word, 8* (1952): 39–41.

16] E. L. Kelly, "An Experimental Attempt to Produce Artificial Chromesthesia by the Technique of the Conditioned Response," *J. Exp. Psychol., 17* (1934): 315–341.

17] T. H. Howells, "The Experimental Development of Color-Tone Synesthesia," *J. Exp. Psychol., 34* (1944), 87–103.

18] O. Ortmann, "Theories of Synesthesia in the Light of a Case of Color Hearing," *Human Biol., 5* (1933): 155–211; L. A. Riggs and T. Karwoski, "Synaesthesia," *Brit. J. Psychol., 25* (1934): 29–41; M. J. Zigler, "Tone Shapes: A Novel Type of Synaesthesia," *J. Gen. Psychol., 3* (1930): 277–287.

19] C. C. Pratt, *The Meaning of Music,* N.Y., McGraw-Hill, 1931; "The Design of Music," *J. Aesth., 12,* No. 3 (1954): 289–300. Essentially the same position is taken by O. K. Bouwsma in Chapter 5 of *Aesthetics and Language,* W. Elton, ed., N.Y., Philosophical Lib., 1954.

20] W. V. Bingham, *Mood Music,* Orange, N.J., Thomas A. Edison, 1921.

21] A more recent study along the Edison lines is that of A. Capurso, *et al., Music and Your Emotions,* N.Y., Liveright, 1952, pp. 56–86. Sixty-one pieces were found which provided listener agreement (1075 nonmusical students were the listeners) of 50 per cent or more when the task was to sort the compositions into six categories.

22] Thus S. and R. L. Fisher, in "The Effects of Personal Security on Reactions to Unfamiliar Music," *J. Soc. Psychol., 34* (1951): 265–273, report that a large percentage of those who react to "dramatic" music with unusually extreme favorableness or unfavorableness seem to possess marked personal insecurity.

23] M. Schoen and E. L. Gatewood, Chapter 7 in *The Effects of Music,* M. Schoen, ed., N.Y., Harcourt, Brace, 1927; H. K. Mull, "A Study of Humor in Music," *Amer. J. Psychol., 62* (1949): 560–566.

24] R. E. Dreher, "The Relationship between Verbal Reports and Galvanic Skin Responses to Music," Doctoral Thesis, Indiana U., 1947.

25] P. J. Hampton, "The Emotional Element in Music," *J. Gen. Psychol., 33* (1945): 237–250.

26] I. G. Campbell, "Basal Emotional Patterns Expressible in Music," *Amer. J. Psychol., 55* (1942): 1–17; B. Shimp, "Reliability of Associations of Known and Unknown Melodic Phrases with Words Denoting States of Feeling," *J. Musicol., 1,* No. 4 (1940): 22–35.

27] K. Hevner, "Expression in Music: A Discussion of Experimental Studies and Theories," *Psychol. Rev., 47* (1935): 186–204; "Experimental Studies of the Elements of Expression in Music," *Amer. J. Psychol., 48* (1936): 246–268. (The Hevner Adjective Check List is reproduced by permission of the *Psychological Review* and the American Psychological Association). A. L. Sopchak, "Retest Reliability of the Number of Responses to Music," *J. Psychol., 44* (1957): 223–226.

28] P. R. Farnsworth, "A Study of the Hevner Adjective List," *J. Aesth., 13* (1954): 97–103.

29] The mood expressed by the adjectives of cluster A resembles most closely the mood of clusters B and I, and resembles least the mood of clusters E and F. The adjective "frustrated" describes a mood which only cluster F reflects, and even here the affect is expressed with little precision.

30] K. Hevner, "Studies in Expressiveness of Music," *Mus. Teach. Nat. Assoc. Proc. 1938*, pp. 199–217. See also Hevner's "Experimental Studies of the Elements of Expression in Music," *Amer. J. Psychol., 48* (1936): 246–268; "The Affective Value of Pitch and Tempo in Music," *Amer. J. Psychol., 49* (1937): 621–630; "Expression in Music," *Psychol. Rev., 42* (1935): 186–204.

31] The tables that follow, reproduced by permission of *The American Journal of Psychology*, are from R. Gundlach, "Factors Determining the Characterization of Musical Phrases," *Amer. J. Psychol., 47* (1935): 624–643; "A Quantitative Analysis of Indian Music," *Amer. J. Psychol., 44* (1932): 133–145. See also S. DeGrazia's attempted analysis of Shostakovich's *Seventh Symphony*. His descriptive categories are intra-opus repetition, short and symmetrical themes, figurative background, simplicity of fugal form, regular chord progressions, rhythmic background, and correlative description ("Shostakovich's *Seventh Symphony*: Reactivity-Speed and Adaptiveness in Musical Symbols," *Psychiat., 6* (1943): 117–122).

32] Factor analysis is a method for resolving a set of interrelated variables or tests into a few "factors" which are regarded as being the fundamental variables underlying the original complex of variables.

33] R. W. Brown, R. A. Leiter, and D. C. Hildum, "Metaphors from Music Criticism," *J. Abn. Soc. Psychol., 54* (1957): 347–352.

34] R. I. Henkin, "A Factorial Study of the Components of Music," *J. Psychol., 39* (1955): 161–181; "A Reevaluation of a Factorial Study of the Components of Music," *J. Psychol., 43* (1957): 301–306.

35] R. V. Fay points out that music tensions are produced by "dissonance and diminution of dissonance, intensification of a rhythmic pattern, intensification of a note or chord, sequential building of phrases or motives, change in dynamics, alternation of unfamiliar material with familiar material, enlargement and elaboration of material already presented, addition of new harmonies or of melodic and rhythmic counterpoints" ("Tension and Development as Principles in Musical Composition," *J. Musicol., 5* (1947): 1–12).

36] Actually, only a portion of the Hevner list was presented.

37] G. O. Rogge, "Music as Communication, with Special Reference to Its Role as Content," Doctoral Thesis, U. of California at Los Angeles, 1952, pp. 66–67.

38] G. O. Rogge, *op. cit.*, p. 76.

39] A. Pepinsky, "The Contribution of the Frequency Factor to the Psychological State of Tension," *Mus. Teach. Nat. Assoc. Proc. 1939*, pp. 134–143.

40] R. Morey, "Upset in Emotions," *J. Soc. Psychol., 12* (1940), 333–356.

41] T. F. Karwoski, H. S. Odbert, and C. E. Osgood, "Studies in Synesthetic Thinking: II. The Role of Form in Visual Responses to Music," *J. Gen. Psychol., 26* (1942): 199–222; L. Omwake, "Visual Responses to Auditory Stimuli," *J. Appl. Psychol., 24* (1940): 468–481.

42] J. T. Cowles, "Experimental Study of Pairing Certain Auditory and Visual Stimuli," *J. Exp. Psychol., 18* (1935): 461–469.

43] R. R. Willmann, "An Experimental Investigation of the Creative Process in Music," *Psychol. Monog., 57*, No. 1 (1944).

44] A. Montani, "Psychoanalysis of Music," *Psychoanal. Rev., 32* (1945): 225–227.

45] D. Mosonyi, "Die irrationalen Grundlagen der Musik," *Imago, 21* (1935): 207–226.

46] I. M. Altshuler, "The Case of Horace F.," *Mus. Teach. Nat. Assoc. Proc. 1946*, pp. 368–381.

47] M. Tilly, "The Psychoanalytic Approach to the Masculine and Feminine Principles in Music," *Amer. J. Psychiat., 103* (1947): 477–483.

48] The ancient theorists of China also saw sex qualities in music. In the Lin Lun system of approximately 2700 B.C. in the reign of Emperor Huang-ti there were the *lu* or masculine family of scale notes and the *lui* or feminine. See also the theories of Handschin (p. 52).

49] P. R. Farnsworth, J. C. Trembley, and C. E. Dutton, "Masculinity and Femininity of Musical Phenomena," *J. Musicol., 9* (1951): 257–262; C. H. Rittenhouse, "Masculinity and Femininity in Relation to Preferences in Music," Thesis, Stanford U., 1952; P. R. Farnsworth, "The Musical Taste of an American Musical Elite," *Hinrichsen Musical Year Book, 7* (1952): 112–116.

50] I. A. Berg, in "Observations Concerning Obsessive Tunes in Normal Persons under Stress," *J. Clin. Psychol., 9* (1953): 300–302, has made a study of clients who were plagued by obsessive songs and song lyrics. Interestingly enough, he found that their conflicts, while severe, were largely nonsexual. This was true even though the lyrics of these obsessive tunes were filled with what the Freudians traditionally term sexual symbols, e.g., bananas, coconuts, pistols, and the like.

51] A cleverly written article on art and Freudianism is that by R. Arnheim, "Artistic Symbols—Freudian and Otherwise," *J. Aesth., 12*, No. 1 (1953): 93–97. Other articles on the same general topic can be found in this issue of the *Journal of Aesthetics*.

52] A. R. Chandler, *Beauty and Human Nature*, N.Y., Appleton-Century, 1934, p. 213, by permission of the publisher.

53] Thus, persons who possess tonal-visual associations which differ markedly from those of Walt Disney and his staff may have found his *Fantasia* extremely distasteful (H. B. English, "*Fantasia* and the Psychology of Music," *J. Aesth., 7* (1943): 27–31).

54] The calling up of imagery is certainly not essential to the musical enjoyment of adults. Evidence is at hand that this generalization also holds true for children 10 to 14 years of age (J. H. Higginson, "The Associational Aspect of Musical Response in School Children," *J. Educ. Psychol., 27* (1936): 572–580.)

CHAPTER SIX

The Nature of Musical Taste

A PERUSAL of the current definitions of musical taste would lead one to believe that there is no definition which can be taken as authoritative. Even Runes's *Dictionary of Philosophy*[1] offers two statements which are quite different in meaning. His first is "the faculty of judging art without rules, through sensation and experience." The second, "the ensemble of preferences shown by an artist in his choice of elements from nature and tradition, for his works of art," would appear to be acceptable if the term "artist" is broadened to include *all* men making judgments in the field of art. The term "preferences" should not be limited to momentary pleasures, but should refer to an over-all, average set of emotionally oriented attitudes, even including the strivings for appreciations not as yet gained. Thus, the person who is endeavoring to achieve an appreciation of Bach's music, but who so far does not enjoy contrapuntal music, has taste different from that of his friend who casts Bach aside as the mere creator of tinkly sounds.

Musical taste can be very roughly described as the over-all attitudinal set one has toward the phenomena which collectively

Note: The material in this and the following chapter is reprinted (with adaptations and revisions) from *Musical Taste: Its Measurement and Cultural Nature* by Paul Randolph Farnsworth with the permission of the publishers, Stanford University Press. Copyright 1950 by the Board of Trustees of Leland Stanford Junior University.

comprise music. The communication expectancies one has, the attitudes built up in one toward modal, finality, key, and other effects, all quite clearly form a part of musical taste. In the present chapter we shall examine this larger attitudinal picture called taste in an effort to understand at least a little of its nature.

Whimsey or Law?

The fact that several of one's friends may enjoy only jazz and other colleagues receive their greatest pleasure from the music of Bach is often brushed aside with an airy "What's one man's poison, *signor*, is another's meat or drink." The assumption seems implicit in this statement that taste is whimsical, and so without pattern of any sort. But the diametrically opposed view—and the more common one— is that musical taste obeys some absolute and unchanging set of laws. According to this view, the musically elite—the critics, the genius-composers, and the musicologists—have discovered, or are on their way to discovering, what constitutes "good taste." One's jazz-loving friends have taste of a low order; a higher order of taste is possessed by the man who loves the music of Mendelssohn but not that of Bach; and a still higher status has been reached by those who are more attracted to the works of Bach than to those of Mendelssohn.

Laws can be either absolute, eternal, and unchanging, or relative, culturally derived, and stable for only limited areas and periods of time. The professor of music who attempted to keep his students from being "polluted" by the music of Mahler and Bruckner—which really happened—was following the absolutist's conception of musical taste. His colleague was more of a relativist when he said to his students: "I much prefer the music of the early nineteenth century to that of later periods. Yet it might be well if you would become familiar with music of later periods, since who can tell what level of regard this newer music will have achieved by the days of your grandchildren."

The absolutist in musical theory holds that musical creations are good because they follow metaphysical rules, or are in line with certain of the principles of natural science. For a sample of the metaphysical approach, we can refer to the classical Chinese, who justified their pentatonic scale on the grounds that there were five, and only five, elements—metal, wood, water, fire, and earth; five social and political relationships—father and children, husband and wife, brothers, friends, and ruler and subjects; and five political terms—king, official, people, governmental affairs, and wealth.[2]

Closer to our own culture was the Western European sixteenth-century taboo against music ratios employing prime numbers not in the series 1–6.[3] The reason offered, as we saw in Chapter 2, was that space has six directions—above, below, fore, after, right, and left. To make use of a prime not in this series was thought to be contrary to the Will of God. Even in our own time there are many who believe that "good" aesthetic taste is inherent in those of us who happen to have been born under a propitious sign of the zodiac, but these astrology-lovers are often a little vague as to just which sign is most influential in predetermining taste. Whatever the astrological answer, however, it does not check with experimentally tested facts. For it has been demonstrated that the distribution of the birthdays of the musically great is not different from that of the less gifted.[4] In their birthdays, the artistic and the inartistic have been favored by the same astrological signs.

Although it is quite probable that only the more credulous today would believe in such metaphysical principles as the above, the idea that a law of physics or of some other natural science underlies taste is still held by many theorists. We have already noted (p. 21) that a number of the important textbooks persist in describing the scale of just intonation as the scale of nature and our contemporary equally tempered scale as a compromise affair, simply because the former can be derived, in theory at least, from the overtone series,

while the latter cannot be so rationalized. These overtone enthusiasts seem to forget that other cultures have enjoyed equally
tempered scales, some of them even farther removed than ours from
the possibility of such rationalization, e.g., the Siamese and the
Javanese. Although the physics of horns, reeds, and strings did help
condition the early use of the octave, and perhaps a few of the other
intervals with simple ratios, it seems unjustifiable to restrict our
explanations of present-day taste to physical principles.[5]

Attention has already been called to the interesting neurological
speculations of Meyer and to the theories of Mursell, particularly as
they relate to finality effects (pp. 42, 53). So long as these theories
are not formulated to exclude habituation they would not appear un-
tenable, although in the present primitive state of neurology they do
not seem currently to furnish much help to the understanding of the
nature of taste. A firmer statement can be made about the relation
between the true beat in music and body pulse-rate (p. 5), for
there are experiments to show that the latter cannot possibly account
for the diversities of true beat. It is obvious that the capacities of the
biological organism set the general limits within which man's ears
and his muscles react. But that they can affect his taste without the
mediation of cultural forces has never been demonstrated. All the
facts so far accumulated by the musicologists and social scientists
seem to point in a different direction, toward a cultural explanation
of taste.

The hypothesis that contemporary taste in music is, at least in
large measure, culturally derived, can be demonstrated through
the data of anthropology, history, and experimental psychology. It
has been shown that the Occidental love for simple rhythms, careful
tuning, fixed tonal steps, harmonies, the tonic effect, and the
diatonic scale is not shared the world over. As we saw earlier, the
African predilection for complicated rhythmic patterns was so far
out of line with the taste and perceptual abilities of many of the early

missionaries that they commonly reported the Africans to be arhythmical. The Chinese often appear oblivious to mistunings; they love music which has little harmony in the Western sense of the word. Yet Orientals can learn to love Occidental music and, indeed, with continued residence in America come to appreciate Western musical principles, and gradually to develop facility in the perception of small auditory differences. Conversely, the people of the Western world often learn to love alien music forms, and to master more complicated rhythmic patterns. When constantly subjected to poor tuning, the American slowly loses his pitch sensitivity and his need for pitch exactitude.

It is well known that the people of each culture area are likely to regard their art forms as God-given and superior to those of their neighbors. But the theorist who would accept the mythology of racism and believe that the composers of his group alone have discovered the "true" standards of musical taste will receive no support from the social sciences.

Some form of the absolutist view is often accepted by professional musicians. It is among the relatively untutored, on the other hand, that the whimsey view of taste is more likely to be found. As a matter of fact, the evidence which can be gathered supports neither of these conceptions. But before indicating what theoretical position the facts force us into, let us see why we cannot accept the idea that taste is without pattern. We shall first note the degree of agreement to be found in judgments on relative eminence.

Eminence

The most eminent composer is not necessarily the best known, or even the man whose works are most preferred. Yet the relationship between these three categories—eminence, knowledge, and preference—is a close one. Moreover, while eminent composers are assumed to be geniuses or at least near-geniuses, not all geniuses can be called eminent. Only a few live up to their potentialities, or create that which is honored by their fellows. Others have traits of character or are subjected to situational pressures which preclude great achievement; or perhaps they are not born at the "right moments" in the development of their art.[6] We can readily accept the traditional, dictionary view of eminence as "an elevated condition among men; a place or station above men in general," adding that the elevated status is the result of social evaluations which are relative to particular times and places.

The patience of the listener, along with the conventions of the classroom and lecture hall, force each lecturer on music history to confine his talk to an hour or two. Similarly, written work is restricted to what the author and editor, if no one else, consider a reasonable number of pages. These limitations function to reduce the number of composers who can receive critical attention, and to decrease the extent to which those of lesser importance can be treated. By these means, eminence hierarchies are in effect created, with as many such lists appearing as there are musicologists at work. Each scholar has his individual biases, produced out of national, school, and teacher loyalties, and occasional illogical reasoning, to mention what are perhaps the most obvious influences. If eminence as a measured entity is to have stability, each selection of the eminent must be balanced by the choices of many others. Fortunately, the polling of individual decisions furnishes just such a balancing mechanism, and cancels out many of the eccentricities in the choices.

EMINENCE RANKINGS. The unsoundness of the view that taste is just a matter of whimsey can be demonstrated in a variety of ways. Our first evidence is that the members of the American Musicological Society, one group of elite, agree among themselves extremely well in their selections of eminent musicians. In 1951 these specialists were asked to consider a long list of composers born since 1870 and to check the names of the ten whose contributions to music appeared to be of greatest importance.[7] As the ballot sheets were received, they were put alternately into two piles, the first ballot going into pile 1, the second into pile 2, the third into pile 1, etc. Thus, with two piles of the same 'size, two rankings of eminence could be constructed by tabulating the number of checks each composer received from the ballots in each pile.

The table below shows that the first seven names chosen by the two subgroups of musicologists were identical. The eighth and ninth of the one subgroup were the ninth and tenth of the other. Of course, if the table had been lengthened to include composers who received relatively few votes, the two columns would not resemble each other quite as much as they do now. For just as almost all of us relish roast beef and apple pie but disagree more with regard to tripe and cottage-cheese pie, so practically all musicologists treat with high regard Stravinsky and Bartók, but do not agree quite as well on the importance of composers of the order of Mason and Lockwood.

FIRST NINE EMINENCE CHOICES OF MUSICOLOGISTS
POLLED IN 1951
COMPOSERS BORN SINCE 1870

Rank Order	Pile 1	Pile 2
1	Stravinsky	Stravinsky
2	Bartók	Bartók
3	Hindemith	Hindemith
4	Ravel	Ravel
5	Schönberg	Schönberg
6	Prokofiev	Prokofiev
7	Vaughan Williams	Vaughan Williams
8	Copland	Rachmaninov
9	Britten	Copland
11	Rachmaninov	10 Britten

Note: The name appearing below the line in any one of the columns appears among the first nine in one of the other columns.

The musicologists were also asked in 1951 to scrutinize lists of composers whose birth dates were before 1870. They were to check the 25 they deemed most worthy to be called to the attention of their children and their lay contemporaries. When the two-pile scheme was employed, the top names were found to be the following:

FIRST NINE EMINENCE CHOICES OF MUSICOLOGISTS
POLLED IN 1951
COMPOSERS BORN BEFORE 1870

Rank Order	Pile 1	Pile 2
1	Beethoven	Beethoven
2	Bach	Bach
3	Haydn	Brahms
4	Brahms	Mozart
5	Mozart	Haydn
6	Debussy	Schubert
7	Handel	Debussy
8	{ Schubert	Handel
9	{ Wagner	Wagner

The members of the American Musicological Society were first consulted in 1938 and were asked at that time to list the ten musicians of history whom they regarded as having contributed most to music.[8] A total of 92 composers were named in this survey. Letters were again sent to the AMS members in 1944 and, as we have already noted, once more in 1951.[9] The ballots received in 1944 were placed randomly into two sets. Special attention was paid to the ranks achieved by the 92 names mentioned in the original (1938) survey. The correlation (*rho*) between the two-pile orders came to the high value of ·97.[10] The same technique employed on the 1951 data yielded *rho*'s of ·96 for those born since 1870 and ·98 for those born before this date. It is thus apparent that even at the lower levels of eminence there was considerable agreement between the two sub-groups of contemporary musicologists. It can safely be said, then, that the judgments of this group of the musically elite are following some sort of principle or lawful pattern.

The reader may say, however, that it is one thing to prove that considerable agreement in taste exists among musical specialists, and quite another to demonstrate it among lay groups. To answer this reasonable objection, the procedures which were employed with the musicologists were used in 1945 with 250 college students taken from psychology classes at Stanford University, with 105 nearby senior high-school students, and with 100 sixth-graders and 100 fifth-graders. Here, again, each group was split into two and the scheme was followed of correlating two eminence lists compiled from the ballots cast for the 92 composers voted as most eminent in 1938. While no correlations quite as high as the ·98 of the musicologists appeared, the college value was found to be ·95, the high-school ·93, the sixth-grade ·93, and the fifth-grade ·87.[11] It is not assumed that these groups are typical of all college, senior-high, or grade-school groups, even in California. But it is logical to believe that since all the above groups showed marked communality of taste, other fairly similar lay groups would also show fair agreement among themselves.

For illustrative purposes, the nine names receiving the highest number of college votes from a 1953–54 balloting are shown below.[12]

FIRST NINE EMINENCE CHOICES OF 120 COLLEGE STUDENTS POLLED IN 1953–54 COMPOSERS BORN BEFORE 1870

Rank Order	Pile 1		Pile 2
1	Beethoven		Beethoven
2	⎰ Bach		Bach
3	⎱ Chopin		Chopin
4	⎰ Mozart		Mozart
5	⎱ Tchaikovsky		Wagner
6	⎰ Brahms		Brahms
7	⎱ Liszt		Tchaikovsky
8	⎰ Wagner		Handel
9	⎱ Schubert		Liszt
10	Handel	10·5	Schubert

The fact that musically elite, college students, and even high- and grammar-school students agree so well in their selections of eminent composers can only be interpreted as showing that this facet of taste is patterned and is not a matter of whimsey.

Eminence hierarchies of great stability also appear when people of similar culture are queried about the composers of the "popular classics." The next table shows the top nine names given by two college groups of approximately 40 each, questioned in 1954. Each subject had been given a list on which were the names of 108 composers and had been told to rank the ten most eminent from 1 to 10.[13]

FIRST NINE CHOICES OF 80 COLLEGE STUDENTS, POLLED IN SUMMER OF 1954
COMPOSERS OF "POPULAR CLASSICS"

Rank Order	Pile 1		Pile 2
1	George Gershwin		George Gershwin
2	Cole Porter		Irving Berlin
3	Jerome Kern		Jerome Kern
4	Irving Berlin		Richard Rodgers
5	{ Richard Rodgers		Cole Porter
6	{ Stephen Foster		Stephen Foster
7	Hoagy Carmichael		S. Romberg
8	S. Romberg		{ Hoagy Carmichael
9	J. Strauss		{ Sir Arthur Sullivan
10·5	Sir Arthur Sullivan	10	J. Strauss

CHANGES IN EMINENCE RANKINGS. If taste behaves as do other folkways it should be possible to perceive changes over the years. That such changes do occur is shown by the fact that although the eminence ranks yielded by the votes of the American Musicological Society's members in 1951 correlated ·95 with the ranks obtained in 1944, they correlated only ·85 with the 92 ranks derived from the polling of 1938. (The comparisons concerned the 1938 poll's 92 eminent names.)

EMINENCE RANKS OF THE MUSICOLOGISTS

Rank Order	1938		1944		1951
1	Bach		Bach		Beethoven
2	Beethoven		Beethoven		Bach
3	Wagner		Mozart		Brahms
4	Mozart		Wagner		Haydn
5	Palestrina		Haydn		Mozart
6	Haydn		⎰ Brahms		⎰ Schubert
7	Brahms		⎱ Palestrina		⎱ Debussy
8	Monteverdi		Schubert		Handel
9	Debussy		Handel		Wagner
10	Schubert	10	Debussy	10	Palestrina
11	Handel	25	Monteverdi	15	Monteverdi

Stanford college students similarly polled showed the following agreements: 1953 and 1945, a *rho* of ·88; 1953 and 1938, a *rho* of ·81.

EMINENCE RANKS OF COLLEGE STUDENTS

Rank Order	1938		1945		1953
1	Beethoven		Beethoven		Beethoven
2	Bach		Wagner		Bach
3	Wagner		Mozart		Chopin
4	Mozart		Bach		Mozart
5	Brahms		Chopin		⎧ Wagner
6	Tchaikovsky		Tchaikovsky		⎨ Tchaikovsky
7	Schubert		Brahms		⎩ Brahms
8	Chopin		Mendelssohn		Liszt
9	Mendelssohn		Schubert		Schubert
11	Liszt	10	Liszt	17	Mendelssohn

REVERENCE FOR THE PAST. One occasionally hears a cynic remark that "the older a composition the more highly will it be regarded," or, "Music of the quality of Mozart's compositions but written in the twentieth century will not receive wholehearted acceptance." Unfortunately, the complete facts which could prove or contradict these statements are not at hand. Yet data are available which bear at least indirectly on the problem. They refer, however, to the eminence of composers rather than to the acceptability of the compositions.

In one pertinent study, the time which had elapsed since the birth of each of the 92 composers mentioned as most eminent in the 1938 polling of the American Musicological Society was carefully tabulated.[14] The rank order which these time periods yielded was then correlated successively with each of more than 20 eminence ranks obtained through a variety of methods. The coefficients of correlation were found to range from $+ \cdot 21$ to $- \cdot 36$, with the median coefficient falling at $- \cdot 15$, a value not significantly different from zero. Had time from death been used in the tabulations instead of time since birth, the values would have been almost precisely the same, since the two time series correlate $\cdot 99$ one with the other. The over-all picture, then, disclosed no significant relationship between the relative eminence of the men in this highly selected list and elapsed time since birth or death.

In a second study, the relation of the year of birth to eminence was observed by plotting the birth years of the 92 selected composers, and then finding the central tendency. The median birth year was found to fall in the decade of the 1720's.[15] Next, the birth years of a larger number of less rigidly selected musicians were analyzed to determine the effects of broadening the concept of "high eminence." For this part of the research the original list of 92 composer names was expanded to include 118 other composers mentioned as eminent by current musicologists in their articles and books. The median birth year of this less highly selected group fell in the first decade of the 1800's. Finally, to study the effect of broadening the selection still more, the birth years of all the musicians mentioned in two current encyclopedias of music, the *Oxford Companion to Music* and the *International Cyclopedia of Music and Musicians*, were examined. For these two large groups the median birth years were in the late

1820's and the early 1850's, respectively. In each of the four lists examined, the mode was found to fall several decades after the median.

Another view of the working of the same principles can be obtained by studying the birth dates of the hundred or so who ranked highest in the American Musicological Society's eminence lists. The 5 persons who achieved top status in the 1944 survey were found to have a median birth year of 1756. For the top 11, the median figure was 1770; for the top 15, 1809; top 25, 1813; top 100, 1820. The comparable medians compiled from the data of the 1951 survey were astonishingly similar: top 5, 1756; top 11, 1770; top 15, 1797; top 25, 1810; top 100, 1818. The analyses were not carried beyond the first hundred ranks because of the poorer reliability of the lower rank positions.

From the data of these researches we can conclude that, in considering musicians of great eminence, there is little or no tendency to bestow most honor on those who have been longest dead. It is clear, however, that the higher the selection of those we call eminent, the greater the chance that they will not be of our own day. In fact, the data show that it is far easier for a composer of a century or so ago to achieve a placement in a music encyclopedia than it is for one born toward the end of the last century or later. The composer of recent years has not had the requisite time to become familiar to his listeners, to build up a school of supporters. His peer of many centuries ago is also at a disadvantage, for his works are too far removed, stylistically, from the contemporary scene. The latter's chances of being rediscovered become progressively slighter as his birth date recedes farther and farther from the 1700's. The most honored, then, must be the between-groups, the composers of the eighteenth and nineteenth centuries.

Enjoyment

For those who refuse to believe that the measurement of eminence is an adequate measurement of contemporary taste, there is pertinent information to be considered which concerns the closely related variables of enjoyment and knowledge. Enjoyment and eminence ratings are positively correlated. But their degree of relationship varies with the musical sophistication of the subjects.

Data on enjoyment have been obtained from students of the San Francisco City College.[16] These subjects were asked to check a list of 225 names and to indicate the ten composers whose music they most enjoyed. The *rho* between the rank orders of two subgroups was ·66, showing fair agreement. It should be noted that Bach falls lower in this sort of ranking than in the eminence listings.

FIRST NINE PREFERENCES OF 126 JUNIOR-COLLEGE
STUDENTS POLLED IN 1954

Rank Order	Pile 1		Pile 2
1	Chopin		Chopin
2	Beethoven		Beethoven
3	Tchaikovsky		Schubert
4	Brahms		⎧Tchaikovsky
5	Mozart		⎩Mozart
6	Rimsky-Korsakov		Brahms
7	⎧Sousa		R. Strauss
8	⎨Debussy		⎧Sousa
9	⎩Bach		⎩Foster
10·5	Foster	11·5	Debussy
12·5	Schubert	11·5	Bach
15·5	R. Strauss	15·5	Rimsky-Korsakov

The well-known West Coast critic Alfred Frankenstein has also found Bach relatively lower in the enjoyment lists he assembled by interviewing many college students in different areas of the United States.[17]

As another example of how similar groups will show similar preferences, let us examine the ballots collected from members of the Philadelphia Orchestra and the Boston Symphony Orchestra in the early 1930's by Folgmann, a former symphony player.[18] The members of these orchestras were asked to exclude from their preference ratings of composers any biases based on their knowledge of the relative greatness of the composers. As can be seen from the accompanying table, the first nine names are identical, although the order is somewhat dissimilar for the members of these two great orchestras.

PREFERENCES OF SYMPHONY PLAYERS

Rank Order	Boston	Philadelphia
1	Beethoven	Beethoven
2	Wagner	Brahms
3	Bach	Bach
4	Mozart	Mozart
5	Brahms	Wagner
6	Debussy	Schubert
7	Schubert	Haydn
8	Haydn	Debussy
9	Schumann	Schumann

The enjoyment of sections of compositions,[19] of the simpler phrases, and even of chords and intervals, is also rather consistent for similar groups. Let us compare the order of preference established for college students at the University of Minnesota in the years before 1929[20] with the order found at Stanford University in 1933.[21] While there is some slight variation in the order of preference, there is essential agreement as to which intervals are preferred, which are regarded as neutral, and which are disliked.

Some years ago, while making studies of the *Measure of Consonance* from Seashore's well-known music-test battery and of Kwalwasser's *Melodic and Harmonic Sensitivity* tests, an analysis was run of the "errors" made by two large groups of subjects.[22] In these experiments, the *Measure of Consonance* was treated as a tonal-preference test, just as were the two Kwalwasser records. The "errors" (i.e., the disagreements with the "correct" choices) of two groups of 100 subjects each correlated in this order: Consonance, ·96; Melodic Sensitivity, ·98 ; Harmonic Sensitivity, ·99. A later, similar study of the Kwalwasser-Dykema *Test of Melodic Taste* yielded coefficients of correlation of ·78 for fifth-graders, ·92 for eighth-graders, and ·91 for college students.[23] The corresponding values for the Kwalwasser-Dykema *Test of Tonal Movement* were ·91, ·91, and ·98, respectively. Here again we see almost perfect agreements, this time in the liking for intervals, for simple phrases, and for certain resolutions as well.

PREFERENCES FOR INTERVALS

Rank Order	Minnesota	Stanford
1	Major Third	Major Third
2	Minor Third	Minor Third
3	Minor Sixth	Minor Sixth
4	Major Sixth	Fourth
5	Fourth	Octave
6	Tritone	Major Sixth
7	Fifth	Tritone
8	Octave	Fifth
9	Major Second	Major Second
10	Minor Seventh	Minor Seventh
11	Major Seventh	Major Seventh
12	Minor Second	Minor Second

Knowledge of Composers

Like enjoyment, knowledge of composers seems to be a factor in musical taste. The best known composers, however, do not always appear at the top of the eminence listings, and when knowledge and eminence ranks are correlated, the value may run as low as ·65. The next table shows the top nine composers as they appeared on certain college ratings of professed knowledge. When 212 names were considered, the rank orders of the two piles correlated at ·75.[24]

131

FAMILIAR NAMES, JUDGED BY 126 JUNIOR-COLLEGE STUDENTS POLLED IN 1954

Rank Order	Pile 1	Pile 2
1	Chopin	Chopin
2	Beethoven	⎰ Beethoven
3	Mozart	⎱ Mozart
4	Schubert	Schubert
5	Brahms	Tchaikovsky
6	Tchaikovsky	Brahms
7	R. Strauss	⎧ Schumann
8	Schumann	⎨ Bach
9	Bach	⎩ Mendelssohn
10	Mendelssohn	10 R. Strauss

Programs

By this time the reader may be saying to himself: "So far the behavior under observation has been purely verbal. Why not discuss taste from the standpoint of action? Does any one of our great orchestras, for example, ignore many of the more eminent composers and concentrate consistently on playing the music of certain others? Do the programs of the several great symphony orchestras of the world tend to resemble one another?"

To give a partial answer to the first of these queries a study was made of the frequencies with which the compositions of each of the 92 world-famous composers have been listed in the programs of the Boston Symphony Orchestra. The tabulations, made by decades, show rank-order correlations from one decade to the next averaging in the nineties (·87 to ·98). In the table below are given the names of the nine composers whose music was played most frequently in each of two decades. And again we can make the statement that the names are practically the same. In fact, the first ten names are identical.

PROGRAM CHOICES OF THE BOSTON
SYMPHONY ORCHESTRA

Rank Order	1925–1935	1935–1945
1	Beethoven	Beethoven
2	Brahms	Brahms
3	Wagner	{ Mozart
4	Bach	{ Sibelius
5	R. Strauss	R. Strauss
6	Ravel	Ravel
7	Mozart	Wagner
8	Sibelius	{ Stravinsky
9	Stravinsky	{ Tchaikovsky
10	Tchaikovsky	10 Bach

Furthermore, supplementary information shows that the programs of the great orchestras do resemble each other in large part. Mueller and Hevner have constructed a "popularity pyramid" from the programs played during 1936–41 by seven of our leading American symphony orchestras.[25] Note that nine of the top ten names of their pyramid appear among the ten played most often by the Boston Symphony Orchestra during the decade starting in 1935.

SEVEN AMERICAN SYMPHONY ORCHESTRAS, 1936–1941

Rank Order	Composers
1	Beethoven
2	Brahms
3	Mozart
4	Wagner
5	Tchaikovsky
6	Sibelius
7	{ R. Strauss
8	{ Bach
9	{ Ravel
10	{ Schumann

Thus it appears that this operational or action aspect of taste shows consistencies just as does the more verbal side, which is studied through balloting.

To learn whether or not the broadcast programs of recorded music also show consistency, an analysis was made by the author of the Pacific Gas and Electric Company's programs, which, for a period of years, were broadcast nightly over KYA from 8.00 until 10.00 P.M. The years 1941, 1942, and 1943 were chosen for study.[26] Ranks for each of these years were constructed by counting the number of times the works of the great composers were broadcast. Great consistency was found, shown by the fact that the average of the intercorrelations of the three ranks was ·95. If, then, other radio hours of this type show similar program hierarchies, and there is no reason to suspect that they do not, it can be said that the choice of recorded music for broadcasting purposes also follows some sort of lawful pattern.

PACIFIC GAS AND ELECTRIC COMPANY BROADCASTS

Rank Order	1941		1942		1943
1	Beethoven		Beethoven		Beethoven
2	Tchaikovsky		Tchaikovsky		Brahms
3	Brahms		Bach		Mozart
4	Mozart		Mozart		Bach
5	Sibelius		Brahms		Tchaikovsky
6	Bach		Sibelius		Wagner
7	Wagner		Wagner		Schubert
8	Schumann		Debussy		Sibelius
9	Schubert		R. Strauss		Debussy
11	R. Strauss	10	Schubert	10	Schumann
37·5	Debussy	11	Schumann	11	R. Strauss

CHANGES IN PROGRAMS. Fluctuations in musical taste can be seen clearly in program trend lines. If taste were a matter of the slow discovery of absolute values, one might reasonably expect that the great orchestras would gradually discard from their programs the works of all but the "best" composers. This progressive elimination would show itself in upward swings on the curves of the chosen few. However, when Mueller and Hevner examined the 1876–1941 programs of several of the great American symphony orchestras, curve fluctuations and plateaus rather than persistent climbs or falls seemed to be the rule.[27] It is true that Brahms was shown to be slowly climbing in favor. But the curves for Mozart and Bach were quite flat. Beethoven, who started at the top in favor, is still in this position, though his curve dropped speedily at first, then less rapidly and now has leveled off. Wagner started second in popularity, then had a dip in the late 1880's, climbed back into second place with a peak about 1910, and since has fallen markedly. Tchaikovsky's curve appeared to resemble Wagner's, but at a lower level of popularity.

These researchers have conducted many other interesting studies on taste, among them an analysis of the relative popularity of Beethoven's nine symphonies as program material. For illustrative purposes, it will probably suffice to describe the popularity curves of the *Fifth* and *Ninth*. The former had fairly high status in the earliest years, dropped a bit in the late 1880's, climbed in popularity rather rapidly until World War I, and has since fallen slowly though it is still much preferred to any of the other symphonies. The *Ninth* started somewhat below the *Fifth* and has rather steadily fallen in rank until it now is lowest in favor.

In the course of a later study, Mueller assembled additional data to show the cultural nature of taste.[28] Just as social attitudes tend to strike different world areas at somewhat different times, so, he finds, do trends in musical taste. Thus, while Beethoven's curve of popularity is much the same whether plotted for the London or the New York orchestras, any given position on the curve is reached by the New York orchestras approximately five years after the London body. For Wagner the lag appears to be in the same direction, but is fifteen years in length.

We have seen that the relative frequencies with which the works of eminent composers appeared on the programs of the Boston Symphony Orchestra for the decade beginning in 1925 are similar to those for the next decade. The data of the following table indicate that the resemblances tend to be greatest between contiguous decades. The program shifts are slow and irregular, but definitely present. The correlation values shown below were obtained from comparisons of the relative frequency of appearance of the works of 92 composers on the programs of this orchestra.

DECADE INTERCORRELATIONS FOR THE BOSTON SYMPHONY ORCHESTRA

Period	1905	1915	1925	1935
Decade Starting in 1895	·87	·82	·81	·81
Decade Starting in 1905	...	·92	·83	·83
Decade Starting in 1915	...	...	·98	·90
Decade Starting in 1925	...	...	...	·90

Space Allocations

Another operational or action aspect of taste concerns the relative amounts of space allotted to composers in histories of music and in general and music encyclopedias. As it is obviously out of the question to permit the insertion in these books of articles of considerable length on all of the world's musicians, there must be selection in considering the composers to be mentioned and the amount of space each composer is to receive. Our children cannot be informed about the lives and works of all who have composed. Are selections made, then, in accordance with some principle, or is it largely a matter of chance which composers are included in a history or an encyclopedia?

To throw light on this problem, histories and encyclopedias of the early 1900's were studied, as well as others published in each decade from 1920 on. It was found that the publications, some 22 or more in each decade, agreed among themselves quite well, that is, they devoted almost the same relative amounts of space to the musicologists' favored 92 composers.[29] The coefficients of correlation ranged from ·94 to ·96, demonstrating considerable communality of

way. That is, even if musical taste obeys social principles, individual differences of considerable magnitude will of necessity be present in this behavioral area, just as they are in all other socially significant realms of human response. In any social group there will be those who respond to a particular social pressure with almost complete passivity and compliance. Others will be more resistant, and a few will be extremely unconventional.

Although the pooling of items is necessary if trends are to be established, this process tends to mask whatever differences are present, and may give an erroneous impression of the extent of the agreement between people, books, programs, or whatever the items may be. To avoid all possibility of misinterpretation, it might be wise to study the diversity of the elements which make up a typical pool. To illustrate this process, 126 randomly selected college students were presented, late in 1946, with a list of over 200 composers born since 1860. They were asked to rank on a scale of 10 to 1 the names of those they regarded as the ten leading composers. The response sheets were divided by simple alternation into two equal piles, labeled A and B.

The table shows the detailed distribution of the votes cast for each of the twelve composers who received the greatest number of votes. The number at the top of each column shows the ascribed rank, and the numbers below (opposite the names of the composers) show the number of votes cast for each composer under each rank. Thus, twelve of the students in Pool A gave Debussy a rating of 10, five a rating of 9, etc. To figure the final ranks, the number of votes received by each composer was multiplied by the respective rank-value, the products were totaled, and the sums so obtained were arranged in order of size and ranked. For Debussy (Pool A) the figuring proceeded as follows: 12 times 10 plus 5 times 9 plus 12 times 8, etc. Note that even Debussy, who achieved the top position in each pool, received a number of 4-, 3-, 2-, and 1-order votes.

Thus the examination of the inner structure of the two pools reveals enormous individual differences among the judgments of the raters. Yet a view of the two rank orders shows almost unanimity of opinion when the voters are considered as groups rather than as individuals.

POOL A

ORDER OF CHOICE

Composer	10	9	8	7	6	5	4	3	2	1	Sums	Rank
Debussy	12	5	12	4	5	4	3	2	3	1	364	1
Kreisler	1	0	3	4	2	3	4	2	4	1	120	11
Sibelius	7	7	9	6	1	2	6	2	0	4	297	3
Ravel	1	8	3	2	2	4	4	2	1	0	176	9
R. Strauss	7	8	3	5	4	4	3	3	1	0	268	5
Paderewski	4	2	6	2	2	5	4	1	3	4	186	7
Prokofiev	0	3	1	4	7	2	2	2	1	1	132	10
Rachmaninov	7	12	6	11	5	2	1	3	0	2	358	2
Shostakovich	6	4	4	4	8	5	3	1	2	3	251	6
Stravinsky	2	2	3	5	5	1	4	8	4	3	183	8
Gershwin	7	6	7	1	4	5	3	4	3	5	271	4
Schuman, W.	0	0	0	1	1	4	4	1	3	2	60	12

POOL B

ORDER OF CHOICE

Composer	10	9	8	7	6	5	4	3	2	1	Sums	Rank
Debussy	16	7	10	5	1	5	3	3	2	1	395	1
Kreisler	1	1	4	1	4	1	5	4	5	5	134	11
Sibelius	7	7	5	5	2	4	2	4	8	0	276	5
Ravel	0	8	6	5	8	4	5	2	4	3	260	7
R. Strauss	9	7	5	5	2	4	2	4	8	0	296	4
Paderewski	0	8	7	6	3	1	1	6	5	4	229	8
Prokofiev	1	3	6	7	3	1	2	2	3	0	177	10
Rachmaninov	14	8	8	4	10	2	3	2	0	1	393	2
Shostakovich	5	5	3	5	6	5	9	3	1	2	264	6
Stravinsky	2	7	2	4	2	8	7	2	5	2	225	9
Gershwin	9	3	5	9	7	6	7	3	2	1	334	3
Schuman, W.	0	2	1	1	1	1	2	3	4	3	72	12

It has just been shown that individual musical tastes differ much as do other individual behaviors governed by social pressures. Moreover, characteristic differences as well as similarities also can be

detected among the programs of the leading American symphony orchestras. In their careful study of orchestral idiosyncracies, Mueller and Hevner have given us a wealth of information, from which are presented here a few illustrations of the characteristic program styles their researches have disclosed.[30]

During its years under Koussevitzky, the Boston Symphony Orchestra changed from lowest to highest place in the amount of Russian music it presented. But this great organization has never, except for a five-year period under the batons of French conductors, favored French music. Moreover, it has given little attention to Wagner. And, sur-prisingly enough when its foreign-born personnel is considered, it has always been a proponent of American music. Since 1920 it has been an outstanding leader in the presentation of music of the modern period.

Since the time of Stransky, the programs of the New York Philharmonic Orchestra have reflected less interest in Russian music than have the programs of the other leading American orchestras. But they have indicated more than average interest in German music, an interest held to throughout World War I. French and American music, on the other hand, have been rather neglected. The program trends of the sister organization, the New York Symphony Orchestra, are the most irregular and difficult to characterize of the entire study. The programs of this orchestra have been weak in German and American music, but strong in French.

The programs of the Philadelphia Orchestra have reflected almost an average interest in the music of all the chief Occidental nationali-ties, with the exception of the British. There is less than average interest indicated for the music of Beethoven, Mozart, Mendelssohn, Liszt, Handel (except from 1925 to 1930), Schumann, D'Indy, Rachmaninov (except from 1915 to 1920, 1925 to 1930, and 1937 to 1940), Saint-Saëns, Berlioz, and Glazunov. In contrast, more than average attention has been paid to Haydn, Bach (up to 1936), Brahms, Wagner, Debussy, Stravinsky, Sibelius, and Mahler.

The opera in New York and Chicago also has been scrutinized by these two researchers, with the result that certain characteristics for each geographic area have been uncovered. This research on the opera companies and that on the orchestras make it clear that while the hierarchy of composer prestige is roughly similar from one organization to another, conductors, directors, critics, and perhaps others stamp their individualities on the programs.

Criteria and Conditioners of Taste

With C. E. Seashore's dictum that beauty consists in artistic deviations from the regular or rigid no one need quarrel, for illustrations of this phenomenon are legion in all of the arts.[31] The painter never paints with completely photographic accuracy; the vocalist and the violinist make great use of that deviation from the regular known as the vibrato. But if one should desire to make specific use of this generalization in forecasting which future compositions will be accepted and which will be rejected, he will find it of little help. For what is considered an artistic deviation in one generation may not be so regarded in another. To be called artistic, a deviation must be acceptable to some particular culture group. And the reasons for its acceptance may be difficult to ascertain.

Howes and others have maintained that taste in music is good whenever one chooses the sincere; avoids the shallow, the sentimental, and the cliché; and is not deceived by base motives and emotions.[32] Some writers have implied that somehow the listener comes to appreciate the composer's motives, and so eventually develops good taste.

A careful examination of this position shows that no one can ever be absolutely certain of a composer's motives—not even from a study of his life, and certainly not from a mere scrutiny of his music. In fact, the musical genius often does not understand his own impulses, and if asked about them will answer with rationalizations of the most unrealistic sort. Was Wagner's music insincere because Wagner hoped it would bring him fame, and because he forgot his earlier democratic ideals? Is boogiewoogie shallow and sentimental per se, or because of the associations we have with it? These terms, it is clear, are not of much help to one who desires to study taste.

And as for the cliché, it need only be said that while there is a tendency to eschew the hackneyed, clichés are matters of personal experience, and the cliché of one period may become acceptable music in the next (and vice versa). Thus, parallel fifths were popular at one time, but became clichés later. Their excessive use in this second period brought on a ban which is only now being gradually lifted. To the listener born in this century, parallel intervals do not constitute hackneyed material but may be regarded as alluring and strange. Thus Howes's criteria, we are forced to conclude, are too subjective for our purposes. Only the cliché has utility as an explanatory concept, and even it has very definite limitations.

In considering the phenomena which are basic to the appreciation of music, E. H. Staffelbach has stressed the feeling tone he believes to be implicit in rhythms and auditory sensations; the associations formed between music and persons, places, things, and previously expressed affective states; the lure of the familiar and the novel; the stimulation of the imagination; the possibilities of self-expression; and the pleasures to be derived from the genius and good craftsmanship of composers and performers, from facts about the lives and works of these artists, and from the belief in one's ability to interpret what artists are attempting to express. [33] C. E. Seashore, a pioneer in the scientific study of music, has said:

> Why then do we love music? Among other things we love it because it creates a physiological well-being in our organism; it is built from materials which are beautiful objects in themselves; it carries us through the realms of creative imagination,

thought, actions, and feelings in limitless art forms; it is self-propelling through natural impulses, such as rhythm; it is the language of emotion, a generator of social fellowship; it takes us out of the humdrum of life and makes us live in play with the ideal; it satisfies our cravings for intellectual conquest, for isolation in the artistic attitude of emotion, and for self-expression for the joy of expression.[34]

Whether or not we agree with all of these carefully considered reasons for the love of music, it should be clear that the topic needs further review. It is time, then, to examine in some detail the theories which purport to explain the reasons behind some of our current preferences. The facts of the situation are still quite unclear. But sufficient data have already been assembled to prove the great importance of both formal training and incidental learning in the building up of taste norms.

CULTURAL DERIVATIONS. If taste is culturally derived rather than innate, one would expect to find the taste of the child approximating more and more closely that of the adult as he grows older. Such a convergence does occur in judgments of eminence. In one study in which several groups had been asked to assess the relative eminence of 92 composers, a group of fifth-graders was found to agree only slightly with the members of the American Musicological Society (a *rho* of ·33). But a group of sixth-graders was somewhat closer to the musicologists in its judgements (*rho* of ·52); the similarity was more marked for some high-school students (·68), and still more for Stanford University sophomores (·79). Musicologists surveyed in 1951 and college students polled in 1954 agreed to the extent of a *rho* of ·77. Here we see a steady climb in the degree of agreement as the groups become more alike in age and in training.

In 1913 Valentine reported on some of his experiments with British school children.[35] He found that by age twelve or thirteen there tended to be a decided change in the preferences for tonal intervals, so that the intervals preferred by adults were also enjoyed by adolescents. Another psychologist, Dashiell, observed that, although kindergarten children did not have precisely the adult preferences for the diatonic intervals, they already rated the thirds high and the sevenths and seconds low.[36] Aizawa, who had examined the songs most enjoyed by Japanese school children, noted that agreements in preference of children and adults increased as the school year advanced, being particularly marked among children of the upper classes.[37]

The Kwalwasser-Dykema *Test of Melodic Taste*, in which 20 items are considered for their suitability as concluding phrases, can be employed to yield data which reflect the learning of folkways. While the college subjects in one study of this test showed agreement with the "correct" responses on 15·4 out of 20 items, eighth-graders gave the "correct" responses 13 times, and fifth-graders only 12·2 times on the average. Similarly, when data of the Kwalwasser *Test of Harmonic Sensitivity* were analyzed, it was found that an unselected group of college students averaged 25·4 "correct" scores out of a possible 35, eighth-graders 24·1, and fifth-graders 21·2. As the ages became more similar the responses became more like those of the experts, i.e. more like the "correct" responses.

In the areas of tempo and rhythm, it is noteworthy that subjects show consistent preferences, but differ considerably among themselves.[38] Although one writer feels that this "intra-individual consistency" is the result of inheritance,[39] there are the previously mentioned data (p. 9) which clearly show that tempo preferences are in part functions of cultural conditioning. Foley, it will be recalled, found that subjects studying trades in which activity proceeds at a slow pace, e.g., dressmaking, favored andante tempo; those working with power machines, a slow allegro; while his typists preferred a fast allegro bordering on presto.[40] Other experimenters

(p. 69) have found that college students prefer their waltzes to be played at about the speed they have heard them rendered traditionally. In fact, these students have demonstrated a sort of absolute or positive tempo quite comparable to absolute pitch.

Somewhat similar to the work of Foley, but broader in its scope, was the study by Schuessler.[41] Eight phonograph recordings were played to large groups of subjects who had been divided according to occupation into six job levels. On the five-point preference scale which Schuessler employed, great differences of scores appeared.

CLIMATIC CYCLES AND TASTE. According to one of the climatic determinists, R. H. Wheeler, world climate fluctuates "in rhythms within rhythms which tend to follow multiples of the sun-spot cycle of 11·3 years."[42] Whether long or short, these rhythms "tend to follow a similar pattern of phase sequences, the phases being cold-dry, warm-wet, warm-dry, cold-wet, then cold-dry again, in that order." Phases of warm weather are supposed to bring into being musical taste for (and so creativity in the area of) the serious opera, the symphony, the sonata, the concerto, chamber music, swing, jazz syncopation, masses, anthems, oratorios, dissonance, and atonality. Warm weather is also said to be conducive to the rise of choruses, orchestras, and bands. Cold spells, on the other hand, somehow put us temperamentally in tune with light and comic operas, program music, tone poems, folk music, ballads, madrigals, and counterpoint—according to the Wheeler doctrine. During cold periods occur the heyday of Castrati and musicology! However, the "golden ages" of music were neither warm nor cold, but were rather periods of transition from cold to warm.

Wheeler holds that we are now in a cold-wet phase which we will not leave until 2000 or 2010 except for a ten-year warm period in this decade or the 1960's. Our last previous cold phase began around 1830; the last warm period about 1900. Since such swings are held by Wheeler to be the rule of nature, he believes that we need merely to study weather cycles to forecast the taste of any future time period. The only escape from these predetermined swings would seem, he says, to be in universal air-conditioning.

No scientist would dare say that the Wheeler doctrine may not eventually be found to have some very slight validity. Yet it would be surprising, to say the least, if the relatively insignificant temperature changes the world has endured during the past few centuries should have caused huge changes in aesthetic interests and taste while the far greater climatic differences of, say, Minnesota and California are apparently unrelated to musical taste.

TASTE CREATED BY THE STATE. It is becoming increasingly popular to believe that good taste in music is indicated by special reverence for those compositions which mirror the times. Some would go so far as to say that good taste insures the honoring of only that type of music which has a propaganda value for the furthering of "good" causes. Ordinarily, little is done to promote the acceptance of compositions which are so regarded. In lands under police control, however, this doctrine is often so rigidly enforced that only compositions which are felt to mirror the times or which follow the state's approved pattern can be heard.[43] The fact that the leaders may be deluding themselves as to the timeliness or propaganda worth of their approved compositions is beside the point. If only certain musical works can be heard, and it is healthier to honor these than to laugh at them, they will quite likely come to be accepted by the masses.[44] This is one way to create taste.

TRAINING. Little by little, data are being accumulated which demonstrate the potency of both auditory and visual training in the creation of musical taste.[45] As Tyler[46] and C. L. Stone[47] have shown, we are trained to think of music in terms of stereotypes. Even the

147

relatively unsophisticated college student has been taught to tie the names of Mozart, Beethoven, and Schubert to certain styles of composition. Italian music he associates with the light and the airy, Russian music with the somber and the gloomy, and German music with the heavy and the philosophic. The studies reported in previous chapters also tell of training in stereotyped thinking. For American grade-school children surely have few facts to go on when they place Beethoven and Bach so high on their eminence lists. They answer not from deep conviction, but rather in accordance with their teaching. The situation is analogous to their placing of Jesus, Washington, and Lincoln at the top of their lists of the most eminent men of all time.

J. Stone[48] and W. Robinson[49] have studied the sociopsychological aspects of war music. Stone points out that during the American Civil War, the soldiers' songs reflected their common traditions and not their war alignments. Although noting that each war to some extent mirrors the times, Robinson stresses the common subjects soldiers of all wars sing about: bad food, insect pests, war terrors, the enemy, sweethearts and other loved ones, and the desire to return home.

Gardner and Pickford have demonstrated by experiment what absolutists have difficulty in understanding: that perceived dissonance varies with (1) the listener's experience, training, and traditions, and (2) the musical "intent" of the passage as a whole, as well as (3) the physical composition of the chord.[50] The effect of the listener's recent experiences on enjoyment has also been shown in an experiment in which Beethoven's *Fifth Symphony* and Stravinsky's *L'Histoire du Soldat* were presented to several groups of college sophomores. When the playing of the Beethoven composition preceded that of the Stravinsky, the professed enjoyment-ratings were 73·8 and 27·4 respectively (a rating of 100 equaled "greatest possible enjoyment"). When the order was reversed, the values became 34·5 for the Stravinsky number, and 79·1 for Beethoven's *Fifth*. Note the depressive effect on the less enjoyed when it followed the better liked, and the enhancement of the latter when it was played second.

Wiebe found that the extensive playing of popular songs over the radio did not appear to increase his student subjects' liking for them.[51] However, lack of "plugging" seemed to result in a decrease of preference. Suchman concluded that the broadcasts of radio station WNYC have done much to develop an interest in music among its listeners and to establish taste norms.[52] The broadcasts make music more accessible; they extend the range of musical experience; they repeat the musical stimuli; they supply commentators and, on occasion, program notes[53] and other educational literature. A possible liability which may be inherent in radio taste training is the development of a dependent attitude of listening attentively only to compositions which are sponsored by the broadcasters of the favored radio station.

A number of researchers have attempted to telescope history by forcing their subjects to hear the same musical stimuli many times within a relatively short period.[54] Although the conclusions of the several studies are not in complete agreement, it seems safe to say that a composition with little variety reaches maximum acceptance quickly, and then as speedily declines in popularity. Music with more complexity tends to gain acceptance more slowly and to become hackneyed less rapidly. In one paper it has been suggested that the continuous repetition of musical material has a stronger effect on the listener than would the same number of well-spaced hearings.[55] Mull has made the interesting discovery that the preferred parts of musical compositions tend to become larger on rehearing.[56] Since the spread of preference usually is greater at the anterior end of the focal region, Mull has suggested that this phenomenon may be a case of what psychologists call "goal gradient." As she phrases it: "Might it not be that learning to like a composition has features similar to those involved in an animal's learning to run a maze—that is to say, in the case of our experiment, an original high spot (corresponding to the maze goal) may be thereafter anticipated and a pleasure gradient extend backward? Thus, pleasure would actually spread from a focus, rather than appear *de novo*. Once the climax is reached, there would be relaxation of interest and some tendency for the pleasure to drop off."

A peculiar situation has developed in the area of phonograph and radio listening, in which tones of relatively "poor" quality, i.e., with timbres unlike those of the "live" instruments, are at present preferred to those of more realistic quality. Apparently, long-continued, informal training is the responsible agent. We have developed one set of taste habits for listening to the phonograph and the radio, and another to function when in the presence of orchestral instruments.[57] Chinn and Eisenberg, two of the investigators of this phenomenon, have shown that this type of preference is found among the musically sophisticated as well as the naïve, and persists even when the listener is told that a wider tonal band yields tones closer to the sounds of real life.[58] Until recently the lay preference has been for an unusually strong emphasis on the bass. Presumably this preference arose from the fact that the engineers early achieved reasonable realism in the lower tonal ranges but have only recently brought in the very high frequencies. As a matter of fact, the early attempts of RCA Victor to produce "high fidelity" led to such poor audience response that this manufacturer continued for some years with an overloaded bass. However, with "high fidelity" now an essential for all music lovers, one might guess that there will shortly appear an equally extreme taste for an overloaded treble.

The Hi-Fi Hall, with its incredibly short reverberation time, necessitates further taste adjustments.[59] Long accustomed to the deadening effects of most auditoriums, the listener is here called upon to react to greater brilliance, to tone that is "acoustically naked." While the hi-fi enthusiast has little difficulty in learning to appreciate this "drier" effect, persons more attuned to the older home sets are at first somewhat startled, to say the least.

Some of us learn to pay more attention to the associations music can call up than to the music itself. Schoen terms this extreme sort of response "extrinsic" listening,[60] Myers "associative,"[61] and Ortmann "imaginal."[62] Those who pay more attention to the music than to its associations Schoen calls "intrinsic" listeners. Such persons are often said to have taste of a high order. Myers subdivides this group into "objective," if there is great concern with the objective features of the music, "intrasubjective," if the attention is on real or apparent changes within the listener's own body, and "character," if the listener imputes moods, traits, and activities to the music itself. Ortmann divides this group into "sensorial" and "perceptual." While these classifications may to some readers look suspiciously like fixed types, it is clearly not the intent of these theorists to create typologies. They are, rather, emphasizing the different things people have learned to "see" in music and they realize full well that few if any listeners belong to a single category.

We hardly need proof to be certain that taste develops out of experiences gained in home, church, club, and school, and out of contacts with the concert stage, recordings, the radio, and the printed page. These agencies of education, propaganda, and censorship force us to revere certain composers and their compositions, and to take less seriously other men and their works. We come to have several standards of taste: for the concert stage, for the dance hall,[63] for church, and for school—to mention some of the more important. Age, intelligence, and special training are important variables in this process of taste formation.[64] But it is difficult to be specific about all this since there seems to be a great difference between taste as it is observed in everyday life and the sort of taste people are willing to admit they possess.[65]

If we take as our aim the inculcation in our children of the standards of taste that adults of our culture regard as "good," checks on the success of this endeavor with groups of children can be made through the use of taste and attitudinal tests, interviews, and operational methodologies. Care should be taken, however, that the standards set up are not made too narrow, and that they are not thought of as absolute and unchangeable. For if taste training is to be directed toward the widening of the possibilities for the enjoyment of music, it would seem obvious that a standard of taste which embraces only a few composers of top eminence will be less effective than a more catholic standard which leads to an interest in many styles of composition.

Summary

The first thesis considered in this chapter was, "Is musical taste a matter of whimsey or is it in some way lawful?" The answer was clear—taste is lawful. It was noted that the musically elite have surprisingly similar tastes in their selections of eminent composers. Even more surprising is the high agreement on eminence found to exist among college and high-school groups. Enjoyment, too, is shared, with the music of certain composers given top billing by the elite and the lay public alike. And, if knowledge of composers is accepted as forming at least one facet of musical taste, knowledge also must be mentioned as lawful, for a man known well to one segment of the population tends to be equally well known to the members of other similarly chosen samples. Analyses of musicians' nonverbal behavior further attest to the fact that musical taste is not whimsical. Thus, the composers whose works are most recorded and appear most often on the programs of symphony orchestras are, with few exceptions, those regarded as most eminent. Moreover, they are likely to be the men whose biographical sketches occupy most space in histories of music and in general and music encyclopedias.

The second question the chapter posed was that of learning whether the laws of taste are absolute or relative. Here, too, the answer was unequivocal. Taste follows no absolute, metaphysical rules. And even if natural science variables are among the determiners of taste—as they may well be—their importance must be slight at best. All the evidence so far gathered points rather to the relativity of taste, to the fact that it is culture-bound, not culture-free. The descriptions sociology gives of mores fit taste most exactly. Change with training and individual differences in the acceptance of standards, both characteristics of musical taste, are earmarks of mores and folkways. The teaching of taste, then, is essentially a process of indoctrination, and the material to be learned differs somewhat from culture to culture and from period to period.

Notes

1] D. D. Runes, ed., *The Dictionary of Philosophy*, N.Y., Philosophical Library, 1942.

2] M. F. Meyer, *The Musician's Arithmetic*, p. 109.

3] *Ibid.*, p. 81.

4] P. R. Farnsworth, "Aesthetic Behavior and Astrology," *Char. and Person.*, 6 (1938): 335–340.

5] The reader who enjoys speculations based on physics and neurology is referred to the interesting articles by N. Rashevsky, "Suggestions for a Mathematical Biophysics of Auditory Perception with Special Reference to the Theory of Aesthetic Ratings of Combinations of Musical Tones," *Bull. Math. Biophysics*, 4 (1942): 27–32; "An Alternate Approach to the Mathematical Biophysics of Perception of Combinations of Musical Tones," *op. cit.*, pp. 89–90.

6] See Chapter 4 of A. Einstein's *Greatness in Music*, N.Y., Oxford U. Press, 1941.

7] P. R. Farnsworth, "The Musical Taste of an American Musical Elite," *Hinrichsen's Musical Year Book*, 7 (1952): 112–116.

8] P. R. Farnsworth, "Stereotypes in the Field of Musical Eminence," *Genet. Psychol. Monog.*, 24 (1941): 347–381; "Musical Eminence," *Sch. and Soc.*, 50 (1939): 158–160.

9] P. R. Farnsworth, *Musical Taste*, Stanford, Calif., Stanford U. Press, 1950.

10] When it is desired to find the degree of correspondence between two sets of measurements, each is ranked and an index of relationship is figured. This value may vary from 1·00 (which shows the rank orders to be identically arranged) through 0 (where there is no correspondence) to − 1·00 (where the two rank orders are inversely arranged; the highest name in one array is lowest in the other). The *rho* of ·97 indicates that the two piles were ordered very similarly. Unless otherwise designated the *rho*'s are all to be regarded as positive.

11] Unless otherwise stated, it is to be assumed that wherever coefficients of correlation are mentioned the rank method was employed, and that the 92 names mentioned in the 1938 survey formed the list of items to be correlated.

12] In these tables, the nine top names are offered with no thought that the number nine has any particular significance. The number is kept constant only for the sake of uniformity.

13] For a discussion of how jazz experts regard the contemporary performers of jazz music, see the annual polls in *Down Beat* (the first of which was in 1953), or *Metronome*'s "All-Star" polls.

14] P. R. Farnsworth, "Musical Eminence and Year of Birth," *J. Aesth.*, 4 (1945): 107–109.

15] When the birth years of a group of composers are arranged in order from most remote to most recent, the middle birth year is the *median*. That year which more than any other contains birth dates of composers is the *mode*.

16] These data were gathered through the courtesy of Dr R. Granneberg, of the San Francisco City College.

17] Alfred Frankenstein, "What People Think They Should Think," *San Francisco Chronicle*, February 2, 1941. During the spring of 1947 A. F. Michaelis, the program manager of the (California) Standard Oil Company's "The Standard Hour," conducted a survey among the listeners to this regular NBC Sunday evening broadcast. The 8000 who returned their questionnaires voted Beethoven the most popular composer. The next few in descending order of popular regard were Tchaikovsky, Gershwin, Chopin, Wagner, and Johann Strauss. The most frequently requested of all compositions was Gershwin's *Rhapsody in Blue*. Beethoven's *Fifth Symphony* came a close second, followed by Tchaikovsky's *Nutcracker Suite* and Chopin's *Polonaise Militaire*.

18] E. E. E. Folgmann, "An Experimental Study of Composer-Preference of Four Outstanding Symphony Orchestras," *J. Exp. Psychol.*, 16 (1933): 709–724.

19] H. K. Mull, "Preferred Regions in Music Compositions and the Effect of Repetition upon Them," *Amer. J. Psychol.*, 53 (1940): 583–586; G. Märill and H. K. Mull, "A Further Study of Preferred Regions in Musical Compositions and the Effect of Repetition upon Them," *Amer. J. Psychol.*, 55 (1942): 110–111.

20] W. S. Foster and M. A. Tinker, *Experiments in Psychology*, rev. ed., N.Y., Holt, 1929, p. 316.

21] P. R. Farnsworth, "Studies in the Psychology of Tone and Music," *Genet. Psychol. Monog.*, 15, No. 1 (1934): 24–30. See also O. W. Eagleson and L. E. Taylor, "A Study of Chord Preference in a Group of Negro Women," *J. Exp. Psychol.*, 26 (1940): 619–621; and "The Preference of Twenty-five Negro College Women for Major and Minor Chords," *J. Exp. Psychol.*, 28 (1941): 439–442.

22] P. R. Farnsworth, "An Historical, Critical, and Experimental Study of the Seashore-Kwalwasser Test Battery," *Genet. Psychol. Monog.*, 9, No. 5 (1931): 291–393.

23] P. R. Farnsworth, "Studies in the Psychology of Tone and Music," *Genet. Psychol. Monog., 15,* No. 1 (1934): 50–84.

24] The subjects were asked to check all names they were certain they recognized. The scoring was the simple procedure of tabulating the number of votes each name received.

25] J. H. Mueller and Kate Hevner, "Trends in Musical Taste," *Indiana U. Publ., Humanity Ser.,* No. 8 (1942), p. 59. Reproduced by permission of the Indiana University Press. See also J. H. Mueller's *The American Symphony Orchestra, a Social History of Musical Taste,* Bloomington, Indiana U. Press, 1951, and D. Nash's "The Construction of the Repertoire of a Symphony Orchestra," Thesis, U. of Washington, 1950.

26] These broadcast programs were obtained through the courtesy of R. R. Gros, an official of the company.

27] J. H. Mueller and Kate Hevner, *op. cit.*

28] J. H. Mueller, "Methods of Measurement of Aesthetic Folkways," *Amer. J. Sociol., 51,* No. 4 (1946): 276–282. See also the more recent orchestral data in Chapter 4 of Mueller's *The American Symphony Orchestra.* For data on social roles within the orchestra see M. Kaplan, "Telopractice: A Symphony Orchestra as It Prepares for a Concert," *Soc. Forces, 33* (1955): 352–355.

29] In the case of certain of the histories where the space technique could not be followed, the score was based on the relative number of page mentions the composer received.

30] J. H. Mueller and Kate Hevner, "Trends in Musical Taste." Further data can be obtained in Mueller's article, "Methods of Measurement of Aesthetic Folkways."

31] C. E. Seashore, *Psychology of Music,* N.Y., McGraw-Hill, 1938, p. 267. According to L. Vernon, pianists play at least one-half of their chords asynchronously ("Synchronization of Chords in Artistic Piano Music," *U. of Ia. Stud. Psychol. Mus., 4* (1936): 306–345). See also W. H. Lichte's "One Man's Preferred Fifth," *Amer. J. Psychol., 68* (1955): 312–315.

32] F. Howes, *The Borderland of Music and Psychology,* London, Kegan Paul, 1926.

33] E. H. Staffelbach, "The Psychology of Music Appreciation," *School Musician, 29* (1928): 9–13.

34] C. E. Seashore, *Why We Love Music,* Philadelphia, Ditson, 1941, p. 9.

35] C. W. Valentine, "The Aesthetic Appreciation of Musical Intervals among Children and Adults," *Brit. J. Psychol., 6* (1913): 190–216.

36] J. F. Dashiell, "Children's Sense of Harmonies in Colors and Tones," *J. Exp. Psychol., 2* (1917): 466–475.

37] M. Aizawa, "The Musical Taste of School Children," *Tohoku Psychol. Folia, 6* (1938): 111–126.

38] T. W. Harrell, "Factors Influencing Preference and Memory for Auditory Rhythm," *J. Gen. Psychol., 17* (1937): 63–104.

39] I. Frischeisen-Kohler, "The Personal Tempo and Its Inheritance," *Char. and Person., 1* (1933): 301–313.

40] J. P. Foley Jr., "The Occupational Conditioning of Preferential Auditory Tempo," *J. Soc. Psychol.*, 12 (1940): 121–129.

41] K. F. Schuessler, "Social Background and Musical Taste," *Amer. Sociol. Rev.*, 13 (1948): 330–335. For a study of age, sex, regional, educational and urban-rural differences in the preference for popular music during 1942, see J. G. Peatman, "Radio and Popular Music," in *Radio Research 1942–43*, P. F. Lazarsfeld and F. Stanton, eds., N.Y., Duell, Sloan and Pearce, 1944.

42] R. H. Wheeler, "Climate and Human Behavior," in P. L. Harriman, ed., *The Encyclopedia of Psychology*, N.Y., Philosophical Library, 1946, pp. 78–86; R. H. Wheeler and T. Gaston, "The History of Music in Relation to Climatic and Cultural Fluctuations," in *Mus. Teach. Nat. Assoc. Proc. 1940*, pp. 432–438.

43] An example of a governmental determination of taste can be seen in the official "advice" given a number of the leading composers of the USSR, February 10, 1948. Translations of the governmental pronouncement and the composers' answering statements appear in the American Russian Institute's pamphlet, *On Soviet Music*, published in May 1948, in Hollywood.

44] The task of an officially constituted committee on musical standards is made easier by the tendency of the masses to accept what the "experts" claim is "good music." For an experiment on the effect of expert opinion on musical taste see H. T. Moore, "The Comparative Influence of Majority and Expert Opinion," *Amer. J. Psychol.*, 32 (1921): 16–20.

45] M. J. Keston and I. M. Pinto, "Possible Factors Influencing Musical Preference," *J. Genet. Psychol.*, 86 (1955): 101–113.

46] L. E. Tyler, "An Exploratory Study of Discrimination of Composer Style," *J. Gen. Psychol.*, 34 (1946): 153–163.

47] C. L. Stone, "Identification of Nationality in Music," *Psychol. Bull.*, 35 (1937): 756.

48] J. Stone, "War Music and War Psychology in the Civil War," *J. Abn. Soc. Psychol.*, 36 (1941): 543–560.

49] W. Robinson, "War Songs of America," in *Writers Congress, Proceedings*, Berkeley, U. of Calif. Press, 1944, pp. 284–304.

50] P. A. Gardner and R. W. Pickford, "Relation between Dissonance and Context," *Nature* (London), 154 (1944): 274–275. For a study of the effects on appreciation of playing Bach and jazz in the same program see G. D. Williams, "The Effect of Order of Appearance on the Appreciation of Musical Selections," *J. Gen. Psychol.*, 27 (1942): 295–310.

51] G. Wiebe, "The Effect of Radio Plugging on Students' Opinions of Popular Songs," *J. Appl. Psychol.*, 24 (1940): 721–727.

52] E. A. Suchman, "Invitation to Music: A Study of the Creation of New Music Listeners by the Radio," in *Radio Research 1941*, P. F. Lazarsfeld and F. Stanton, eds., N.Y., Duell, Sloan and Pearce, 1941.

53] For an experiment on the effectiveness of program notes see G. D. Williams, "The Effect of Program Notes on the Enjoyment of Musical Selections," *J. Gen. Psychol.*, 29 (1943), 261–279.

54] H. T. Moore, "The Genetic Aspect of Consonance and Dissonance," *Psychol. Monog.*, 17 (1914): 1–68; M. F. Washburn *et al.*, "The Effects of Immediate Repetition on the Pleasantness or Unpleasantness of Music," in *The Effects of Music*, N.Y., Harcourt, Brace, 1927, Chap. 10; A. R. Gilliland and H. T. Moore, "The Immediate and Long-time Effects of Classical and Popular Phonograph Selections," *J. Appl. Psychol.*, 8 (1924): 309–323; H. E. Krugman, "Affective Response to Music as a Function of Familiarity," *J. Abn. Soc. Psychol.*, 38 (1943): 388–392; J. E. Downey and G. E. Knapp, "The Effect on a Musical Programme of Familiarity and of Sequence of Selections," in *The Effects of Music*, Chap. 12; H. K. Mull, "The Effect of Repetition upon the Enjoyment of Modern Music," *J. Psychol.*, 43 (1957): 155–162.

55] E. M. Verveer, *et al.*, "Change in Affectivity with Repetition," *Amer. J. Psychol.*, 45 (1933): 130–134.

56] H. K. Mull, "Preferred Regions in Musical Compositions and the Effect of Repetition upon Them," *Amer. J. Psychol.*, 53 (1940): 583–586. For further data on the gradient conception as it applies to music, see G. H. S. Razran's "Studies in Configurational Conditioning. VII: Ratios and Elements in Salivary Conditioning to Various Musical Intervals," *Psychol. Rec.*, 2 (1938): 370–376.

57] This suggestion is supported by a study by H. F. Olson, who found that when an all-acoustic filter was placed between sound and audience the preference was for a full frequency range. ("Frequency Range Preference for Speech and Music," *J. Acoust. Soc. Amer.*, 19 (1947): 549–555.)

58] H. A. Chinn and P. Eisenberg, "Tonal Range and Sound-intensity Preferences of Broadcast Listeners," *Inst. Radio Eng., Proc.*, 33 (1945), 571–581.

59] "The new sound," *Time*, 66, No. 26 (1955): 40.

60] M. Schoen, "The Aesthetic Attitude in Music," *Psychol. Monog.*, 39 (1928): 162–184. See also P. E. Vernon, "The Phenomena of Attention and Visualization in the Psychology of Musical Appreciation," *Brit. J. Psychol.*, 21 (1930): 50–63.

61] C. S. Myers, "Individual Differences in Listening to Music," *Brit. J. Psychol.*, 13 (1922): 52–71.

62] O. Ortmann, "The Sensorial Basis of Music Appreciation," *J. Comp. Psychol.*, 2 (1922): 227–256.

63] J. E. Eggen, "A Behavioristic Interpretation of Jazz," *Psychol. Rev.*, 33 (1926) 571–581.

64] G. Rubin-Rabson, "The Influence of Age, Intelligence, and Training on Reactions to Classic and Modern Music," *J. Gen. Psychol.*, 22 (1940): 413–429; E. G. Plotkin, "An Experimental Study of the Factors Involved in the Appreciation of Standard Music," Thesis, Columbia U., 1931; M. J. Keston, "An Experimental Evaluation of the Efficiency of Two Methods of Teaching Music Appreciation," *J. Exp. Ed.*, 22 (1954): 215–226. For an experiment on increasing tolerance with age, see P. R. Farnsworth, "Changes in Musical Taste," *J. Musicol.*, 1 (1939): 1–4.

65] R. L. Fisher, "Preferences of Different Age and Socio-economic Groups in Un-structured Musical Situations," *J. Soc. Psychol.*, 33 (1951): 147–152.

CHAPTER SEVEN

The Measures of Musical Taste

W<small>E</small> have seen that taste, in its several manifestations, has considerable stability. Moreover, it has been shown that taste behaves like other social phenomena of our culture and not as if it were obeying some absolute law.[1] It is now time to consider the measurement of taste, the problem of the current chapter.

A Variety of Measures

Experience has shown that no one measure of musical taste can hope to tap the ensemble or totality of preferences. Several procedures, then, are needed, each to paint a partial picture. Though the measures we are about to describe are of many different types, they can for convenience be divided into two main categories— (1) the formal tests, and (2) the approaches which do not employ such standardized procedures. The tests, in turn, can be split into the auditory and the purely paper-and-pencil types. The less standardized methods include the techniques discussed in the previous chapter—the interview and the counting of ballots, the measurement of space allocations,[2] and the analysis of programs—as well as the tabulation of phonograph record listings.

Auditory Tests

One of the earliest of the standardized music tests was Columbia record number A7539, designed by C. E. Seashore as a measure of the "sense of consonance," rather than as a test of taste.[3] However, the directions proved to be impossible of execution, and the term "consonance" was seen to be so ambiguous that the test was dropped from the later revision of the Seashore battery. The record has since been more suitably employed by some researchers as a preference test for tonal intervals. In giving the test, 50 sets of simultaneous dyads are presented in pairs, with the second of each pair to be judged as "better" or "worse" than the first. As the reliability of the measure is, by a very conservative estimate, only in the neighborhood of ·65 for adults and considerably lower for children, its use should be limited to group work.[4] It should be noted, however, that this reliability figure, low as it is, at least equals the values reported for a number of the other tonal appreciation tests.

The early Kwalwasser battery consists of two tests of 35 items each. The *Melodic Sensitivity Test* presents two-measure melodic progressions, and the *Harmonic Sensitivity Test* presents harmonic progressions of three chords each. The stimuli are to be rated as "good" or "bad."

> Bad melodic progressions result from the following: bad resolutions, incompatible tones, awkward rhythms, failure to turn after a wide skip, lack of design or purposiveness, distorted balance, incompleteness of melody or rhythm, etc. Authorities agree that bad harmonic effects result from parallel fifths and octaves, wrong doublings, bad-sounding voice movement, bad part omissions, digressions, unprepared modulations, unresolved dissonances, voice distribution over too wide a range, etc.[5]

Scores on these two Kwalwasser tests intercorrelate best at the fifth-grade level with a value of ·40. The corresponding value for the eighth grade is ·29, and for college, ·24. With reliabilities of only ·42 and ·21 (adult level), these two tests must be rated as of questionable value, except possibly for studying group trends. The tests have the disadvantage of offering stimuli which are completely out of musical context and of scoring the answers on the basis of rules from a day now past. To a greater or lesser extent many of the other tests described below suffer similarly.

The later Kwalwasser-Dykema battery has among its tests two that appear to be directly concerned with taste. The *Melodic Taste Test* measures, "on the basis of general music appeal, sensitiveness to structure, balance, and phrase compatibility."[6] Each test item consists of two melodies of two phrases each. The opening phrases of the two melodies are identical, but the second ones are unlike. The latter are to be compared for their suitability as concluding phrases. The test has only 10 items. As this number of stimuli is too small to allow the test much reliability, its usefulness is definitely limited.[7] The second test having to do with taste, the measure of *Tonal Movement*, offers 30 patterns, each consisting of four tones. The patterns are incomplete melodically, and the listener must supply mentally a fifth tone, reporting whether it is *above* the fourth tone or *below* it. With its reliability for adults in the ·80's, this test is statistically the best of the K-D battery. There is a correlation of ·40 between the scores of college students on the two K-D tests, and the scores of grade-school children show only chance resemblances.

One of the earliest tests of appreciation which employed music is the one by Courtis, in which the child is asked to recognize moods and rhythmic movements. Typical of the directions is the following:

> It was Saturday morning and the sun was shining. John's mother gave him a pail and sent him into the woods to pick berries. The music will tell you how John felt about going. Listen to the selection and underline the words which best express how the music says John felt.[8]

After listening to approximately 30 seconds of Victor record number 74711 (*Sérénade Mélancolique*) or 25 seconds of number 74581 (*Perpetual Motion*), the child states whether he thinks that John felt glad, sorry, angry, or busy. The test is very short, and so has little reliability. However, for training purposes it may have a real function.

A higher-level test with somewhat the same basic idea is the Schultz *Test of Listening Power in Music*.[9] Admittedly more than a taste test, it calls for the playing of phonograph discs followed by 32 multiple-choice questions similar to those in achievement tests. Reliabilities range from ·75 for junior high-school students to ·81 for college adults. Another test along these lines, which "seeks to show...awareness of tonal-rhythmic configurations," is the *Gaston Test of Musicality*.[10]

Themes from 20 selected works constitute the *Gernet Music Preference Test*.[11] The compositions include both "serious" music and jazz. The electrically transcribed stimuli are arranged in pairs for simple preference judgments, forming a test which has a reported reliability of ·55.

Themes from 20 selected works are also the elements of the *Bower Musical Moods Test*.[12] The items of this test, which was arranged for seventh- and eighth-graders, were prejudged by 17 music instructors, whose answers are assumed to be the correct ones. The task is to designate the one or more sets of adjectives which describe each of the themes. No reliability data are reported for this test, which has little relation to the so-called "tonal capacity" tests.

A similar measure is the *Keston Music Preference Test*, in which 120 musical excerpts, 45 seconds in length, are arranged for judging in groups of four.[13] Twelve "music authorities" decided the relative worth of each excerpt. As was to have been expected, the twelve rated the "serious classics" as best and the swing as worst. In the *Keston Music Recognition Test*, the subject is asked to match a list of 34 composers with 30 snatches of "serious" music.

The *Adler Music Appreciation Tests* present compositions by Brahms, Chopin, Mozart, Rameau, Ravel, and Weber, recorded on player-piano rolls.[14] Besides the original version of each piece there are three distorted forms—a sentimental, a dull, and a chaotic version. The subject indicates which are his most and least preferred versions, and attempts to guess the names of the composers.

Phonograph records give the stimuli for the *Mohler Scales for Measuring Judgment of Orchestral Music*.[15] Sixteen compositions of jazz and serious music, prejudged as to merit by 368 critics, were assembled into groups, whose small size precludes a reliability of more than ·51. The measure is now of historic interest only, as several of the record discs are unavailable. Semeonoff, following the Mohler procedure, has also offered sets of phonograph records for preference judgment.[16] In one study he also asked his subjects to check from four possible interpretations the mood intended by the composer.

An ambitious attempt to measure musical taste has been made by R. B. Cattell and D. R. Saunders.[17] Snatches of 120 compositions, averaging 20 seconds in length, were given to 188 persons confined to a mental hospital and to 196 who were assumed to be normal. The data were factor analyzed and eleven factors were teased out. Unfortunately, the phonograph recording was badly done. But if it can be assumed that this imperfection did not unduly affect the subjects' judgments, and if it can be further granted (as many will not grant) that the emerging factors all have meaning, the data become of interest. One factor was found to concern liking for popular jazz-like structure, rhythmical emphasis, fast tempo, individual interpretation, discordant harmonies, and joyful but agitated mood. A second factor apparently involved "an attachment to classical music, of a sentimental, introspective but cheerful nature, with a tendency to color harmonies." Another factor seemed to stress a liking for "warmth and gentleness," and another a preference for "lush, romantic, fairly conventional harmonies, with a flourish." The nature of still other additional factors was not entirely clear.

The easier of the *Oregon Music Discrimination Tests* (constructed by Kate Hevner and J. L. Landsbury) can be used to learn whether or not a subject can differentiate between short musical compositions deemed to possess merit, and versions of these compositions with distorted melody, rhythm, or harmony.[18] The test consists of 48 pairs of "meritorious" and altered compositions. Scoring credit is given for recognition both of the unaltered versions and the type of distortion to the altered version. The reliability of this measure ranges from ·47 for children of the fifth and sixth grades, to ·63 for junior high-school groups, ·78 for pupils in the senior high-school, and ·86 for adults. A second, more difficult test comes in two forms, each of which contains 40 items. The subject indicates his preferences and his degree of confidence, the latter being taken into account in the scoring. The test's reliability has been found to fall in the neighborhood of ·80 (college population). Both of these tests are by all odds the best of the formal auditory tests of taste so far developed.

Hevner has constructed another measure, the *Test for Musical Concepts*, to assess the subject's comprehension of compositions as complete wholes.[19] While hearing a rendition of Tchaikovsky's *Sixth Symphony*, for example, the listener answers a set of true-false questions of this type: "The melody of the middle section is taken from the original theme; it is varied, however, and is played in faster tempo." After three hearings of the symphony, the listener checks one statement in each of four pairs of statements which have largely to do with mood. Preliminary forms of this test have reliabilities which run as high as ·81.

Wing has devised four tests which have to do with judging the appropriateness of the style of playing a tune.[20] In each test a recorded tune is repeated either in identical or altered style. The notes played by the left hand in the "harmony" test may or may not be altered during the second rendition. The subject must listen for the possibility of a change, and then decide which of the two harmonizations (if there are two) is the more appropriate. In the test of "rhythmic accent" the accents may or may not fall in a different place in the second rendition. The possibility of change and, if there is a change, the more appropriate style of playing are to be checked. The two other tests in this series concern loudness patterns and phrase groups. The four tests are individually not very reliable. But when they are taken as a battery and combined with several other tests of music ability, a reliability in the neighborhood of ·90 is achieved. The Wing battery appears to be having considerable use in Great Britain.

Tests of taste have been constructed by Schoen,[21] Lowery,[22] Drake,[23] and others.[24] Schoen's *Tonal Sequence Test* supposedly reveals the listener's sensitivity to the fitness of the tones of a melody. For fitness, Schoen suggests five criteria: balance, "belonging-togetherness," unity, variety, and finality. In the test, each phrase is followed by four terminal phrases, which must be assigned values of 0, 2, 4, or 6 for fitness. In Lowery's *Cadence Test*, the second of each pair of cadences heard must be judged as more or less complete. Drake's *Test of Intuition* probes for the ability to supply endings to unfinished themes. This ability is thought to be concerned with phrase-balance, key-center, and time-balance. The listener judges whether or not the second phrase of each stimulus pair makes a satisfactory ending to the first phrase. Lowery, Drake, and Schoen have constructed other measures of abilities which border on the area of taste.

Practically nothing is known about the degree of overlap among the areas covered by these formal, auditory tests. However, with the stimuli often quite divergent and the test philosophies occasionally rather dissimilar, it would be surprising if all of the test inter-correlations were found to be very high, i.e., for all of the tests to be measuring very similar variables. Moreover, it should be remembered that the criteria of the tests for "correct" answers are based on social judgments. Naturally, then, a fraction of the "correct" answers of today will be "incorrect" tomorrow.

Paper-and-Pencil Tests

On the theory that general musical information should be related to appreciation, Kwalwasser has published a *Test of Music Information and Appreciation*.[25] Its arrangement is that of the typical school-subject achievement test, with queries about composers and compositions, the production of tone by orchestral instruments, etc. The test requires some 40 minutes for its administration. Its reliability for adults has been found to be approximately ·84 for Stanford students. A more difficult form of this test has been constructed by M. Young,[26] and another modification of it is by Semeonoff.[27]

A novel sort of measure, with a reliability around ·85, is the *Test of Musical Taste* developed by Vernon.[28] Here the subject is asked to record his reactions to 30 wholly imaginary programs of music. On the assumption that the experts Vernon has chosen to prejudge the programs possess taste (he has chosen as experts a panel of six musicians), the score is defined in terms of the resemblances between what the subject records and what the experts have previously checked as the ideal.

Using a slight modification of the Thurstone method for the construction of attitude scales, Kate Hevner and R. H. Seashore have developed a *Test of Attitude Toward Music*.[29] While this measure is not, strictly speaking, a test of taste, it bears rather closely on the problem. The test is composed of statements about music with which the subject is asked to agree or disagree. An example of an item whose acceptance would indicate a fairly favorable attitude toward music is,

"I believe strongly in the beneficial and pleasurable effects of music, but do not care to take an active part in it myself." As each test item has been prejudged by a large group of people, and so may be placed on an attitudinal continuum, the testee's verbal attitude can readily be assessed by this instrument.[30] The reliability as reported for college students is exactly ·90.

Self-rating scales have been developed to measure interests in "serious" music and in several sorts of "popular" music.[31] An important feature of these scales is the placing of prejudged behavioral characterizations along the rating lines as points of reference. Thus, in the case of one scale 24 cm. in length, where a check at the extreme left indicates "extreme dislike of music" and one at the right end "strongest possible interest in music," the two most extreme characterizations are, "I listen to music only when my parents or teachers make me listen to it" (placed 2·7 cm. from the extreme left) and, "I spend most of my free time listening to or playing music" (placed 21·3 cm. from the left end). In an assessment of one of the scales, seventh-graders and their mothers were asked to check independently the musical interests of the former. The coefficient of correlation between the ratings of the mothers and their children was found to be ·80, indicating a fair degree of validity for the scale. It should be added, however, that the mothers believed their children to have more interest in music than the latter admitted to having.

Another, more informal measure of taste involves the use of the list of 200 composers described in Chapter 6.[32] Those whose taste is to be assessed are given this list with the request that they check the most eminent ten, fifteen, or so. The extent of the agreement with the ordering made by the members of the American Musicological Society determines the score. It should be noted that any such list becomes out of date in the course of time. To be of worth it must reflect contemporary attitudes.

The more formal tests are obviously concerned with individual taste. With their reliabilities and validities generally mediocre or poor, they would appear to have a rather limited future. So far, they seem to have stimulated little interest or research. The techniques next to be discussed are in no sense rivals, for they aim to measure what might be termed "collective" taste.

Polling

This book has already considered at some length data obtained through polling, which is obviously not the perfect psychological tool.[33] Samples polled in past studies have sometimes proved to be but poor representatives of the populations with which the researcher was really concerned. The questions which have at times been asked have all too often been shown to be ambiguous or impossible to answer. And pollsters have occasionally misinterpreted their own data. These are among the most frequently encountered difficulties where polling is used. Yet, polling data, inaccurate as they sometimes are, have been found to yield roughly the same picture of contemporary taste as have the more operational procedures. Polling would appear to possess, then, a degree of validity and research utility.

Orchestral Programs

Attention has been called to the fact that the Boston Symphony Orchestra favors approximately the same composers decade after decade. It is of interest, too, that this orchestra's top choices[34] tend to be the ones also favored by the musicologists (*rho*[35] of ·81 in 1944, ·75 in 1951) and by a group of presumably typical Stanford sophomores (*rho* of ·79). These same composers are, by and large, the ones who have received the greatest amount of attention in the music encyclopedias of the 1940's, in the general encyclopedias of

167

the same decade, and in the histories of music. The *rho*'s here run
·82, ·73, and ·75, respectively. Had the orchestral choices been
limited to the 1940's, the *rho*'s would have been even higher.

MUSICOLOGISTS' AND BOSTON SYMPHONY'S FAVORITES COMPARED

Order of Choice	Boston Symphony Orchestra		Musicologists (1944)		Musicologists (1951)
1	Beethoven		Bach		Beethoven
2	Brahms		Beethoven		Bach
3	Wagner		Mozart		Brahms
4	Mozart		Wagner		Haydn
5	R. Strauss		Haydn		Mozart
6	Bach		Brahms		Debussy
7	Sibelius		Palestrina		Schubert
8	Tchaikovsky		Handel		Handel
9	Debussy		Schubert		Wagner
11	Haydn	10	Debussy	10	Palestrina
13	Schubert	13	Tchaikovsky	18	R. Strauss
16	Handel	20	R. Strauss	19	Tchaikovsky
66	Palestrina	30·5	Sibelius	30	Sibelius

Note: The names appearing below the line in any one of the columns appear among the first nine in one of the other columns.

Unusual features of the Boston Symphony's order of favorites are the high status of R. Strauss and Sibelius, and the low position of Palestrina. The idiosyncrasies of the Boston Symphony's list, however, are relatively few. Hence, we appear to have at hand a fair barometer of taste, particularly if the data gathered from this organization are pooled with those from the other leading orchestras of the land.[36]

Broadcasts of Recordings

When the Pacific Gas and Electric Company's broadcasts (p. 134) were analyzed in an effort to learn whose compositions were most often played, it was found that the favorites over a three-year period coincided remarkably well with those of the Boston Symphony Orchestra (*rho* of ·90). Here, again, Sibelius achieved unusually high status. Tchaikovsky's broadcast rank was the most markedly out of line (using the musicologists' ballots as the frame of reference). The rank order of composers favored in the broadcast programs correlated fairly well (*rho* of ·85) with the eminence ranks established from the votes of the musicologists (1944) but somewhat less well (*rho* of ·71) with the eminence ranks derived from the ballots of a group of Stanford sophomores. The hierarchies based on the relative amounts of attention paid the musicologists' 92 composers in the histories and in the music and general encyclopedias of the 1940's yielded *rho*'s of ·81, ·81, and ·68 when correlated against the rank order derived from the utility company's programs. Thus, a glimpse at the table will give approximately the same picture of current taste as will an inspection of some of the other barometers.

PACIFIC GAS AND ELECTRIC COMPANY'S BROADCASTS

1941, 1942 AND 1943

Order of Frequency	Composers
1	Beethoven
2	Tchaikovsky
3	Brahms
4	Mozart
5	Bach
6	Sibelius
7	Wagner
8	Schubert
9	Schumann

Record Listings

The composers favored in the programs of the Boston Symphony Orchestra and the Pacific Gas and Electric Company broadcasts tend also to be the ones with the most recordings to their credit. Thus, the rank order of the record-listing frequencies of the early 1940's correlates ·88 with the symphony's rank order, and ·91 with that of the utility company's broadcasts. When compared with the eminence ranks obtained from the histories, the music encyclopedias, and the general encyclopedias of the 1940's, the correlation values were found to be ·87, ·88, and ·69, respectively. The musicologists agreed to the extent of a *rho* of ·90, but the college students' value was lower, ·75.

The scores for the disc listings were obtained by noting the distribution of recordings mentioned in each of four books. Those used in counting the discs were I. Kolodin's *A Guide to Recorded Music* (1941), D. Hall's *The Record Book* (1943), B. H. Haggin's *Music on Records* (1943),[37] and *The Gramophone Shop Encyclopedia of Recorded Music* (1942). The four books agree very well among themselves on the number of recordings associated with the 92 composers. The pool of any two of the book lists against the pool of the other two yields a *rho* of approximately ·95. Incidentally, the agreement between the 1936 and 1942 and between the 1942 and 1948 editions of the *Gramophone Shop Encyclopedia* is roughly of the same order of magnitude. Here, then, we have a reliable index which checks well a number of the other barometers of taste.

Scholarly Texts

Since histories of music and encyclopedia articles on the composers are written by musicologists or their peers, it is not too much to expect that the allocations of space in scholarly works will follow the taste patterns of the authors' cultures. Of course, the editors of encyclopedias must usually limit the over-all space, and this necessity must in turn lead to a restriction of the number of composers whose names can appear in such publications. But the relative amounts of space devoted to the names which do pass the selection will tend to reflect cultural attitudes.

It must be granted, of course, that the allocations will mirror more than taste. The perfectionist who composes relatively little and the important composer whose life-span is short may both receive less space than they deserve, while the controversial and notorious character, particularly if blessed with a long life, may receive undeserved space. Moreover, the author of the history or article may possess biases of his own which at times can reach serious proportions. But if the data of many histories and encyclopedias are pooled, the author-biases will tend to cancel, or at least will distort the picture less.

Before the turn of this century, J. McKeen Cattell employed the space-allocation method in an attempt to discover the thousand most eminent men of history.[38] Although the names of the encyclopedias he used cannot now be determined, it may be guessed that the *Encyclopaedia Britannica* was one. There are some ambiguities in his list because no initials were given to aid in distinguishing which of the several famous Webers and Strausses Cattell intended. Hence some of the composers who bear these names may or may not have been in the list. Of those whose identities cannot be questioned, Mozart is the first musician, with a rank of 93 in the general array (Napoleon topped the list with a rating of 1). Beethoven had a rank of 220, Handel 261, Haydn 300, Rossini 326, Wagner 337, Mendelssohn 404, Palestrina 471, and Bach 475. No other composers appeared among the first 500.

It was to have been expected that the editors of the general encyclopedias would allocate less space to composers than to the military heroes and to the eminent of certain other fields. Hence, the absolute ranks of these musicians tell us very little. Yet the fact that these nine composers received the lion's share of attention is surely indicative of their relative status during the period just prior to that of Cattell's researches. It is of interest that all of these names, with the exception of Rossini's, appear high on the later lists compiled by the present author. The space devoted to this Italian composer has decreased slowly but steadily in both the music and general source books written in the English language during this century.[39] Rossini was not mentioned by a single musicologist in the 1938 survey and received few votes from the 1944 and 1951 memberships. Bach, on the other hand, improved in status rapidly and soon became one of the top-ranking masters.

In the allocation studies reported in this book, the pooling of several works published in each time span has been the practice. The general encyclopedias under scrutiny numbered five standard works for each period except for the 1940's, for which only three were employed. Seven standard music encyclopedias were examined for the period 1900–19, six for the decade of the 1920's, and five each for the 1930's and 1940's. Ten to twelve histories of music were studied for each of these same periods.

Although an eminent composer is normally discussed in but one section of any given encyclopedia, histories typically mention a number of composers on a single page and repeat mention of the same composer on a number of widely separated pages. Hence, space measurements are usually not possible in work on histories, and the only practical technique so far found to be serviceable is that of the tabulation of page-mentions. Fortunately, the number of page-mentions and the amount of space have been found to correlate so highly (*rho*'s in the ·90's) that for most purposes they may be considered as a single technique.[40]

It has already been demonstrated that the rankings of composers determined on the basis of space-measurement and page-mention frequencies are quite similar to the eminence rankings obtained from the ballots of musicologists and college students, to the preference orders taken from the programs of the Boston Symphony Orchestra and the Pacific Gas and Electric Company, and to the order of frequencies secured from record listings. Furthermore, the three sorts of scholarly endeavor—the histories of music, the music encyclopedias, and the general encyclopedias—devote rather similar amounts of attention to our group of 92 composers. When the decade of the 1940's is considered, the rank order obtained from the histories correlates ·81 and ·70, respectively, with those constructed from the music and the general encyclopedias. The ranks secured from the two kinds of encyclopedias agree to the extent of a *rho* of ·77. The intercorrelations between the data of the other time periods have been found to be of approximately the same order of magnitude.

While these space values and the related ones described in this chapter are not as high as might be desired, it would appear safe to consider the space- and page-mention procedures as yielding a fairly good picture of taste at any given place and time.

Boredom

While no one has probably ever attempted seriously to measure taste by testing for musical boredom, the *New York Herald Tribune*, during March of 1954, asked its readers to name the ten compositions they regarded as most boring.[41] It would seem, however, that the New York list is unique, that it should in all probability not resemble one assembled either in Minneapolis or in San Francisco since local conditions would be quite dissimilar in these three locales. Each area would have its own particular irritations, brought on in part by the too-frequent hearing of certain pieces and by the fact that other compositions may have recently been badly played.

But one wonders if it is not a relatively small number who would react so strongly to clichés and nuances of rendition. As the critic Alfred Frankenstein says in the April 4, 1954, issue of the *San Francisco Chronicle*, there is a considerable group of listeners who are passive followers and honor what they have been taught to honor. For them, boredom, even if present, would have little effect on basic taste. Only the sophisticated listeners might be seriously affected. Of course, most persons tire rather rapidly of jazz pieces and other examples of less serious music. And Rachmaninov's *Prelude* must be shelved occasionally to keep it reasonably in favor. But such reactions to specific compositions have relatively little to do with basic musical taste.

In a somewhat broader sense of the term, however, boredom is related to taste. Any school of musical composition, no matter how much it is in favor at any one time, sooner or later begets a reaction against itself. Although it may later return to favor, at least in modified form, it must pass through a period of partial eclipse. Here is a phenomenon found in all but the most static cultures, a sort of collective boredom. The sociologist W. I. Thomas has called this human tendency "the wish for new experience."

Summary

In this chapter attention was first called to the formal tests and to the fact that, in general, they measure individual taste with relatively poor reliability and validity. To disclose the taste of classes and interest groups, other techniques have been more successful. Thus, polling, program analyses, the counting of recordings, and examinations into the relative amounts of attention paid composers in scholarly works[42] on music all have disclosed similar group favorites among the composers. These barometers have been found to be internally consistent. They furnish ways of studying collective taste as it exists here and elsewhere, and even as it existed decades ago.

Notes

1] Hungerland has reviewed the problem of aesthetic standards in the field of painting and has offered a relativistic view which is consonant with that expressed throughout this book. See Helmut Hungerland, "Suggestions for Procedure in Art Criticism," *J. Aesth.*,

5, No. 3 (1947): 189–195. A more recent rejection of the absolutistic position can be seen in T. Munro's "The Concept of Beauty in the Philosophy of Naturalism," *Rev. Intern. Phil., 31* (1955): 1–43.

2] The page-mention method can be considered as a variety of the measure of space allocations.

3] C. E. Seashore, *Manual of Instructions and Interpretations for Measures of Musical Talent*, N.Y., Columbia Graphophone, 1919.

4] The reliability of a test is its degree of self-consistency, the extent to which it is uninfluenced by factors intrinsic to or associated with it. For most purposes, a reasonable reliability is one in the high ·80's or low ·90's. As a test is lengthened (but not so much as to induce boredom or fatigue) it tends to become more reliable.

5] J. Kwalwasser, *Tests and Measurements in Music*, Boston, Birchard, 1927, p. 26.

6] J. Kwalwasser and P. W. Dykema, *Manual of Directions, K-D Tests*, N.Y., Fischer, 1930, p. 18.

7] The authors realize that a 10-item test tends to have poor reliability and suggest a repetition under conditions such that the subjects believe they are hearing a 20-item test. But even with 20 items the test is quite unreliable.

8] S. A. Courtis, *Courtis Standard Research Tests, Series M, Music*, Detroit, S. A. Courtis, 1922, p. 5. Before the days of formal psychological tests an even earlier attempt to study music moods was that by B. J. Gilman, "Report on an Experimental Test of Musical Expressiveness," *Amer. J. Psychol., 4* (1892): 42–83; 5 (1893): 558–587.

9] E. J. Schultz, "Testing Listening Power in Music," *Mus. Superv. Nat. Conf. Yearb.*, 1933, 306–312.

10] E. Gaston, *A Test of Musicality, Manual of Directions*, 2nd ed., Kansas City, Streep, 1944.

11] S. K. Gernet, *Musical Discrimination at Various Age and Grade Levels*, College Place, Washington, College Press, 1940.

12] L. B. Bower, "A Factor Analysis of Music Tests," Thesis, Catholic U., 1945.

13] M. J. Keston and I. M. Pinto, "Possible Factors Influencing Musical Preference," *J. Genet. Psychol., 86* (1955): 101–113.

14] M. J. Adler, "Music Appreciation: An Experimental Approach to Its Measurement," *Arch. Psychol., 17*, No. 110 (1929): 1–102.

15] M. R. Trabue, "Scales for Measuring Judgment of Orchestral Music," *J. Educ. Psychol., 14* (1923): 545–561.

16] B. Semeonoff, "A New Approach to the Testing of Musical Ability," *Brit. J. Psychol., 30* (1940): 326–340; "Further Developments in a New Approach to the Testing of Musical Ability, with Special Reference to Groups of Secondary School Children," *Brit. J. Psychol., 31* (1940): 145–161.

17] R. B. Cattell and D. R. Saunders, "Music Preferences and Personality Diagnosis," *J. Soc. Psychol., 39* (1954): 3–24; R. B. Cattell and Jean C. Anderson, "The Measurement

175

of Personality and Behavior Disorders by the I. P. A. T. Music Preference Test," *J. Appl. Psychol.*, *37* (1953): 446–454.

18] John H. Mueller, *et al.*, "Studies in Appreciation of Art," *U. Oregon Publ.*, *4*, No. 6 (1934): 115–130.

19] *Ibid.*, 131–137.

20] H. Wing, "Tests of Musical Ability and Appreciation," *Brit. J. Psychol.*, *Monog. Suppl.*, No. 27 (1948).

21] M. Schoen, "Tests of Musical Feeling and Musical Understanding," *J. Comp. Psychol.*, *5* (1925): 31–52.

22] H. Lowery, "Cadence and Phrase Tests in Music," *Brit. J. Psychol.*, *17* (1926): 111–118.

23] R. M. Drake, "Four New Tests of Musical Talent," *J. Appl. Psychol.*, *17* (1933): 136–147; *Drake Musical Aptitude Tests*, Chicago, Science Research Associates, 1954.

24] The difference between a test of taste and one of musical "capacity" is sometimes slight. See Chapter 9 for a discussion of the latter type of measure.

25] J. Kwalwasser, *Tests and Measurements in Music*, 90–98.

26] M. Young, "A Study of the Kwalwasser Test of Music Information and Appreciation, and the Construction for this Field of a More Reliable and Advanced Test," Master's Thesis, Stanford U., 1932.

27] B. Semeonoff, *op. cit.*

28] P. E. Vernon, "A Method for Measuring Musical Taste," *J. Appl. Psychol.*, *14* (1930): 355–362.

29] John H. Mueller, *et al.*, "Studies in Appreciation of Art," pp. 138–142.

30] The scale value of the example just given was found to be 4·2 where 11 is the most unfavorable end of the continuum and 1 the most favorable.

31] P. R. Farnsworth, "Rating Scales for Musical Interests," *J. Psychol.*, *28* (1949): 245–253.

32] P. R. Farnsworth, "Agreement with the Judgments of Musicologists as a Measure of Musical Taste," *J. Psychol.*, *28* (1949): 421–425.

33] Q. McNemar, "Opinion-Attitude Methodology," *Psychol. Bull.*, *43* (1946): 289–374.

34] These values were obtained through a tally of the musical items listed in the "Boston Symphony Orchestra Programmes" for the seasons 1895–96, 1904–5 through 1907–8, 1912–13 through 1918–19, and 1920–21 through 1944–45.

35] This *rho* and those which follow have as their number of items the 92 names offered by the members of the American Musicological Society in the 1938 poll (see p. 123).

36] For extremely interesting program analyses which are too technical (in a mathematical sense) for review here, see G. K. Zipf, "On the Dynamic Structure of Concert-programs," *J. Abn. Soc. Psychol.*, *41* (1946): 25–36.

37] Because of the peculiar arrangement of the Haggin book, it proved necessary to employ the page-mention technique.

38] J. McKeen Cattell, "A Statistical Study of Eminent Men," *Pop. Sci. Month.*, 62 (1903): 359–377. Cattell's data were gathered many years before they were published.

39] Under the direction of R. S. Tangeman of the University of Indiana, space measurements have been taken from five sets of general-interest encyclopedias, each written in a different language. It is worth noting that Rossini was given the second largest amount of space in *Enciclopedia Italiana*. He achieved eighth place in *Enciclopedia Universal* (Spanish), a rank of 8·5 in *Larousse du XXe Siècle*, a rank of 18 in the *Encyclopaedia Britannica*, and one of 22·5 in *Meyers Lexikon*. G. H. Stempel, who has reported these studies, has found that in the *Encyclopedia Americana* Rossini was seventh in space allocation. (Note that this allocation is completely out of line with what Rossini is given in other English-language encyclopedias.) When Stempel combined his data with those of Tangeman, Rossini's placement was seventh. From these data, then, comes the hint that Rossini may be regarded far more favorably in Italy and Spain than in Germany and the Anglo-Saxon countries. (G. H. Stempel, "C Sharp Minor," *The Bloomington* [*Ind.*] *Star*, August 6, 1943.)

40] It can be taken as axiomatic that the greater the variability in the lengths of the encyclopedia articles the more exact will be the differences in eminence that can be expressed. If it is found that the largest encyclopedias possess articles with the greatest range in length it would seem to follow that these massive treatises can supply the most adequate material for work on eminence. Support for this possibility can be seen in the *rho* of ·54 which obtains between the sizes of the encyclopedias and the spread in the lengths of the articles.

41] From most to least boring these compositions were said to be: Rimsky-Korsakov's *Scheherezade*, César Franck's *Symphony*, Ravel's *Bolero*, Wagner's *Parsifal*, Beethoven's *Missa Solemnis*, Brahms's *German Requiem*, Dvorak's *New World Symphony*, Beethoven's *Ninth Symphony*, Wagner's *Tristan und Isolde*, Tchaikovsky's *Fifth Symphony*.

42] That the music encyclopedias make more reliable barometers of taste than the general encyclopedias has recently been demonstrated by the author. His researches show that the *Encyclopaedia Britannica* no longer keeps abreast of changes in musical taste. See "The Limitations of Cattell's Space Method of Studying Eminence," *J. Psychol.*, 44 (1957): 169–173.

CHAPTER EIGHT

The Nature of Musical Abilities

In the preceding chapters, the notion of capability has been freely employed but in rather loose fashion. To discriminate between intervals, to differentiate major from minor, to sense strain or relaxation in a melody, or even to develop a taste for a particular kind of music, presupposes musical abilities of some sort. But whether these capabilities are largely inborn and whether only one general ability or several must be assumed are questions which have so far not been considered. It is time, then, that these and other important questions about the functioning of our musical capabilities be examined.

Ability—an Appropriate Descriptive Term

In their work of describing musical capabilities, the psychological testers have employed a variety of terms without complete agreement as to exact meanings. To some authorities musical talent has meant innate capability for musical performance. Others have used the term more broadly to include musical appreciation. Talent in this latter area has sometimes been called "musicality." The term "capacity" also seems to bear the connotation of innate ability. Capacities, of course, are never directly observed, but are inferred from behavioral manifestations such as test scores. The term "aptitude" is somewhat less controversial in that the inferred ability is assumed to be only in part innate. It tends to imply potentiality rather than achievement, ability undeveloped before formal training has taken place. The term "ability," suggesting the power to act but indicating nothing about the hereditability or congenitalness of the inferred potentiality is the broadest and safest of all of these terms; for as we shall soon see, nature and nurture invariably function jointly, and it is erroneous to say that any act is the sole result of either the one or the other. Hence, in the discussions of the present chapter, conservative usage will be followed and musical ability will be the focus of attention.

Generality of Ability

Almost everyone who has attempted to forecast musical success has met persons who show great promise along some musical lines and extreme weakness in other areas. Here is a sixth-grader who scored in the top percentile on standardized tests of tonal memory and of pitch and intensity discrimination but had only chance scores on measures of time and rhythm. A monotone of mature years who came to the laboratory for aid in overcoming his disability was found to score quite well on time, intensity, and rhythm tests. But his pitch weakness was so complete that he could detect only a slight difference between the highest and lowest tones of the piano. And the vocalist Galli-Curci, while proficient in most musical endeavors, had such a poor "musical ear" that she needed an accompanist who could be called upon to transpose at a moment's notice. There also are weaknesses in the affective realm, e.g., a kettle drummer in one of America's great symphony orchestras who privately admitted that he abhorred all music in which the kettle drums were not frequently called into action. It was his abnormally strong interest in rhythms which early led him to work with the percussion choir. Cases such as these would seem to yield evidence for the existence of several rather independent musical abilities rather than a single all-embracing one.

Certain of the statistically minded have attempted to answer the question of the generality of ability through recourse to tables of intercorrelations and to the findings of factor analysis. They point out that most music tests now at hand intercorrelate very poorly indeed. Hence, if it can be assumed that the tests are valid measures of musical capabilities, this evidence also tells against the notion of a single musical ability.

The factor analysts have tried to probe more deeply into the problem. Unfortunately, however, the several different methods of factor analysis now available are based on somewhat dissimilar philosophies and therefore do not always lead to identical conclusions. It is hardly an exaggeration to say that the English, who are prone to believe in the existence of general factors, tend to find them in almost every set of test intercorrelations, while the Americans, with their different theories, more commonly find several group factors but no general one. Thus, the British-trained Drake found a general musical factor when he studied tests covering the areas of tonal memory, pitch, rhythm, intensity, tonal movement, and general intelligence.[1] While scrutinizing his own English-made music tests, Wing also found a general factor which accounted for 40 per cent of the total variance.[2] There were two additional group factors, one being bipolar and apparently having to do with analysis and synthesis, and the other concerned with harmony and melody. Another Briton, McLeish, who gave both the Wing and the Seashore music batteries to some 100 students, found the same general cognitive factor in each.[3] Still another Briton, Vernon, feels that the American-built tests of Seashore which stress sensory capabilities (p. 237) have little to do with music ability.[4] He quotes the data of Manzer and Marowitz to bolster this view.[5] He himself has studied tests such as the Hevner-Landsbury (p. 163) which make use of actual musical materials. These, he thinks, test a general factor. Vernon's attitude toward the sensory tests is partly shared by Franklin, who has recently factor analyzed a battery of tests including several of the Seashore, the Wing, tests of intelligence and vocabulary, some visual perceptual tests, and his own music test (p. 246). A study of the factors which emerged convinced him that music ability has two aspects, one being the mechanical-acoustic (e.g., pitch, timbre, time, and intensity discrimination) and the other, on a far higher level, he terms the judicious-musical. The latter reaches its highest levels in creative musical talent.[6]

The most extensive study of basic music abilities so far undertaken has been that of Karlin, an American, who factored 32 tests and found eight group factors.[7] No general factor emerged from the statistical manipulations. The most important factors involved pitch, memory for musical passages as a whole, and recall for isolated musical elements. A still later American study by Bower also disclosed no huge general factor but rather three group factors.[8] Bower's first factor was a complex one which had to do with tonal memory, pitch discrimination, melodic taste, and rhythm discrimination. Her second concerned mood, loudness, and time discrimination. Her third featured rhythm discrimination and tonal memory.

The reader will probably agree that conclusions based on factor analysis must be quite tentative. Factors are obviously products of the tests used. Therefore, if there is no test covering some important area of musical activity, the picture disclosed by the factor analysis will reflect this imbalance. When two studies employ different sets of tests, it is quite possible that they will report different factors. For, after all, factor analysis is only a way of describing with some economy a matrix of correlations. Since the factors depend upon the measures used, they will be meaningful only as the tests are meaningful. With present-day music tests still in a primitive state, it follows that factor analysis can yield no definitive answers. We are left, then, with whatever conclusions case studies and intercorrelational analyses can yield, and with the notion that there probably are several poorly correlated music abilities.

Ability in Music and the Other Arts

Another aspect of the problem of general musical ability has to do with the hypothesis that there may exist a broad ability which embraces all the arts. But here again, the experimental evidence is largely opposed. In an extensive study with a variety of special aptitude and taste tests, Morrow could find no correlations of any size between the music and art measures.[9] Although Strong found that artist score as measured by his well-known *Vocational Interest Test* correlates ·57 with musician score, he also noted that the former correlates higher with a number of other occupational interests: ·61 with mathematician, ·62 with dentist, ·70 with psychologist, ·79 with physician, ·84 with author-journalist, and ·85 with architect. Music interest correlates ·60 with interests in both psychology and the ministry.[10] White, in a study of the versatility of 300 eminent men, could find no general aesthetic type of interest or ability.[11]

One small area in which musicians do resemble artists is in the average length of life of their eminent fellows. In one study, the life span for both musicians and artists was found to be approximately 67·5 years. That of eminent engineers, on the other hand, was slightly over 71, and for educators it was somewhat more than 72·5 years.[12] Just why artists and musicians should be alike and musicians and educators different in this regard is not clear. But the fact that two occupational groups have similar longevities is most certainly no justification for hypothesizing a commonality of abilities.

Academic Intelligence and Musical Ability

It has been argued that academic intelligence is an important component of musical ability.[13] At least the fact has been established that the musically great men of history possessed far better than average intelligence. J. S. Bach, for example, had an estimated I.Q. somewhere between 125 and 140, Beethoven's was between 135 and 140, Haydn's between 120 and 140, Handel's between 145 and 155, and Mozart's between 150 and 155.[14] And there are studies which show children with high music-test scores to be significantly brighter than their low-scoring colleagues.[15] But, for the other side of the argument, it must be said that scores on the better-standardized music tests, when given to groups of limited age range, show little correlation with those on tests of academic intelligence, although the slight correlations which are found are usually positive.[16] It should also be noted that children of high I.Q. tend to yield music test scores appropriate to their chronological ages but not to their I.Q.'s.[17]

Other evidence against the notion that intelligence and musical ability are invariably related can be seen in data gathered on those peculiar individuals, the idiot savants. Traditionally this term has been applied to persons who test low in intelligence but who possess some well-developed special ability. Typical is an idiot of four years who could barely articulate "papa" and "mama" but was able to sing over 50 melodies. It is now believed that many of the cases thought earlier to fit the idiot-savant classification could better be called schizophrenics. Others have been found to be much higher in I.Q. than had first been estimated,[18] while still others, admittedly low in intelligence, have been shown to be musical or artistic in only a relative sense. That is, they were imbeciles or idiots, perhaps, in academic intelligence but morons or border-line in the special ability, not really superior. There seem, however, to be at least a few cases who come close to fitting the classical picture of the idiot savant. When Rife and Snyder addressed inquiries to 55 American institutes for the feeble-minded they unearthed eight mental defectives who appeared to show somewhat better than average musical ability.[19]

True idiot savants, while small in number, are sufficiently numerous to refute the hypothesis that better-than-average musical ability must invariably be accompanied by high intelligence. And, as we have seen, the music test data indicate that within the range of school populations, academic intelligence and the several tonal abilities have at best only a slight positive relationship.[20] Yet the fact remains that if one is to reach the highest level of musical success one needs an intelligence considerably above that of the average.[21]

The Hereditability of Musical Abilities

The present-day formulation of the nature-nurture relationship is not one which would have appealed to the extremists of a few decades ago. Whether they were hereditarians or environmentalists, the older theorists blinded themselves to the obvious in their attempts to maintain their one-sided positions. It is now clear that neither nature nor nurture can alone make a musician. Both must be present before musical and other abilities can emerge. The person who has excellent tonal and rhythmic sensitivities but who is in unmusical surroundings will not be as likely to achieve in music as will another with similar sensitivities who finds himself in a more propitious environment. Questions which ask for the relative potencies of nature and nurture in creating a musician are unanswerable. They are as meaningless as questions on how much of the speed of a particular automobile is due to the gasoline and how much to the make of car, or what percentage of the area of a rectangle is attributable to its length and what percentage to its width.

Certain people seem to be so constructed that they react far more positively than most to tonal stimuli. But even for these cases there must be fertility of environment if the early interest is not to be turned in other directions. Erwin Nyiregyhazi, a prodigy who was studied most carefully by Révész, sang melodies before he could speak and began to improvise during his third year.[22] Yet he has not achieved the renown which might reasonably have been forecast for him. But Mozart, who "learned" the clavier before age four and composed little pieces at age five, although perceptibly no more precocious, reached musical heights almost no one else has attained. The differences in the successes of Mozart and his fellow prodigy must be due, at least in part, to dissimilarities in environmental pressures.

A warning should be given on the possibility of confusing musical ability with motor skills. History reveals youngsters whose hands were excellently formed for piano work, who were willing to practice long hours and so mastered many difficult piano techniques, and who had parents or teachers to tell them precisely what to play and when and how to vary their playing from the mechanically exact. These children admitted to no real love of music or yearning to perform or to compose. The "performance expressiveness" of their playing was not their own but was imposed on their playing by others. Were these children musical geniuses, then, or were they merely persons of unique build on whom optimal pressures from the surrounding environment led to the development of remarkable motor skills?

The more tonal abilities[23] appear in the child at an earlier age than do the rhythmic.[24] With practice, preschool children make spectacular gains in singing tones, intervals, and phrases, but less improvement in time-keeping. Greatly enhanced skill in the last mentioned appears with training at a somewhat later period, as soon as better motor coordination permits. Some of the unevenness in musical growth, then, is apparently due to differences in maturational readiness for the activities in question.

It is reassuring to know that pitch sensitivity can be improved by training. Wyatt and a number of others have shown that enormous changes can be produced by the use of proper training procedures.[25] After training, Wyatt's music-school students had moved on the Seashore pitch norms (p. 235) from the seventh up to the second decile. Her subjects who were not enrolled in a music school had with pitch training risen from the seventh decile to the third or fourth. This growth in sensitivity was not just a coaching effect but was apparent at tonal ranges where no training had been attempted. But is the improvement so far demonstrated a matter of enhanced attention and mental concentration, a mere upping of cognitive limits as Seashore has maintained,[26] or is it something more basic? If the Seashore thesis were valid, one would expect children of high I.Q., with their better powers of concentration, to score higher than their more normal fellows on tonal tests. But, as we have already noted, the two groups make similar scores.[27] Hence, it seems safe to assume that the effects of pitch training on ability are rather basic. It might, of course, be added that even if sensitivity changes had not been demonstrated so dramatically there would still be no reason to suppose that training methods developed later might not be effective.

The view of nature and nurture to which our considerations so far have led us is, in brief, that an ability is always the resultant of the interplay of heredity and environment. The organism limits or facilitates achievement in many ways. The environment likewise aids or inhibits. From these two sets of interacting limitations and facilitations abilities develop. Musical abilities seem in general no more nor less inherited than abilities in many other areas.

MUSICAL ABILITIES AND FAMILY LINES. Like begets like only to a limited extent. But even where the offspring closely resemble the progenitors in abilities, it is impossible to determine the exact causes of the resemblance. D.A.R.-like studies of family stock are of little or no value to the problem of unscrambling the roles played by heredity and environment in the creation of musical abilities.[28] It should come as no surprise to find that where a man has had two wives, only one of whom was musical, his two broods of children resemble, on the average, their own mothers more than their step-mothers. But whether the resemblance is due to the biological inheritance of genes transmitting musical potentiality, to a complex of mother fixations or stepmother rejections, or to some combination of biological and sociopsychological causes, the analyses cannot disclose.[29] Whether a person is wedded to the idea that musical ability is wholly a matter of inheritance or entirely due to excellent training he can be made happy by the same family line analyses. If the genealogical research proceeds far enough back in time, the musician who believes in heredity can always find a musical ancestor from whom his musical ability may have come, while the environmentalist can relish the absence of musical abilities among his immediate ancestors and point to some unrelated musician or teacher as the "source" of the environmental pressures which have antedated the musical achievements.

The musical Bachs and the members of other families of famous virtuosos have been carefully counted generation after generation but with no great benefit to science.[30] For who can tell whether the eventual eclipse of certain of these families was due to dilution of the musical heritage; to changes in the social, economic, and political milieu which made other occupations more attractive to the members of later generations; or to some combination of biological and economic forces? Genealogical research may indeed be quite necessary for those who crave to belong to the socially elite. But it throws no light on the problem of the origin of special abilities.

Abilities and Body Structures

Much of the folklore about the effects of physique on ability is an outgrowth of "common sense" and primitive logic.[31] One such folktale is that angular ears predispose the owner to unmusical existence since sound waves are not angular but curvilinear. A person fortunate to be gifted with long, thin, muscular fingers and wide hand-span has, per se, the ability to be a violinist, a pianist—or a thief. Extremely even front teeth and certain textures of lip are allegedly related to the ease of playing one or more sorts of wind instruments.

So far no one has bothered to check on the relation of ear shapes to musical abilities. But work has been done on finger length and slenderness, tooth evenness, and thickness of lips.[32] Admittedly it is easier to play the violin or the piano if the hands are "properly" constructed. Yet no correlations of moment have been found between finger, lip, or tooth measurements and ability to master violins, horns, or clarinets. Although the pianists and violinists of college age so far examined do have slightly wider than average hands and longer fingers,[33] a study of still younger pianists showed these beginners to have shorter than average fingers.[34] Apparently a dedicated musician like the great violinist Ysaye, who had extremely stubby fingers, simply works harder at his task and may manage to reach skills as great as those his better-fingered colleagues more easily achieve.

The racial determinists have had much to say about musical abilities.[35] .Ordinarily Nordic-lovers, they have been willing to grant the Alpines, Mediterraneans, Semites, and sometimes the Negroes prominence in one or more of the nonliterary arts because they regard ability in literature as belonging to a higher order of creativity than capability in music, painting, and the other arts. Most racists base any alleged superiority on obscure elements of physique presumably caused by differences in genetic structure. A very few have offered sociopsychological explanations, e.g., the musical achievements of the Negro and the Jew are overcompensations for their unhappy minority status.

It would seem wise to check on the facts of race before searching for reasons for the supposed superiority of some one "racial" group. It is true, of course, that music has blossomed at certain times and places, and has withered at other periods and in other areas. But is the blossoming correlated with the rise or fall of any particular race? The question would have more meaning if there were general agreement as to what constitutes a race. After decades of argument, the physical anthropologists are in the process of discarding the term except, perhaps, for use in separating Caucasians, Mongoloids, and Negroids. The ancestry of most Europeans and Americans shows such diverse strains that it can be described only in terms of national and cultural unities. To explain a person's musical abilities by saying "X is musical because he is a Slavic Jew" can mean little more than that X probably came from a culture area where there were excellent teachers and where music was especially honored and furnished one of the few outlets for occupational success.[36]

As was mentioned earlier, research in music testing has proved of little worth for "racial" assessments,[37] even for the comparisons of whites and Negroes.[38] In the several studies on racial difference, sometimes one and sometimes the other of these two American groups has achieved the higher mean test score. The most that can be said is that whatever the mean score differences are, they appear to be due largely if not entirely to factors of the testing situations and not to basic differences associated with racial stock.

The explanation of sex differences in musical ability is much the same as that for "racial" differences except, of course, that there is less difficulty with the term. Music tests cannot be guaranteed to award the higher mean score consistently to either sex.[39] On the achievement side there is no question but that the male has so far taken almost all prizes. In a man's world this is hardly to be wondered at, for the environmental pressures to succeed are largely exerted in his direction. Such observations, however, have not dissuaded Vaerting,[40] Schwarz,[41] and others from the thought that woman is naturally less creative and is inherently defective in whatever may be the biological bases for the several musical abilities. Moreover, the eminent psychologist and determined hereditarian Carl Seashore has declaimed: "Woman's fundamental urge is to be beautiful, loved, and adored as a person; man's urge is to provide and achieve in a career."[42]

The statements of the hereditarians are not backed by evidence of any strength. Far more basic data must be gathered before sex differences can be properly explained. And, unfortunately, these cannot be gathered until there emerges a culture in which the two sexes have equal opportunity and equal motivation to achieve in the arts. Then and only then will the comparisons have real meaning.

It probably would not occur to most musicians that there might be a connection between handedness and musical abilities. Yet the psychiatrist Quinan has maintained that musicians display more than the normal amount of sinistrality.[43] Sikes, a music teacher, has also considered the presence of left-handedness a cue for the prognostication of later musical achievement, in this case success with the piano.[44] However, there is little support from piano teachers for Sikes's theory.[45] There was the feeling that Sikes may have been unduly affected by the skillful left-hand work of her more promising students. In piano playing the left hand has an important load to carry, a fact which most beginners fail to realize. A more nearly ambidextrous person or one who early recognizes the inadequacies of his left hand and assiduously practices this weaker member would have an advantage although he was not left-handed.[46]

There is the implication in the writings on sinistrality that left-handedness is associated with mental and emotional abnormality and that musicians have more than their proper share of such deviant behavior. It is true that an occasional musician may assume a Hollywood-like personality which has many deviant elements, but there is no reason to believe that one must have an unstable nervous system before he can achieve in music.[47] In one study, elementary-school children were rated by their teachers and music supervisors for promise in music, handedness, and speech adequacy.[48] The data showed that those rated as most musical possessed only the normally expected number of speech troubles and amount of left-handedness. In another, unpublished study of college students, the most musical and most unmusical were compared on standard personality tests. Here, again, there was no evidence that musical abilities are in any way tied to mental or emotional abnormality. Moreover, the work of Miles and Wolfe on the early life histories of fifty of the great geniuses of history discloses no unusual concentration of mental or emotional abnormality.[49]

Keston has recently compared the personality profiles of students who score high on a music preference test of his own construction with others who score low.[50] His two groups of female subjects made quite similar mean scores on the Minnesota Multiphasic Personality Inventory. But his more musical men scored significantly higher than did their less musical fellows on four of the sub-scores (F, Mf, Sc, and Ma). Keston speculates that with music looked upon in America as a relatively feminine interest area only men with slightly deviant personality patterns can be expected to show great interest in this art. It is too early to know whether further researches along the line of Keston's work will yield similar findings. But even if they do it is not to be expected that the deviations will be large enough to justify the branding of male musicians as psychoneurotics.

Adlerian Views on Ability

It is well known that defects often spur an individual to extraordinary achievement. The stuttering Demosthenes of antiquity became a famous orator. The illegitimate Smithson showed the world that though he suffered from social inferiority he was superior to the majority of his generation in many areas of achievement. And the partially deaf Beethoven, perceiving that his affliction was progressive, composed at a faster and faster rate in an attempt to hear his own compositions before complete deafness could overtake him.

The theories of at least a few of the more dedicated followers of Alfred Adler go beyond the simple idea described above.[51] It is granted that man may be spurred by his inferiorities to new heights. But instead of seeing this mechanism as one of the many wellsprings of virtuosity, these Adlerians see it as one of few, often as the major wellspring. Thus, Rosenthal views the Jew as possessing a "racial tendency" toward defective hearing and becoming through his overcompensation to this sort of inferiority far more musical than his fellow Gentile.[52] And the deafness of the genius Beethoven is looked upon as antedating all signs of his musicality. Had he not been deaf he would not have become a musical giant, these extremists declare. Needless to say, Rosenthal's "proofs" are of the anecdotal sort. Moreover, it is quite well demonstrated that Beethoven was well on the road to musical success when infection led to his hearing difficulties.[53]

Apparently there has so far been but little experimentation on the subject of the Adlerian theory of musical ability.[54] In 1937 comparisons were made of the auditory acuities of two groups of school children chosen by their teachers as either the most musical or the most unmusical of a group of 1169. The acuities were measured at seven pitch levels, for each ear alone, and for both ears together. Of the 21 comparisons, only one, that for the right ear at 1900 d.v., was what one might regard as a really significant difference and this favored the Adlerian formula, that is, the unmusical group showed more acuity for this pitch with the right ear. With all other comparisons showing insignificant differences it was concluded that these two groups of young children had very similar acuities.[55] The acuities of college students were tested at the same seven pitch levels some years later.[56] At this age the more musical had consistently better acuities. Along with the acuity tests, the students were also given the older Seashore battery of music measures (p. 235). The acuities of those who fell at 67 percentile or above on the Seashore were compared with the hearing scores of those who scored at 33 percentile or lower. Except in the areas of rhythm and consonance the higher Seashore scorers had the better acuities. A similar study of junior high-school students but undertaken in a different context was that by Bower.[57] She states: "There is some evidence here that those with superior and average hearing did better in the tests of pitch, rhythm, and tonal memory than those with defective hearing."

The data gathered in these studies are not incompatible with the notion that *occasionally* a somewhat deaf person may overcompensate in a musical direction. But this is not to say that *all* musical persons (or "races" which show a high incidence of musical achievement) are musical because of overcompensations to felt auditory defects. More often the more musical possess the better acuity.

Jungian Views on Ability

A onetime collaborator of Freud, C. G. Jung, has written extensively of what he has termed "archetypes." These are primordial images, psychic residua of experiences which have happened not to the individual but to his remote ancestors. These psychic residua act as unconscious forces which are basic to the appearance of musical and other artistic abilities, say the Jungians.[58] Unfortunately for the Jungians, the theory of the collective unconscious is out of line with the thinking of all present-day biologists, except perhaps those in the USSR, since it involves the concept of the inheritance of acquired characteristics. In other words, it can be subsumed under the now discredited Lamarckian theory of evolution.

It was Jung who gave the world the terms "introvert" and "extrovert." The introvert is introspective. He tends to be preoccupied with his own attitudes and mental processes. The extrovert attends more to external events and objects, according to the definition. These terms have had a difficult history, and contemporary American psychologists are employing them less and less often. But the Europeans who think more in terms of typologies have seen the several artistic abilites as closely linked to mental types. Thus, Szucharewa and Ossipowa hold that the extreme extrovert is rarely musical although he may possess a good sense of motor rhythm.[59] Gross and Seashore found quite the reverse to be true, at least in America.[60] Here the more musical college students they tested, and ten American composers as well, were found to be more extroverted than were the less musical. Keston and Pinto paint still a different picture of the extrovert.[61] They find him not unmusical per se, but preferring popular to serious music. Such a marked disagreement between research findings is not surprising at a time when the various measures of extroversion now available agree so poorly with each other. What is really needed is a better way of describing personality.[62]

Freudian Views on Ability

Music has received less attention from the Freudians than have its sister arts, but the basic psychoanalytic assumptions seem similar throughout the aesthetic fields. The perplexing problem of the Freudian symbol was considered in Chapter 5. The other elements of

Freud's system are equally difficult to handle.[63] Little is described in an operational form which would permit of ready experimental verification. Explanations in terms of instincts tend to be tautological, and Freud's explanations seem to be no exception. Moreover, such concepts as sublimation are slippery.[64] The Freudians, and everyone else for that matter, can see sex in the cancan, but in explaining this dance form there is no need for the concept of sublimation. Where sex is not obvious, the only "proof" that the energy source is basically sexual comes from the process of psychoanalyzing. And, unfortunately, the psychoanalytic interview is, in great part at least, a process of indoctrination, a putting into the mind of the analysand what the analyst later takes out as his proof. Such a process, of course, adds up to no proof at all. So, while psychoanalysis, at its present stage, may have therapeutic utility, it has not as yet provided a consistent set of scientifically verified explanations for the origin of the several artistic abilities. It must, if it is to be accepted, be taken largely on faith.

Imagery as a Source of Abilities

Sir Francis Galton, one of the first scientists to work with mental imagery, thought he had discovered pure image types. But later researches convinced the psychological fraternity that most persons have images of considerable strength in all sense fields, with the strongest in the visual area and the next most vivid in the auditory. Musicians, of course, tend to have more intense auditory images than do the unmusical and may be above average in the tactual and kinesthetic areas as well.[65] Von Weber, for example, was a musician with extraordinarily strong visual and auditory imagery.[66]

One of the most extensive comparative studies of imagery has been that by Agnew who has carefully rated the "mind's ears" of many run-of-the-mill musicians, psychologists, and children,[67] as well as

195

of great composers.[68] She has developed an imagery questionnaire which has enjoyed some use.

The German scientists, particularly, have noted the existence of imagery of hallucinatory intensity, which they have termed "photographic" or "eidetic." Imaginal material appears to the eidetiker almost as in normal perception. Virtually unbelievable tales have been told of the abilities of eidetikers who, by reading a book or a score only once, or by listening to one rendition of a symphony, could then without obvious cues reproduce the material as if rereading or rehearing.[69] Mozart, Gounod, and Berlioz were undoubtedly eidetikers, and so presumably is the contemporary composer Henry Cowell.[70] Mozart's famous "theft" of the *Miserere* after visiting the Sistine Chapel only twice was accomplished through the aid of his eidetic imagery.

The early appearance of strong auditory imagery in the child may serve as a predisposing factor to subsequent ability with, and interest in, tonal materials. The evidence so far collected indicates that images can be cultivated and that the absence of a functional sense organ, e.g., as in complete deafness, is always paralleled by absence of imagery in that sensory area. Eidetic images are known to be far more common among children than among adults, many of the latter having lost their eidetic potentialities through lack of practice.

Developing Abilities

It is possible for the organism to respond to sudden, loud noises even thirty days before birth. Several instances have been observed where the foetus has jerked convulsively when tones of high intensity were sounded close to the mother. Unless there is anatomical impairment, the child normally shows considerable sensitivity to tone shortly after birth, and by the eighth day he will usually stop feeding at the sound of a gong.[71] Quite naturally, the small infant's reactions to tone will depend to some extent on his physiological condition of the moment, e.g., whether or not he is sleepy or hungry.[72]

The first two-note cadences sung by the very young child tend to be descending fourths and major thirds, according to Platt.[73] Werner agrees that the early cadences are the descending ones but feels that the minor third appears first.[74] The octave is less frequently attempted and the ascending and other descending cadences are tried less often. As the child matures and is presented with scale progressions and chord figures, he learns the former with far greater facility than he does the latter.[75]

When singing voluntarily, children four and a half to eight years of age employ mean pitch levels significantly lower than those arranged for them in their song books; the mean of their voluntary pitch range, approximately 9.5 semitones, is smaller than that demanded of them by their printed songs, which average about 10.5 semitones.[76] But, without much strain, young children can, if they really try, cover a considerably greater tonal span, as Fröschels has shown.[77] His four-year-olds had a range of eight semitones, his five-year-olds ten semitones, his six-year-olds eleven, his seven-year-olds fourteen, and his eight-year-olds sixteen semitones. Jersild and Bienstock found even higher values—age four, thirteen semitones; age five, seventeen; ages six and seven, twenty-two; and age eight, twenty-four semitones.[78] These researchers report that with some practice there can be expected at least a 30 per cent gain in the number of tones three-year-olds can sing.[79]

Outstanding musical abilities are often noted considerably before age seven. In fact the studies of Garrison,[80] Cochran,[81] and of Brown [82] would lead one to suspect that by age seven the typical child has matured to the point where piano lessons may be profitably begun. Unusual ability in painting usually appears at a later age, presumably because the motor skills necessary for handling art tools are not sufficiently developed until after the seventh year.

The typical child must be nearly nine before he will show a decided preference for the traditional concordances, and then only if he has been subjected to some Western subculture.[83] But just how old he needs to be before he will get the full import of the major-minor dichotomy is not clear. Walker, who like many Continentals delights in complicated typologies, has drawn a most involved picture of the growth of the modal discriminatory powers.[84] His data at least make it clear that the child only gradually develops a feel for these affective associations. Particular trouble comes with the minor, which at first seems merely dull and perhaps slightly unpleasant. Only much later does it begin to take on a clearly sad affect.

That the growing child steadily improves his discriminatory powers in the several tonal areas is shown by the fact that music testers like C. E. Seashore found it necessary to offer several sets of age norms. In his earlier music test battery, Seashore presented separate norms for the fifth grade, for the eighth grade, and for adults.[85] His current battery offers one set of norms for the fourth and fifth grades, another for the sixth, seventh, and eighth grades, and still another for grades nine through sixteen.[86]

Attention has already been called to the peculiarly thin tone of the preadolescent male soprano, a tone with less than normal vibrato. The female appears to pick up this ornamentation much earlier than the male, possibly because she matures faster than he does.[87] In both sexes there is a change in tonal quality and a widening of the pitch range at the time of puberty, slight in the female and quite marked in the male. It goes almost without saying that puberty in the male is a period of considerable musical strain. Not only is his voice under less firm control as he shifts from a higher to a lower register but his status has changed. He has begun to assume an adult role and will from now on be compared with other adults. Prodigies particularly suffer from this shift in frame of reference and many such exceptional children leave the musical spotlight shortly after this period. For it is one thing to be compared with other child performers but quite something else to be rated on a continuum along with a Heifetz or a Kreisler.

Training Methods: General Problems[88]

Musical learning might be expected to follow in general the rules of all learning. Questions regarding whole versus part learning, motivation, overlearning, prestudy and mental rehearsal, distributed versus massed practice, beta learning, and retroactive inhibition, are encountered here as elsewhere. In addition, there are other problems met solely within the music area.

Under what conditions, for example, is *whole learning* more efficient than *part learning*? Should one go over the material as a whole, time after time, or is it wiser to break it up into smaller sections with practice restricted pretty much to these smaller portions? Research on music materials checks rather well the work in other learning areas. Where the material to be learned seems very long to the memorizer so that he tends to become discouraged and lose morale, the part method is superior.[89] But where the learner's prior habits are not too tied to the part method and he is not over-awed by the length of the score he must learn, the whole method wins out.[90] The student's aim, then, should be to work with as large a portion of his score as makes a manageable unit for him. For most persons this means that as learning proceeds, longer and longer scores can be treated as a single unit.

The literature reveals but one experimental study in the musical area on *motivated* versus *unmotivated* music learning, and this one would appear to be quite limited in applicability. In each section of the Rubin-Rabson study one of three different sorts of incentives was operative.[91] In the first of the experimental situations the only incentive was what the learning process itself provided. No verbal encouragement or other goad was employed. In a second, there were many exhortations from the experimenter. And in a third, there was promise of money payment if improvement became especially good. Rubin-Rabson's data revealed no differences among the three stimulus situations in the number of trials needed to bring the skill up to a previously agreed upon level of achievement.

It should be noted that the Rubin-Rabson study does *not* prove that learning efficiency will be the same irrespective of the type of incentive. What it does demonstrate is that rather forceful incentive changes must obtain before the slope of the learning curve will be much affected, more forceful than any that Rubin-Rabson employed. One is reminded of an adult monotone who was being taught to discriminate pitches. His improvement had been unmistakable and quite steady, but it remained exasperatingly slow until his hat was knocked from his head during the singing of the national anthem. At this point his learning curve swept sharply upwards and maintained for some time much of its new slope. Any music teacher of long standing can undoubtedly recall somewhat similar instances among her pupils where spurts in learning speed occurred as soon as "proper" incentives were come upon.

To learn an act, say the educational psychologists, practice should be continued beyond the trial where the material can for the first time be reproduced correctly. The material, in other words, must be *overlearned*. Valid as this principle seems to be in most areas, it did not hold in the extensive musical studies of Rubin-Rabson, who forced her subjects to practice 50, 100, and even 200 per cent more than was necessary for bare learning.[92] Nothing was measurably gained by all this added effort. Rubin-Rabson explains her finding with the notion that while it is conceivable that overlearning might affect favorably sheer motor performance on the piano, it should not so affect the learning of piano music since the activity here is much more a matter of meaning and insight. Consequently, once memorization is achieved, it "needs only to be restored to its original clarity on subsequent occasions."[93] With no other studies to contradict those of Rubin-Rabson, her conclusions must be at least tentatively accepted.

Although Kovacs, as early as 1915, attempted to ascertain whether careful inspection of a score before keyboard practice actually takes place might not benefit the subsequent learning of the score, his experimental controls were so poor that no generalizations could safely be drawn.[94] Hence, we must rely again upon the researches of Rubin-Rabson as no other psychologist or educator has worked in this area.[95] The questions Rubin-Rabson attempted to answer were, in brief, (1) is *mental prestudy* of benefit to subsequent learning, and (2) if it is, will *mental rehearsal* be of value at other periods in the learning process? Affirmative answers were found to both questions. The best period for mental rehearsal was found to be a time roughly midway among the keyboard practice sessions. Thus, it would appear that the ambitious piano student should not only analyze and study his scores before he starts his formal keyboard practice but should take off time considerably before his top skill is reached to rehearse mentally what has been going on.

The work of Rubin-Rabson must once again be employed for generalizations on the problem of *massed* versus *distributed practice*.[96] With limited time to spend on learning something, is it wiser to allocate all to one continuous session or to split the effort between several sessions? For the learning of all but the easiest material, educational psychologists favor some sort of distribution or spreading of the practice trials, and Rubin-Rabson's data on the learning of piano music fall in line with their generalization. She set an interval of one hour between trials for her first group of students and 24 hours for the second. Admittedly, far more than two time intervals must be experimented with before it can be said just what allocation is best for any given situation. But with some labor, a music student can, if he will, find the optimum time spread for each sort of material he desires to master.

Common sense warns against the practicing of one's mistakes. Repeated again and again, these errors will grow into habits and become difficult to eradicate. But is this belief in the power of practice really sound? Would it not be more accurate to say that almost all practice is a matter not of avoiding but of repeating mistakes? For if an act can be done perfectly, why practice it at all? The fact that practice is needed shows that errors are still being made even though the learner may not recognize them as associated with the individual skills he wishes to acquire. In ordinary learning, then, there is practice of errors along with a rehearsal of the correct elements.

Why not force the practicer to become acutely aware of his errors? asks the psychologist Dunlap.[97] Why not have the learner single out his mistakes and rehearse them alone but do so with the ever-present desire that they can and should be eliminated? This procedure Dunlap calls *beta learning* in contradistinction to the more ordinary form, where the learner does not restrict his practice to his errors but drills himself on a medley made up of both correct acts and mistakes in the hope that the latter will gradually be eliminated. While McGeoch and Irion categorically state that beta learning has proved effective "in correcting errors in piano-playing," they cite no studies to support their contention.[98] Moreover, the only published report of the use of the beta technique in the entire music area, that by Wakeham on the elimination of errors in organ-playing, tells us only of its failure.[99] It might be added that the present writer has twice tried beta practice on musicians who were bothered by persistent performance errors and was quite unsuccessful in both instances. Perhaps Wakeham and the author unwittingly failed to carry out some detail of Dunlap's methodology. Or it may be that performance errors in music are somehow unlike typing errors where the scheme has proved so successful. But, in any event, there is no reason as yet for replacing the more ordinary procedures with the beta variety.

There is the distinct possibility that the learning process may be thrown badly out of gear should the learner practice two tasks more or less concomitantly. Evidence from a number of areas suggests that this possibility becomes practically a certainty whenever the two tasks are quite similar. The learning of the one somehow inhibits the learning of the other task, a phenomenon called *retroactive inhibition*. It behooves the musical educator, then, to ascertain how important this principle may prove to be for keyboard learning.

To obtain at least a partial answer, Rubin-Rabson observed the behaviors of 18 highly trained musicians in a number of situations. Happily, no important inhibitory effects were detectable when two tasks were learned concomitantly. To quote Rubin-Rabson:

> [My] conclusions are not unexpected. The experimental procedure was only a repetition of a learning situation familiar to these subjects for many years. The mechanics of piano study had long since accustomed them to learning much new music concomitantly while retaining material already learned to various degrees. No confusion develops transferable from one learning to the other because the organizational skill of these learners is highly trained and specific and because rarely are two bits of music so similar in key, rhythm, melodic or structural details as to make involuntary transfer feasible. There is here, furthermore, a favorable task-set engendered by the prestige factors implicit for musicians in a music-learning situation.[100]

It would be a bit premature to suggest that the Rubin-Rabson research has completely settled the problem. While its conclusions will most probably be found to hold for well trained musicians generally, they may or may not apply to beginners. Further research at this lower proficiency level, then, must be undertaken before a final answer can be given.

Training Methods: Special Problems

While it has long been known that practice with the right hand will, to some extent, also train the left hand, this fact has certainly led no one to limit his practice to his right hand. Yet certain music teachers have believed that practice first with one hand and then with the other would result in quicker learning than drill with the two hands in coordination. The notion seemed to be that while one hand was resting it would be absorbing more skill from the hand that was practicing than if it continued to practice with its mate and then rested with it. However, the facts do not support this idea. There are at least two studies available which demonstrate beyond question the superiority of the *coordinated* technique as opposed to the *unilateral*.[101] The student, then, is advised to attempt hand coordination from the very beginning of practice.

Proper imagery is most important for music training. The imagery needed for "good" voice quality is particularly difficult to achieve but, according to Bartholomew, training in this area can be effective.[102] The "feel" and "image" of a tonal quality represented by strong resonance at 500 and 2800 cycles are essential for the male singer and around 3200 for the female vocalist. Good kinesthetic imagery is needed by the violinist, particularly when he begins to practice double stops.[103] At this stage in his learning, auditory imagery is no longer as effective a guide as it was when he was learning to play on a single string. For in his earlier practice on the single string he could by careful listening almost instantly adjust his finger position whenever it was incorrect. But with two fingers breaking the strings it becomes difficult to know which finger to change. So now he must rely on kinesthetic images which refer specifically to a single finger.

Too much emphasis, however, must not be placed on imagery. Indeed, direct sensory cues are often more essential. Thus, beginners on the piano learn more slowly if they are kept from looking at their

hands and the keyboard than if allowed to look where they will.[104]
This finding follows the basic learning principle which states that,
other things being equal, the more the sensory cues available the
faster the learning.[105]

Several excellent studies on *sight reading* are available to the reader.
Although space here allows for but few comments, the serious
student will find an examination of the original articles cited in the
references of the next few pages most worthwhile. The exposure of
musical material on cards offers one approach to the study of sight
reading, and photography of eye fixations furnishes another excellent
source of data. In certain of the studies, the moving hands and the
hammers within the piano have been photographed.

Bean warns piano teachers to allow their pupils to gain reading
speed in the early stages of learning even at the expense of occasional
errors.[106] He finds all too many persons reading slowly and attending
to single notes when they should be attending to musical patterns,
that is, to short phrases. Reading individual notes is akin to attention
to individual letters while reading, and this is behavior typical of
extremely poor readers. By the judicious use of flash cards the reading
of most students can, Bean says, be speeded up appreciably and be made
considerably more accurate. Ortmann points out that the teacher
who knows what her pupils' eyes can and cannot do will be better
equipped to suggest proper training methods.[107]

As a result of their researches, Lannert and Ullman believe that the
piano student should be early taught to read ahead of the measure
being played and should be forced into considerable sight-reading
practice.[108] The arrangement of the keyboard must become so well
known that little visual attention need be paid it. Lowery also stresses
the great need for sight-reading practice and the early achievement of
smooth eye-hand coordinations.[109] He notes that reading music is
far more complicated than reading print, since musical symbols are
not arranged on lines or columns but are scattered both horizontally

and vertically. The eye often fixates on areas between notes or even between staves. Music reading is made even more difficult because of our unscientifically arranged staff and symbols. The work of Wheelwright,[110] for example, clearly shows that the spaces between notes and rests should, for purposes of better reading, be proportional to the represented time values.

A wealth of material on the reading and playing of music can be found in the excellent reports of Weaver,[111] of Van Nuys and Weaver,[112] and of Jacobsen.[113] While these studies were not primarily oriented toward training procedures, they do offer helpful suggestions for the improvement of practice. Only a few samples will be given here, however, since this book is not the place for an extended coverage of all that might be found helpful to the music teacher.

The reading of music should start with diatonic intervals and not with chromatics and accidental signs, which are very difficult to perceive. Music in the bass clef and that written on leger lines cause much reading difficulty which can only be overcome by extensive practice. Surprising as it may seem, practice on reading words is often more needed by the beginning music student than practice on note reading. Immature students should be introduced rather early to scale runs and only much later to arpeggios. Emphasis should be on speed reading rather than on accuracy since the habit of slow reading is difficult to break. On the average, it is the fast music reader, not the slow one, who is the more accurate. Jacobsen ends his advice with the pessimistic comment that much note-reading material for beginners is not well adapted to their reading level and should be replaced by scores better geared to their perceptual capacities.

Creativity

No one really understands the intricacies of the creative processes as they function in any particular composer, not even the composer himself. This fact, however, has not stopped several musicians from introspecting and retrospecting on these interesting processes. For example, the modern composer Henry Cowell, stimulated by his psychologist-mentor, L. M. Terman, has described in some detail how he believes he composes.[114] Early deciding to be a composer and for a time having little access to musical instruments, Cowell diligently practiced imagining the timbres he had heard. He was aided in this labor by the possession of eidetic imagery. With practice, he put together in his "mind's ear" many different timbres, finally getting imagined effects not offered by any instrument played in the traditional manner. Later, when a piano was available to Cowell, he experimented with it to elicit some of the bizarre effects he had been imagining. In this fashion were born his tone clusters, his string massage, and the other Cowellian timbre novelties. Whenever Cowell was commissioned to compose, he employed effects which seemed to him appropriate to the occasion, realizing, however, that he was offering his listener no clear-cut musical message.

Research which many composers might not consider entirely realistic was that performed by Benham when, in the interests of an experiment, he composed a series of nine-measure melodies (average time between 60 and 70 seconds).[115] He found his auditory imagery strongest at the emergence of each musical idea. During the development there were motor sensations and other types of imagery. The major danger in this and other similar experiments, of course, is that the overly analytic mental set, necessitated by the experiment, may have interfered with the experimenter's creative powers or have given them rather different qualitative flavor.

Observations somewhat similar to those of Benham were made by Bahle, who sent questionnaires to 32 well-known European composers in an effort to learn how they believe they composed.[116] Their replies were later checked against autobiographical documents left by a number of the greatest European composers of the past three centuries. In one of his many studies on the problem of creativity, Bahle asked his composer respondents to set poems to music and to introspect and retrospect on the process. Unfortunately his data, extensive as they are, have led to few generalizations which could not have been made before the studies were undertaken. In some respects Bahle's problem was like that of asking centenarians about the reasons for their long life. Many and varied are the convictions that are aired—yet no one knows with certainty the degree of validity of any one of the theories offered to explain either the longevity of an individual or his creativity.

By comparing better and poorer students of composition, Gross and Seashore have helped validate the commonly held belief that facility in composition comes in part at least from toil and sweat.[117] Formal and informal training and knowledge of good work habits appeared in this study as extremely important for all who would compose. Whittaker and his associates also found compositions to reflect the particular composer's informal training.[118] Musical creations were shown to be generally in line with the traditional and folk art of the immediate culture and the rather narrow interests of the community in which the composer lived.

The sociologists Lastrucci[119] and Becker[120] have studied the way of life of dance-band musicians and the effects on creativity and performance which stem from their extremely atypical living habits. Dance musicians feel forced to compose and perform in idioms and manners appreciated by their audiences. Such pressures from the "ignorant" lay public they often resent and compensate for by striving to produce, at least in jam sessions, what they regard as higher level material.

It is popular nowadays to point to a reified unconscious as the major wellspring of artistic inspirations. Thus, the great musicologist Max Graf asserts that the greater part of musical formation takes place in the unconscious mind, which to him is a mystical entity that science cannot measure or explain.[121] Graf does admit, however, that the composer's childhood memories and his life-long environmental pressures affect his style of composition.

Jancke makes the point that most if not all creativity is preceded by psychological tensions which are often unconscious.[122] In some degree the act of composing relieves these tensions. To the composer, then, even more than to the listener, music is autistic and personal. Hence, when the composer listens to one of his own earlier compositions, it may take on a quite different meaning from what it originally had for him, since at this time it serves to lessen what is perhaps a rather different tension.

To make his own unconscious at least somewhat recordable, Loar deliberately fatigued himself and went without his normal sleep.[123] Then he attended concerts where he drowsed. When Loar later attempted to record his dreams and reveries he found that no repressed wish or inhibited desire could be recognized among his fantasies. Instead, there appeared in fictionalized form memories which Loar had formed from his reading of the composer's life and times. However, in fairness to analytic theory, it must be admitted that Loar's technique was not one which could uncover repressed wishes.

Why some composers create "beautiful" music and others "unbeautiful" is explained by Ehrenzweig on a Gestalt-psychoanalytic basis.[124] Aesthetically good Gestalts, i.e., beautiful tonal materials, belong to the surface layers of the mind. The "depth mind" or unconscious, on the other hand, is "Gestalt free." Hence it is from the unconscious that the poor Gestalts, the ugly and the distorted, come. Although the modern composer's unpleasant music may seem highly

209

sophisticated, his art, thinks Ehrenzweig, represents a retrogression to the least differentiated modes of infantile "thing perception."

The composer may honestly believe his compositions to be novel, to be born from an unconscious that has had little or no traffic with the music of his contemporaries or of the past. But the fact is that the composer forgets the origins of much of the material he will later use in his creations. This material has come from a variety of sources and is unconscious in the sense that it is not immediately recallable. As time goes on it will be elaborated into the form in which it will later be produced. But just how much of the rearrangement of items goes on below the verbal threshold is not known. However, the amount must often be considerable as certain composers, Haydn and Schumann, for instance, seem to have done their creative work without much effort. But others, like J. S. Bach, typically scratched and erased and followed extremely rigid rules. There would appear to be a continuum, then, along which composers fall—with the "intuitive" at the one end and the "non-intuitive" at the other, with the former yielding his finished product almost without considered thought and the latter only after much careful deliberation and conscious elaboration.

Biographical studies of the great composers usually stress their personality structures, their psychological abnormalities and sociological uniquenesses, as well as the cultural forces which seem to have been in part responsible both for the style of composition they have embraced and for the fact that they chose composing as a career.[125] Luck, special body build, extreme vitality and joy of living, outstandingly good or extraordinarily poor health, pressures from relatives or friends, high intelligence, extreme tonal and rhythmic facility, vivid imagery, abnormally fine memory, past suffering, much greater than average ambition and persistence, ability to make others work on one's behalf, poorly controlled emotions, inherited talent for composing,[126] readiness to forgo present pleasures for future gains, and even willingness to be a melody thief have all been mentioned by one or another biographer as necessary for creative genius. Biographical research is fascinating work, which may indeed pay big dividends in the years to come, yet at present its methods are too crude to allow for valid generalizations. A biographer is all too likely to conclude that some one of his many biographical items has great causal significance simply because his biases encourage him to select out and emphasize this item. It can be expected, perhaps, that over the years biographer biases will in some degree cancel each other. But until that happier day arrives, only hunches and very tentative conclusions can be safely drawn from this type of research material.[127]

It is interesting to note that the period of life when neurolo-muscular coordinations are at their best was found by Lehman to be the time when eminent composers of the past were at the peak of their creativity.[128] Of course, temporal coincidence does not neces-sarily indicate causality. Yet the correspondence between decade of maximum creativity and years of best motor coordination exists in so many areas—athletics, painting, writing, science, mathematics, and philosophy, as well as musical composition—that it may have considerable significance. However, Bjorksten, while agreeing that motor skill and creativity must be somehow related, asks us not to forget that middle-aged and older men, particularly those in academic life, simply do not have as much free time to devote to creative work as do their younger brethren.[129] Hence, the date of maximum creativity is to some extent determined by available time. And Wayne Dennis[130] seems to find that topflight workers who live long keep producing to an advanced age with surprisingly little letup.

In a study by Lehman and Ingerham of the compositions of eminent deceased musicians, the half-decade from age thirty-five to thirty-nine was shown to be the most productive for grand operas, can-tatas, and orchestral and symphonic works of "superior" quality.[131]

This research team continued its study with contemporary American composers, but apparently met with great difficulty in deciding what compositions should be placed in the "superior" category. Perhaps this uncertainty makes less meaningful the finding that the peak creative half-decade for this group fell much later—in the years from fifty to fifty-four. The peak for music of high quality was found in both studies to come earlier than that for sheer quantity.

It must be admitted that the above discussions of creativity leave us with a deplorable lack of closure. It is quite possible that the answers sought in this area have been as unrealistic as they have sometimes proved to be in certain other areas. Rarely is a phenomenon of nature found to have a single cause. If the process in question is broad in scope and appears in many different contexts, it is bound to be related to a host of variables. We now know, for example, that the several sorts of leadership demand different psychological qualities, although for years researchers sought a single set of psychological characteristics that would be typical of all. Without doubt the creative processes, too, show multiple causality.[132] The blossoming of creativity is surely dependent in considerable part on circumstances unique to particular situations. The trigger which actually sets off the creative process in one man may be quite dissimilar from that needed for another, particularly if he is of a different personality or school of composition, or from another culture or age.

Summary

The layman often speaks of his friends as extremely musical, as moderately musical, or perhaps as not at all musical. He implies that there is one general musical or even broader art ability which one may possess to a greater or lesser degree. The evidence, however, points to a contrary conclusion, to the existence of a number of semi-independent musical abilities no one of which seems particularly related to abilities in the other arts. While top achievement in music, just as in most other areas, calls for academic intelligence of a high order, the correlation in the school years between music test scores and I.Q. is slight. In fact a few very stupid persons have been located who are much less stupid in the musical realm. These are the idiot-savants.

In the main, spectacular musical achievement seems unrelated to anomalies of gross body musculature. This should not be taken to mean that there are not neural constitutions admirably suited to musical endeavor. Yet these constitutions are largely wasted if proper environmental pressures are not operative. We are all well aware of the constitutional misfits who struggle in vain toward musical accomplishment. But we are less apt to note the numerous prodigies who sooner or later drop out of the musical picture because of the infertility of their musical surroundings. It is the view of modern science that the course of development of neither group can be predicted from scrutinies of their family lines. Indeed, the interweaving of nature and nurture is far too complicated for the successful use of such a simple device as genealogical analysis. Achievement and potentiality are by no means identical, and the fact that one man has achieved more in music than another, or men in general more than women, or members of one national or racial group more than another cannot be transcribed into capacity terms. A wide range of achievement can be derived from similar potentialities.

To describe a person as "arty" is, in some circles, to brand him as psychoneurotic. It is true, of course, that history reveals musicians who have been neurotic or even psychotic. But the connection between musicality and abnormality, if there is one, is extremely slight. Standard personality tests and ratings disclose no relationship between the two. A possible exception to this generalization concerns the jazz performer, whose way of life typically encourages unstable relations with his family and other deviant behaviors as well.

In this chapter, the claims of Adler, Jung, and Freud have been scrutinized for their bearing on musical abilities. It was concluded that while auditory insufficiencies can facilitate musical creativity, such weaknesses are not essential to composition and performance of high order, even though the Adlerian extremists would have us think so. Jung's view that abilities arise as psychic residua of ancestral experiences was dismissed as out of line with current biological belief, being a variant of the Lamarckian notion of the inheritance of acquired characters. And the extraversion concept was held to be too poorly defined for purposes of quantification. The Freudian notion of sublimation was also regarded as of little explanatory aid. What are needed are operationally sound hypotheses susceptible to eventual verification. Sublimation seems not to be a concept of this sort but rather something to be accepted as an act of faith.

While all musicians have auditory imagery of more than average strength, a few, the eidetikers, possess auditory pictures of hallucinatory intensity. Such imaginal skill could well encourage a child to enter a musical career. He might enter anyway, however, for the possession of eidetic imagery is not a *sine qua non* of musicality.

By and large, the rules of learning as formulated by the educational psychologists are found to hold for the learning of musical materials. But each field of learning has its unique problems, and music is no exception. Overlearning, for example, is not as beneficial to music learning as it has been found to be in many other areas, presumably because the activities here are more a matter of insight and meaning than of sheer motor performance. Music learning is of course facilitated by proper increases in motivation although not by the slighter goadings found of value in many other sorts of learning. Beta learning, the intentional practice on errors, which works so well in the elimination of typing errors, fails with musical materials. And, at least with well-trained musicians, retroactive inhibition does not appear to be the hazard it is in some fields of learning.

Students of musical creativity are gradually giving up the idea that the abilities of the composer come from a common wellspring and are independent of the social setting. Unfortunately, however, most authorities have so far gotten little beyond the stage of enumerating possible essentials to creativity and of playing up a few as special favorites. The more mystically minded theorists sidestep the problem with their positing of the unconscious mind as the receptacle from which creativity is alleged to spring full blown. Gradually, however, at least a few data are being assembled which may later yield a clearer picture of creativity than is now available. Introspection, retrospection, biographical analysis, and statistical treatment of age data—here are techniques now being used.

With all our concern with precocity and creativity we should not forget that every musician must reach at least a minimum of proficiency in a number of basic abilities. In our next chapter we shall consider those capabilities assumed to be needed, since their measurement has long been one of the tasks of the psychological aesthetician.

Notes

1] R. M. Drake, "Factorial Analysis of Music Tests by the Spearman Tetrad-difference Technique," *J. Musicol., 1* (1939): 6–16. Over the years, Drake has convinced himself that his early conclusions were in error. He now feels that there are two important facets to musical ability—music memory and rhythmic ability. See *Drake Music Aptitude Tests*, Chicago, Science Research Associates, 1954.

2] H. D. Wing, "A Factorial Study of Musical Tests," *Brit. J. Psychol., 31* (1941): 341–355.

3] J. McLeish in *The Fourth Mental Measurements Yearbook*, New Brunswick, N.J., Rutgers U. Press, 1953.

4] P. Vernon, *The Structure of Human Abilities*, N.Y., Wiley, 1950, p. 93.

5] C. W. Manzer and S. Marowitz, "The Performance of a Group of College Students on the Kwalwasser-Dykema Music Tests," *J. Appl. Psychol., 19* (1935): 331–346.

6] E. Franklin, *Tonality As a Basis for the Study of Musical Talent*, Göteborg, Sweden, Gumperts Förlag, 1956.

7] J. E. Karlin, "A Factorial Study of Auditory Function," *Psychometrika, 7* (1942): 251–279; "Factor Analysis in the Field of Music," *J. Musicol., 3* (1941): 41–52.

8] L. B. Bower, "A Factor Analysis of Music Tests," Thesis, Catholic U., 1945.

9] R. S. Morrow, "An Analysis of the Relations Among Tests of Musical, Artistic, and Mechanical Abilities," *J. Psychol., 5* (1938): 253–263.

10] E. K. Strong, Jr., *Manual for Vocational Interest Blank for Men*, Stanford, Calif., Stanford U. Press, 1945.

11] R. K. White, "The Versatility of Genius," *J. Soc. Psychol., 2* (1931): 460–489.

12] C. Alexander, "The Longevity of Scientists," *J. Soc. Psychol., 39* (1954): 299–302.

13] M. Schoen, *The Psychology of Music*, N.Y., Ronald Press, 1940.

14] C. Cox, *Genetic Studies of Genius*, vol. 2, Stanford, Calif., Stanford U. Press, 1926.

15] C. F. Lehman, "A Study of Musically Superior and Inferior Subjects as Selected by the Kwalwasser-Dykema Music Tests," *J. Educ. Res., 45* (1952): 517–522.

16] R. W. Lundin, "The Development and Validation of a Set of Musical Ability Tests," *Psychol. Monog., 63*, No. 10 (1949). For a resumé of the studies in this area see J. L. Mursell, "Intelligence and Musicality," *Education, 59* (1939): 559–562.

17] L. S. Hollingworth, "The Musical Sensitivity of Children Who Test Above 135 I.Q.," *J. Educ. Psychol., 17* (1926): 95–109.

18] E. Ehrsam, "Über den Fall einer einseitigen musikalischen Begabung eines blinden Kindes bei hochgradigen Leistungsrückstand," *Psychiat. Neurol. Med. Psychol.*, Leipzig, *7* (1955): 149–154.

19] D. C. Rife and L. H. Snyder, "Studies in Human Inheritance," *Hum. Biol., 3* (1931): 547–559. See also W. A. Owens and W. Grimm, "A Note Regarding Exceptional Musical Ability in a Low-grade Imbecile," *J. Educ. Psychol., 32* (1941): 636–637.

20] I.Q. data from high schools sometimes show music students to be brighter than average. Of course this finding could conceivably mean that music students per se have higher than average I.Q.'s. More plausible is the hypothesis that the surveys were selective and that this superiority is not the rule (D. K. Antrim, "Do Musical Talents Have Higher Intelligence?" *Etude, 63* (1945): 127–128).

21] The claim has been made that it is not academic intelligence per se to which musical ability is related but rather mathematical ability. To check on this persistent belief, G. Révész has surveyed both mathematicians and musicians and has found no unduly large number of musical mathematicians or mathematically minded musicians (*Introduction to the Psychology of Music*, Norman, U. of Okl. Press, 1954; "Beziehung zwischen mathematischer und musikalischer Begabung," *Schweiz. Z. Psychol. Anwend., 5* (1946): 269–281).

22] G. Révész, *The Psychology of a Musical Prodigy*, N.Y., Harcourt Brace, 1925. See also C. Stumpf, "Akustische Versuche mit Pepito Areola," *Zsch. f. Ang. Psychol., 2* (1909): 1–11; F. Baumgarten, "Der Werdegang eines Wunderkindes," *Zsch. f. Ang. Psychol., 41* (1932): 473–498. It is of interest that there have been virtually no child prodigies in 'cello, clarinet, flute, or voice, and but few in composition. The style now is for prodigy conductors. In the past the most fertile areas for prodigies were violin and piano. See N. Slonimsky, "Musical Children, Prodigies or Monsters?" *Etude, 66* (1948): 591–592.

23] R. Updegraff, L. Heiliger, and J. Learned, "The Effect of Training upon the Singing Ability and Musical Interest of Three-, Four-, and Five-year-old Children," *U. of Ia. Stud. Child Welf., 14* (1938): 83–131; A. T. Jersild and S. Bienstock, "A Study of the Development of Children's Ability to Sing," *J. Educ. Psychol., 25* (1934): 481–503; M. S. Hattwick and H. M. Williams, "The Measurement of Musical Development, II," *U. of Ia. Stud. Child Welf., 11* (1935): 1–100; G. E. Moorhead and D. Pond, "Music of Young Children," *Pillsbury Found. Stud.,* 1941, 1942; E. N. Drexler, "A Study of the Development of the Ability to Carry a Melody at the Preschool Level," *Child Devel., 9* (1938): 319–332.

24] H. Christianson, *Bodily Rhythmic Movements of Young Children in Relation to Rhythm in Music,* Teach. Coll. Contrib. Educ., No. 736, N.Y., Teachers College, Columbia U., 1938; A. T. Jersild and S. Bienstock, "Development of Rhythm in Young Children," *Child Devel. Monog., 22* (1935).

25] R. F. Wyatt, "Improvability of Pitch Discrimination," *Psychol. Monog., 58,* No. 2 (1945); A. A. Capurso, "The Effect of an Associative Technique in Teaching Pitch and Interval Discrimination," *J. Appl. Psychol., 18* (1934): 811–818; E. Connette, "The Effect of Practice with Knowledge of Results," *J. Educ. Psychol., 32* (1941): 523–532; M. Wolner and W. H. Pyle, "An Experiment in Individual Training in Pitch-Deficient Children," *J. Educ. Psychol., 24* (1933): 602–608; G. M. Whipple, "Studies in Pitch Discrimination," *Amer. J. Psychol., 14* (1903): 289–309; R. H. Seashore, "Improvability of Pitch Discrimination," *Psychol. Bull., 32* (1935): 546. For training data on other music abilities see G. M. Gilbert, "Sex Differences in Musical Aptitude and Training," *J. Gen. Psychol., 26* (1942): 19–33.

26] C. E. Seashore, *Psychology of Music,* N.Y., McGraw-Hill, 1938, p. 57.

27] See L. S. Hollingworth, "The Musical Sensitivity of Children Who Test above 135 I.Q." *J. Educ. Psychol., 17* (1926): 95–109.

28] H. Koch and F. Mjön, "Die Erblichkeit der Musikalität," *Zsch. f. Psychol., 121* (1931): 104–136; H. Stanton, "The Inheritance of Specific Musical Capacities," *Psychol. Monog., 31* (1922): 157–204; V. Haecker and T. Ziehen, "Beitrag zur Lehre von der Vererbung u.s.w.," *Zsch. f. Psychol.,* 1931, *121,* 1–103; R. S. Friend, "Influences of Heredity and Musical Environment on the Scores of Kindergarten Children on the Seashore Measures of Musical Ability," *J. Appl. Psychol., 23* (1939): 347–357; A. Scheinfeld, *You and Heredity,* N.Y., Stokes, 1939.

29] J. Mjön, "Zur Erbanalyse der musikalischen Begabung," *Hereditas, 7* (1926): 109–128; G. Voss, "Die Familie G.," *Dtsch. Zsch. f. Nervenhk., 83* (1925): 249–263.

30] C. Terry, *The Origin of the Family of Bach Musicians,* London, Oxford U. Press, 1929; K. Geiringer, *The Bach Family,* N.Y., Oxford U. Press, 1954.

31] In the category of folktales is the belief that music ability arises through being born at an astrologically propitious time (p. 118). There is one folktale which says that musicians do not enjoy normal longevity and another which states that they live beyond their "proper" span. These notions, however, have been disproved by the insurance statisticians, who find the lives of musicians to be of normal length. See W. Schweisheimer, "Do Musicians Live Longer Than Others?" *Etude*, 67 (1949): 54–55; A. H. Whittaker, "Occupational Diseases of Musicians" in *Music and Medicine*, N.Y., Schuman, 1948. Note (p. 182), however, that musicians enjoy less longevity than educators, whose life-span is above average. The blood pressure of musicians is slightly lower than that of non-musicians but the difference is not statistically significant (L. F. Sunderman, "A Study of Some Physiological Differences between Musicians and Non-Musicians: I. Blood-pressure," *J. Soc. Psychol.*, 23 (1946): 205–215).

32] C. J. Lamp and N. Keys, "Can Aptitude for Specific Musical Instruments be Predicted?" *J. Educ. Psychol.*, 26 (1935): 587–596.

33] J. H. Taylor, "The Relation between Finger Length, Hand Width and Musical Ability," *J. Appl. Psychol.*, 20 (1936): 347–352.

34] S. Graf, "Measurements of Hand Length, Muscular Control, and Motility Related to Handedness," Master's Thesis, Syracuse U., 1952.

35] E. Bauer, E. Fischer, and F. Lenz, *Human Heredity*, N.Y., Macmillan, 1931; R. Breithaupt, "Pianistic Talent and Race," *Etude*, 42 (1924): 455–456; E. Kretschmer, *The Psychology of Men of Genius*, N.Y., Harcourt, Brace, 1931. A typical racist generalization is that of S. Günther. Western music, says he, is better integrated than that of the Dinaric people but lacks the empathic or emotional potential of the latter ("Rassenseelen-kundliche Beiträge zur musikalischen Stilforschung," *Arch. Musikforsch.*, 3 (1938): 385–427). E. Rittershaus maintains that most creative musicians of the nineteenth century had Nordic features ("Die Vererbung musikalischer Eigenschaften," *Arch. Rass.- u. Ges.-Biol.*, 29 (1935): 132–152).

36] R. Braine, "The Making of a Virtuoso Violinist," *Etude*, 43 (1925): 157–158. Keith Sward, "Jewish Musicality in America," *J. Appl. Psychol.*, 17 (1933): 675–712, points out that in 1932 one-half of American violin virtuosos, maestros, and first violinists of symphony orchestras were of Jewish descent. Ten per cent of American composers were also Jewish. Yet ten- and eleven-year-old Jewish and gentile youngsters score similarly on tests of pitch and intensity discrimination, tonal movement, and tonal memory. It would appear, then, that the presence of so many Jews in American musical life must be due to economic and social factors rather than genetic causes.

37] G. B. Johnson, "Musical Talent of the American Negro," *Mus. Superv. J.*, 15 (1928): 81, 83, 96.

38] The study of D. Van Alstyne and E. Osborne, "Rhythm Responses of Negro and White Children Two to Six," *Monog. Soc. Res. Child Devel.*, 2 (1937): 4, is almost the only research where Negro superiority has seemingly been found. Negro children appeared to be markedly better in motor rhythm, the superiority being greatest for the simplest rhythms and the youngest subjects. But whether these data are to be explained on genetic grounds, are due to errors of selection, or may be attributed to the Negroes being less inhibited or receiving more musical encouragement is not clear. Other studies, e.g., that of R. L. Streep, "A Comparison of White and Negro Children in Rhythm and Consonance," *J. Appl. Psychol., 15* (1931): 53–71, have found slight Negro superiorities but never differences of such impressive magnitude.

39] G. M. Gilbert, "Sex Differences in Musical Aptitude and Training," *J. Gen. Psychol., 26* (1942): 19–33.

40] M. Vaerting, "Die musikalische Veranlagung des Weibes," *Zsch. f. Psychother. Med. Psychol., 7* (1917): 120–127.

41] H. D. Schwarz, "Die Kunst als seelische Kraftquelle für die Frau," *Psychol. Rundschau, 3* (1931): 52–53.

42] C. Seashore, *In Search of Beauty in Music*, N.Y., Ronald Press, 1947, p. 367.

43] C. Quinan, "A Study of Sinistrality and Muscle Coordination in Musicians, Iron-workers and Others," *Arch. Neur. and Psychiat., 7* (1922): 352; "The Principal Sinistral Types," *Arch. Neur. and Psychiat., 24* (1930): 35–47.

44] M. L. Sikes, "Musical Talent and the Left hand," *Ped. Sem., 30* (1923): 156–161.

45] P. R. Farnsworth, "Musical Talent and the Left hand," *Sch. Mus., 32* (1932): 11.

46] For data which picture the ambidextrous as better than average in tongue-agility see J. Kwalwasser, *Exploring the Musical Mind*, N.Y., Coleman-Ross, 1955, p. 132.

47] E. M. East, "Insanity and Genius," *J. Hered., 29* (1938): 275–279; A. Anastasi and J. P. Foley, Jr., "A Survey of the Literature on Artistic Behavior in the Abnormal, I," *J. Gen. Psychol., 25* (1941): 111–142; "II," *Annals, N.Y. Acad. Sc., 42* (1941): 1–112; "III," *Psychol. Monog., 52* (1940): 1–71; "IV," *J. Gen. Psychol., 25* (1941): 187–237. P. E. Vernon believes that composers of the romantic school tend to have been more neurotic than those of the classical school ("The Personality of the Composer," *Music and Letters, 11* (1930): 38–48).

48] P. R. Farnsworth, "Ratings in Music, Art, and Abnormality in the First Four Grades," *J. Psychol., 6* (1938): 89–94.

49] C. C. Miles and L. S. Wolfe, "Childhood Physical and Mental Health Records of Historical Geniuses," *Psychol. Monog., 47* (1936): 390–400. A study by R. V. Burton ("Are Musicians Normal?" *Overture, 35*, No. 5 (1955): 10) on approximately one-third of all musicians employed in the motion picture studios of the Los Angeles area revealed no unusual amount of emotional abnormality. The testing device was the Guilford-Zimmerman Temperament Survey.

50] M. J. Keston, "An Experimental Investigation of the Relationship between the Factors of the Minnesota Multiphasic Personality Inventory and Musical Sophistication," *Amer. Psychol., 11* (1956): 434.

51] A. Adler, "Character and Talent," *Harpers, 155* (1927): 64–72.

52] H. Rosenthal, "Die Musikalität der Juden," *Int. Zsch. f. Indiv.-psychol., 9* (1931): 122–131.

53] P. C. Squires, "The Problem of Beethoven's Deafness," *J. Abn. Soc. Psychol., 32* (1937): 11–62.

54] P. R. Farnsworth, "Auditory Acuity and Musical Ability in the First Four Grades," *J. Psychol., 6* (1938): 95–98.

55] In a parallel study S. Atwell looked for evidence of color weakness among artistic and inartistic children. Her findings were contrary to what might have been expected from the Adlerian doctrine in that it was the artistic youngster who tended to possess slightly better color vision ("Color Vision in Relation to Artistic Ability," *J. Psychol., 8* (1939): 53–56).

56] P. R. Farnsworth, "Further Data on the Adlerian Theory of Artistry," *J. Gen. Psychol., 24* (1941): 447–450.

57] L. B. Bower, "A Factor Analysis of Music Tests," Thesis, Catholic U., 1945.

58] M. Bodkin, "Archetypal Patterns in Tragic Poetry," *Brit. J. Psychol., 21* (1930): 183–202.

59] G. Szucharewa and S. Ossipowa, "Materialen zur Erforschung der Korrelationen zwischen den Typen der Begabung u. d. Konstitution," *Zsch. ges. Neurol. u. Psychiat., 100* (1926): 489–526.

60] B. Gross and R. H. Seashore, "Psychological Characteristics of Student and Professional Musical Composers," *J. Appl. Psychol., 25* (1941): 159–170.

61] M. J. Keston and I. M. Pinto, "Possible Factors Influencing Musical Preference," *J. Genet. Psychol., 86* (1955): 101–113.

62] A number of researchers have attempted to study personality variables through the construction of a tonal equivalent of the famous *Rorschach Ink-Blot Test*. Music is used to elicit imagery and attitudinal sets which are interpreted more or less in the fashion of the Rorschach. For one of the studies in this area, see J. O. Grimmett, "Personality Diagnosis through Music," Master's Thesis, Stanford U., 1950. Personality has also been studied by the aid of musical preference tests.

63] S. Freud, *A General Introduction to Psychoanalysis,* N.Y., Liveright, 1935. See also H. Racker, "Contributions to Psychoanalysis of Music," *Amer. Imago, 8* (1951): 129–163. For a discussion of the Rankian adaptation of Freudianism see A. Michel, *Psychoanalyse de la Musique*, Paris, U. de Paris, 1951. Michel connects the oral stage of sex development with the use of the piano, the anal with the trumpet, and the phallic with the flute.

64] For an attempt to link Mozart's creativity with sublimation see A. H. Esman, "Mozart, a Study of Genius," *Psychoanal. Quart., 20* (1951): 603–612.

65] A. Hartmann, "Untersuchungen über metrisches Verhalten in musikalischen Interpretationsvarianten," *Arch. Ges. Psychol., 84* (1932): 103–193; K. L. Bean, "The Use of Visual, Auditory, and Kinesthetic Imagery in the Transfer of Musical Notation to the Piano Keyboard," *J. Educ. Psychol., 30* (1939): 533–541; J. Mainwaring, "Kinaesthetic Factors in the Recall of Musical Experience," *Brit. J. Psychol., 23* (1932): 284–307.

66] P. C. Squires, "The Creative Psychology of Carl Maria von Weber," *Char. and Pers., 6* (1938): 203–217.

67] M. Agnew, "A Comparison of Auditory Images of Musicians, Psychologists, and Children," *Psychol. Monog., 31* (1922): 268–278.

68] M. Agnew, "The Auditory Images of Great Composers," *Psychol. Monog., 31*(1922): 279–287.

69] R. Kochmann, "Über musikalische Gedächtnisbilder," *Zsch. f. Ang. Psychol., 23* (1924): 329–351; T. Zaworski, "Akustyczne wyobrazenia ejdetyczne," *Kwart. psychol., 13* (1947): 156–203.

70] H. Cowell, "The Process of Musical Creation," *Amer. J. Psychol., 37* (1926): 233–236.

71] H. S. Forbes and H. B. Forbes, "Fetal Sense Reaction: Hearing," *J. Comp. Psychol., 7* (1927): 353–355; K. Fleischer, "Untersuchungen zur Entwicklung der Innerohr-funktion," *Z. Laryngol., 34* (1955): 733–740.

72] M. W. Haller, "The Reactions of Infants to Changes in the Intensity and Pitch of Pure Tones," *J. Genet. Psychol., 40* (1932): 162–180.

73] W. Platt, "Temperament and Disposition Revealed in Young Children," *Char. and Pers., 2* (1934): 246–251.

74] H. Werner, "Die melodische Erfindung im frühen Kindesalter," *Phil.-Hist. Klasse Sitzungsberichte, 182* (1917); T. F. Vance and M. Grandprey, "The Evaluation of the Musical Capacity of Nursery School Children," *Proc. Ia. Acad. Sci., 36* (1929): 321–328. For further data on the music of preschool children see M. G. Colby, "Instrumental Reproduction of Melody by Preschool Children," *J. Genet. Psychol., 47* (1935): 413–430.

75] A. Wells, "A Comparison of Chord Figures and Scale Progressions in Early School Music Learning," *Peabody Bull., 30* (1933): 21–23; D. Doig, "Creative Music: Music Composed for a Given Test," *J. Educ. Res., 35* (1941): 263–275; *35* (1942): 344–355.

76] M. S. Hattwick, "The Role of Pitch Level and Pitch Range in the Singing of Pre-school, First-grade, and Second-grade Children," *Child Devel., 4* (1933): 281–291. See also H. M. Williams, "Immediate and Delayed Memory of Preschool Children for Pitch in Tonal Sequences," *U. of Ia. Stud. Child Welf., 11* (1935): 85–94.

77] E. Fröschels, "Untersuchungen über die Kinderstimme," *Zentralbl. f. Physiol., 34* (1920): 477–484.

78] A. T. Jersild and S. F. Bienstock, "A Study of the Development of Children's Ability to Sing," *J. Educ. Psychol., 25* (1934): 481–503.

79] A. T. Jersild and S. F. Bienstock, "The Influence of Training on the Vocal Ability of Three-year-old Children," *Child Devel., 2* (1931): 272–290.

80] K. C. Garrison, "Psychology of Special Abilities," *Peabody Reflector, 12* (1939):11–13. See also R. Leibold, "Kind und Metronom," *Zsch. Pädag. Psychol., 37* (1936): 317–322; M. Varro, "The Musical Receptivity of the Child and the Adolescent," *Mus. Teach. Nat. Ass. Proc.,* 1943, 77–88.

81] M. Cochran, "Kinesthesis and the Piano," *Austral. J. Psychol., 8* (1930): 205–209.

82] R. W. Brown, "The Relation between Age (Chronological and Mental) and Rate of Piano Learning," *J. Appl. Psychol., 20* (1936): 511–516.

83] C. W. Valentine, "The Aesthetic Appreciation of Musical Intervals among School Children, and Adults," *Brit. J. Psychol., 6* (1913): 190–216.

84] E. Walker, *Das musikalische Erlebnis und seine Entwicklung,* Göttingen, Vanderhoeck u. Ruprecht, 1927.

85] C. E. Seashore, *Manual of Instructions and Interpretations of Measures of Musical Talent,* N.Y., Columbia Graphophone, 1919.

86] C. E. Seashore, D. Lewis, and J. G. Saetveit, *Manual, Seashore Measures of Musical Talents,* N.Y., Psychol. Corp., 1956.

87] For a genetic study of the voices of 44 choir boys see F. J. Hell, "Physiologische und musikalische Untersuchungen über die Singstimme der Kinder," *Arch. Ges. Phonel., 2* (1938): 65–102. Another study which compares the musical productions of children from preschool to adolescence is that by A. Nestele, "Die musikalische Produktion im Kindes-alter," *Beihefte z. Zsch. f. Ang. Psychol., 15,* No. 52 (1930). For still another study of the musical abilities of the adolescent see M. Van Briessen, *Die Entwicklung der Musikalität in den Reifejahren,* Langensalza, Beyer, 1929.

88] The material of this section is largely limited to the work of psychologists. The reader who would know how the professional educator regards the problems of music learning is referred to the text by J. L. Mursell, *Music and the Classroom Teacher,* Boston, Silver Burdett, 1951. Articles which show the insights of both the educator and the psychologist are those by J. Mainwaring, "Psychological Factors in the Teaching of Music, Part I," *Brit. J. Educ. Psychol., 21* (1951): 105–121; "Part II. Applied Musicianship," 199–213. Still another publication worth reading is that by M. E. Wilson, *How to Help Your Child with Music,* N.Y., Schuman, 1951.

89] C. C. O'Brien, "Part and Whole Methods in the Memorization of Music," *J. Educ. Psychol., 34* (1943): 552–560.

90] R. W. Brown, "A Comparison of the 'Whole,' 'Part,' and 'Combination' Methods of Learning Piano Music," *J. Exp. Psychol., 11* (1928): 235–247; G. Rubin-Rabson, "Studies in the Psychology of Memorizing Piano Music, III: A Comparison of the Whole and the Part Approach," *J. Educ. Psychol., 31* (1940): 460–476; L. E. Eberly, "Part versus Whole Method in Memorizing Piano Music," Thesis, Columbia U., 1921.

91] G. Rubin-Rabson, "Studies in the Psychology of Memorizing Piano Music, IV: The Effect of Incentive," *J. Educ. Psychol., 32* (1941): 45–54.

92] G. Rubin-Rabson, "Studies in the Psychology of Memorizing Piano Music, VI: A Comparison of Two Forms of Mental Rehearsal and Keyboard Overlearning," *J. Educ. Psychol., 32* (1941): 593–602; "VII: A Comparison of Three Degrees of Overlearning," *J. Educ. Psychol., 32* (1941): 688–696.

93] G. Rubin-Rabson, "Mental and Keyboard Overlearning in Memorizing Piano Music," *J. Musicol., 3* (1941): 33–40.

94] S. Kovacs, "Untersuchungen über das musikalische Gedächtnis," *Zsch. f. Ang. Psychol., 11* (1916): 113–135.

95] G. Rubin-Rabson, "The Influence of Analytic Prestudy in Memorizing Piano Music," *Arch. Psychol., 31,* No. 220 (1937): 1–53; "Studies in the Psychology of Memorizing Piano Music, V: A Comparison of Prestudy Periods of Varied Lengths," *J. Educ. Psychol., 32* (1941): 101–112.

96] G. Rubin-Rabson, "Studies in the Psychology of Memorizing Piano Music, II: A Comparison of Massed and Distributed Practice," *J. Educ. Psychol., 31* (1940): 270–284.

97] K. Dunlap, *Habits: Their Making and Unmaking,* N.Y., Liveright, 1932.

98] J. A. McGeoch and A. L. Irion, *The Psychology of Human Learning,* N.Y., Longmans Green, 1952.

99] G. Wakeham, "Query on 'A Revision of the Fundamental Law of Habit Formation'," *Science, 68* (1928): 135–136.

100] G. Rubin-Rabson, "Studies in the Psychology of Memorizing Piano Music, VIII: The Inhibitory Influence of the Same and of Different Degrees of Learning," *J. Musicol., 5* (1947): 25.

101] R. W. Brown, "The Relation between Two Methods of Learning Piano Music," *J. Exp. Psychol., 16* (1933): 435–441; G. Rubin-Rabson, "Studies in the Psychology of Memorizing Piano Music, I: A Comparison of the Unilateral and Coordinated Approaches," *J. Educ. Psychol., 30* (1939): 321–345.

102] W. T. Bartholomew, "Imagery in Voice Pedagogy," *Peabody Bull., 31* (1934): 20–28; "The Paradox of Voice Teaching," *J. Acoust. Soc. Amer., 11* (1940): 446–450.

103] P. R. Farnsworth, "Psychology and Double Stops," *Sch. Mus., 27* (1926): 21.

104] R. W. Brown, "A Preliminary Study of the Touch Method of Learning Piano Music," *J. Appl. Psychol., 18* (1934): 516–527.

105] To tie imagery to action rather than to tones, F. Fredrich (*Playing by Seeing,* Medino, Ohio, Lynne, 1950) suggests the use of note pictures where sketches of the piano keyboard are placed over the staff and lines are drawn from the piano keys to their staff notes.

106] K. L. Bean, "An Experimental Approach to the Reading of Music," *Psychol. Monog., 50,* No. 6 (1938); "Reading Music Instead of Spelling It," *J. Musicol., 1* (1939): 1–5; "The Use of Visual, Auditory, and Kinesthetic Imagery in the Transfer of Musical Notation to the Piano Keyboard," *J. Educ. Psychol., 30* (1939): 533–541.

107] O. Ortmann, "Span of Vision in Note Reading," *Mus. Educ. Nat. Conf. Yearb.,* 1937, 88–93.

108] V. Lannert and M. Ullman, "Factors in the Reading of Piano Music," *Amer. J. Psychol., 58* (1945): 91–99.

109] H. Lowry, "On Reading Music," *Diopt. Rev. and Brit. J. Physiol. Opt., 1* (1940): 78–88.

110] L. F. Wheelwright, *An Experimental Study of the Perceptibility and Spacing of Music Symbols,* Teach. Coll. Contr. Educ., No. 775, 1939, N.Y., Teachers College, Columbia U., 1939.

111] H. E. Weaver, "A Survey of Visual Processes in Reading Differently Constructed Musical Selections," *Psychol. Monog., 55,* No. 1 (1943): 1–30.

112] K. Van Nuys and H. E. Weaver, "Memory Span and Visual Pauses in Reading Rhythms and Melodies," *Psychol. Monog., 55,* No. 1 (1943): 33–50.

223

113] O. I. Jacobsen, "An Analytic Study of Eye-movements in Reading Vocal and Instrumental Music," *J. Musicol., 3* (1941): 1–32, 69–100, 133–164; *3* (1942): 197–226.

114] H. Cowell, "The Process of Musical Creation," *Amer. J. Psychol., 37* (1926): 233–236.

115] E. Benham, "The Creative Activity," *Brit. J. Psychol. (Gen. Sec.), 20* (1929): 59–65. For somewhat similar research on children eight to eleven see the series of articles entitled "Creative Music" by D. Doig. Of special interest is number 2 which is to be found *J. Educ. Res., 36* (1942): 241–253.

116] J. Bahle, *Der musikalische Schaffensprozess*, Leipzig, Hirzel, 1936.

117] B. Gross and R. H. Seashore, "Psychological Characteristics of Student and Professional Musical Composers," *J. Appl. Psychol., 25* (1941): 159–170.

118] W. G. Whittaker, W. O. Hutchison, and R. W. Pickford, "Symposium on the Psychology of Music and Painting," *Brit. J. Psychol., 33* (1942): 40–57.

119] C. L. Lastrucci, "The Professional Dance Musician." Thesis, Stanford U., 1941.

120] H. S. Becker, "The Professional Dance Musician and His Audience," *Amer. J. Sociol., 57* (1951): 136–144. A somewhat similar study is being made of contemporary American composers of "serious" music by D. Nash ("Challenge and Response in the American Composer's Career," *J. Aesth., 14* (1955): 116–122).

121] Max Graf, *From Beethoven to Shostakovich; the Psychology of the Composing Process*, N.Y., Philosophical Library, 1947.

122] J. Jancke, "Das Spezifisch-Musikalische und die Frage nach dem Sinngehalt der Musik," *Arch. Ges. Psychol., 78* (1930): 103–184.

123] L. Loar, "An Adventure in Musical Psychoanalysis," *J. Musicol., 2*, No. 1 (1940): 15–23.

124] Anton Ehrenzweig, *The Psycho-analysis of Artistic Vision and Hearing*, London, Routledge and Kegan Paul, 1953.

125] M. I. Stein, "Creativity and Culture," *J. Psychol., 36* (1953): 311–322.

126] G. Révész, in his *Introduction to the Psychology of Music*, Norman, U. of Oklahoma Press, 1954, maintains that there is a single homogeneous talent for composing which manifests itself in very young children much less often than does the reproductive-interpretative talent.

127] Biographical studies by psychologists are the following: J. Bahle, *Eingebung und Tat im musikalischen Schaffen*, Leipzig, Hirzel, 1939; H. Jancke, "Beiträge zur Psychologie der musikalischen Komposition," *Arch. Ges. Psychol., 66* (1928): 437–492; R. Schramek, "Franz Liszt," *Arch. Ges. Psychol., 92* (1934): 45–84; P. C. Squires, "The Creative Psychology of César Franck," *Char. and Pers., 7* (1938): 41–49; P. C. Squires, "The Creative Psychology of Chopin," *J. Musicol., 2*, No. 1 (1940): 27–37; P. C. Squires, "Peter Ilich Tschaikowsky (a psychological sketch)," *Psychoanal. Rev., 28* (1941): 445–465; P. C. Squires, "The Creative Psychology of Carl Maria von Weber," *Char. and Pers., 6* (1938): 203–217; P. E. Vernon, "The Personality of the Composer," *Music and Letters, 11* (1930): 38–48.

128] H. C. Lehman, "'Intellectual' vs. 'Physical Peak' Performance," *Sci. Month., 61* (1945): 127–137.

129] J. Bjorksten, "The Limitation of Creative Years," *Sci. Month., 62* (1946): 94.

130] W. Dennis, "Predicting Scientific Productivity in Later Maturity from Records of Earlier Decades," *J. Gerontol., 9* (1954): 465–467.

131] H. C. Lehman and D. W. Ingerham, "Man's Creative Years in Music," *Sci. Month., 48* (1939): 431–443; H. C. Lehman, *Age and Achievement,* Princeton, N.J., Princeton U. Press, 1953.

132] Most authorities find no evidence for a unitary creative ability in the arts. See J. P. Guilford, "Creative Abilities in the Arts," *Psychol. Rev. 64* (1957): 110–118.

CHAPTER NINE

The Measurement of Musical Abilities

Musical abilities can be measured in a variety of ways. For persons already proficient in some phase of music, achievement tests are appropriate. These may be measures either of verbal knowledge, of appreciation (see Chap. 7), or of nonverbal musical skills. For use before the person to be tested has had much formal training, there are the aptitude tests. In the latter, music is usually broken into its various components and tests are constructed in each of these component areas. In a sense, aptitude tests are also measures of achievement, although they aim to test informal learning and potential ability rather than the effects of formal training.[1]

Tests of Verbal Knowledge

Music achievement tests based on verbal knowledge are generally geared to school performance and attempt to measure how well certain musical abilities have been taught. They tell us nothing about what should be taught and so do nothing toward altering the musical *status quo*. Achievement tests typically possess high reliability.

The earliest published tests of verbal knowledge are the *Beach Standardized Music Tests*, which cover a wide area of musical abilities.[2] There are parts devoted to notation, to the elements of "time and

tune both in isolated form and in melodies," recognition of fundamental structural elements, pitch differences, memory, sight singing,
and to the writing of music. The title is something of a misnomer as
the battery has not been well standardized.

Beach's battery was followed by the *Musical Achievement Test*
developed by Gildersleeve and Soper.[3] This has five parts designed to
measure recognition of compositions from notation and as played by
the examiner; ability to detect changes in pitch, meter, key signature
and meter signature; knowledge of instrumentation, theory, history,
note values, time signatures, and transpositions from one clef to
another; and ability to use accidentals, to locate *la* in six different
keys, and to write key signatures. Designed for grades four through
eight, it has a reliability of over ·90 at each age-grade.

The *Torgerson-Fahnestock Music Test* is another of the older achievement measures.[4] Part A taps knowledge of note and rest values, time
signatures, pitch and syllable names, expressive marks, major and
minor key signatures, repeat bars, slurs, *do* placements, clefs, and
natural and harmonic minor scales. Part B tests ear training through
four subparts which are concerned with the writing of syllable
names, time signatures, and notes, as well as with the detection of
pitch and time errors.

The most used of the early achievement measures was the
Kwalwasser-Ruch Test of Musical Accomplishment.[5] This battery attempts
to test the following phases of public-school music from grades four
through twelve: knowledge of musical terms and symbols, pitch and
letter names in bass and treble clefs, time signatures, key signatures,
note values, rest values, and familiar melodies from notation; and
detection of pitch and time errors in a familiar melody.

An achievement measure very similar in most respects to the
Kwalwasser-Ruch is the *Strouse Music Test*, which covers the same
areas except for detection of pitch and time errors and adds tests of
pitch height and time length.[6] The Strouse measure takes longer to

administer and must be accompanied by a piano or singer. There are three forms which can be used in grades four through twelve.

Number 1 of the *Hutchinson Music Tests* is a measure of tonal imagery.[7] Snatches from 25 well-known melodies are presented along with the names of these and of 25 additional songs. The purpose of Hutchinson's measure is to test "silent reading and recognition." Norms are available for grades seven through twelve.

The *Knuth Achievement Tests in Music* are well characterized by their subtitle, "For Recognition of Certain Rhythmic and Melodic Aspects."[8] In presenting the stimuli for the test, the examiner first strikes a chord to sound the key and then plays four measures which represent one of the four scores the student has in his hands. The Knuth has three levels, one for grades three and four, another for five and six, and the third for grades seven through twelve.

The *McCauley Experiment in Public School Music*, arranged for grades four through nine, is much like the older test by Gildersleeve and Soper, but so much longer that it takes more than one session to give.[9] There are measures of knowledge of syllable and letter names, of note and rest values, meter and key signatures, chromatics, sight and aural identification of melodies, types of compositions, musical instruments, famous names in music, and musical terms.

A somewhat more limited measure is the *Providence Inventory Test in Music*.[10] Its ten sections have to do with naming notes, note values, key signatures, measure signatures, rest values, syllables, melodies, bass-staff syllables, and symbols; and placing *do*. Like most of its rivals, it has but one form. It is intended for grades four through nine.

A rather different kind of achievement test is the musical vocabulary list developed by L. C. Pressey.[11] The so-called "fundamental vocabulary" words appear in capital letters, fairly important supplementary words in italics, and words of no great importance but often found in textbooks are in ordinary type.

Ear Tests in Harmony are measures suitable for use in any standard course in harmony.[12] They test "active musical experience in the world of sound." Sound combinations of many sorts including the rather unusual are treated in this battery.

Among the more recently published achievement batteries is one devised by Kotick and Torgerson.[13] Their *Diagnostic Tests of Achievement in Music* are intended for grades four through twelve. The topics covered include diatonic syllable, chromatic syllable, and number names; time signatures; major and minor keys; note and rest values; letter names; signs and symbols; key names; and song recognition.

A contemporary measure which is enjoying some success is the *Farnum Music Notation Test*.[14] Forty four-measure melodies are presented by means of a phonograph record. The student follows along with a printed score and selects for each melody the one measure in which the pitch, rhythm, or time is handled differently. Sets of norms are available for grades seven, eight, and nine, and for the two sexes separately. The test correlates appreciably with a number of the standard measures of musical aptitude and with scores on certain instrumental performance scales.

Another contemporary measure is the *Aliferis Music Achievement Test*, whose tonal stimuli can be given either by piano performance or tape recording.[15] Intended for use at the college freshman level, this test has melodic, harmonic, and rhythmic sections. The total test is said to correlate with music grades in the ·50's and ·60's. It is quite reliable and has been extremely well standardized with separate T-scores for each of the four major geographical sections of the United States.

In 1951 a music achievement test was added to the well known and much used *Graduate Record Examination, Advanced*.[16] Achievement is measured from the senior year of college through graduate school. Since this battery is part of the Institutional Testing Program, it is not available for general use and cannot be described here.

Tests of Nonverbal Musical Skills

The earliest of the semistandardized tests of musical performance (1923) was the *Hillbrand Sight-Singing Test*, a measure devised for fourth-, fifth-, and sixth-grade pupils.[17] The test contains six songs which the student studies for a few minutes and then sings without help or accompaniment. The examiner listens with an ear to notes wrongly pitched, to transpositions, notes flatted, notes sharped, notes omitted, errors in time, extra notes, repetitions and hesitations.

Hillbrand's scale was followed two years later by the *Mosher Test of Individual Singing*.[18] Twelve exercises, arranged in order of difficulty, are presented and sung back by the pupil. The score is the tally of the measures rendered tonally and rhythmically correct. In 1932 Mosher was co-author of a second performance scale entitled the *O-M Sight-Singing Test*.[19] This measure is structurally like the earlier one. The items "progress through most of the major keys and introduce the minor mode. Some of the exercises in the latter part of the test begin on scale steps other than the tonic." The test has high reliability (odd-even) and is reasonably objective in the sense that any two examiners will agree fairly well on the ratings which should be given.

Watkins's *A Performance Test for the Cornet or Trumpet* consists in a scale of fourteen melodic exercises.[20] Two scores are usually obtained, one as the test is administered to the pupil at sight, and the other after he has had a week's time to practice the material. The scores are built up from a tabulation of pitch, time, change of tempo, expression, and slur errors; and the mishandling of rests, holds, pauses, and repeats. An adaptation of this performance scale for the cornet or trumpet is *The Watkins-Farnum Performance Scale*.[21] This latter may be used for any band instrument. The fourteen exercises are so graded that while the first is intended for those who have had lessons for approximately three months, the fourteenth will be found difficult by the student who has studied for several years. The reliability is good as is also the correlation with teacher ratings.

Relatively unstandardized achievement tests keep appearing from time to time.[22] A few of these owe their birth to the idea that the music curricula of the public schools are still too local to justify national norms. Hence, each large school system can with profit construct its own test battery, although at present the majority of music achievement tests do not meet the standards of good test construction. Without doubt the fluid and uncertain state of school music has made the task of devising achievement tests in music more difficult than in, say, the scientific areas. Perhaps at some later date there will be more general agreement on what children should know about music by the end of each grade. When this time arrives, really first-rate tests can be devised for the area of music.

Unstandardized Aptitude Tests

We have seen that the music achievement tests largely reflect current curriculum practices and give little help in isolating the basic musical abilities. Attention must be shifted, then, to the musical aptitude tests in the hope that they may yield more pertinent information.

Stumpf was one of the first psychologists to interest himself in the basic musical abilities.[23] In his work with the young genius Pepito Areola, he stressed the following: possession of absolute pitch; unusually good pitch and timbre discrimination; excellent musical memory; ease in judging pitch intervals; and ability in transposition, in improvisation, and in producing dissonant chords and series of "unmelodic" tones. Stumpf saw four basic abilities in musicality: to tell whether a clang was composed of one or two tones, to discriminate pitch differences, to judge degrees of consonance as to pleasantness, and to sing correctly. Pear modified Stumpf's ideas very slightly by testing for pitch aptitude, ability to sing, ability to analyze a clang, and consistency in reporting the clang analyses.[24]

Meyer has developed a number of ingenious devices to assess musical talents.[25] His "obe-imeter" measures "how echotheratic (sound-hunting) the subject is." The task in this test is to listen for an auditory stimulus which is not easily followed since it is partially masked by other tones and noises. The "concertometer" shows how well a musician can play with other musicians in concert. The "rhythmometer," which resembles the motor rhythm test R. H. Seashore independently developed (p. 235), measures how well a person can follow a rhythmic pattern and reproduce it. The "terpo-meter" presents major, minor, and mistuned chords which are to be classified as either active, sad, or neutral. The last member of the battery, the "hymnometer," is in essence a tonal memory test. Both the "terpometer" and the "hymnometer" make use of a specially devised quarter-tone reed organ.

During his early research, Révész appeared to regard absolute pitch as the most important element of musicality. Chord and interval recognition; ability to compose, improvise, and to transpose; and keen memory were also deemed to be basic musical abilities. All of these Révész found to be present at an early age in the wonder-child Nyiregyhazi (p. 185), whose achievements he described in *The Psychology of a Musical Prodigy*.[26] In his more recent theorizing Révész has differentiated between (*a*) aptitudes which he feels have to do with fitness for performance and (*b*) talents which refer to capacities far above the average in some special field.[27] Musical talents, for him, are of two distinct types: creative and reproductive-interpretative. The latter type is subdivided into instrumental-virtuoso talent and talent for conducting. Révész would now measure the "lower grades of musicality" through tests of rhythmic sensitivity, regional pitch, ability to analyze two-tone clangs and chords, and ability to grasp and sing a melodic line. For the "higher grades of musicality" he would give tests suited to the measurement of relative pitch, harmonic apprehension and response, creative fantasy, and ability to play familiar melodies from memory.

For Rupp the list of basic abilities included: interval recognition, absolute pitch, chord analysis, harmonic feeling, melodic recognition and reproduction, and sensitivity to rhythms and time differences.[28] Billroth[29] and von Kries[30] had briefer lists. The former's included ability to remember, recognize, and reproduce short melodies. The latter's contained sense of rhythm, musical memory, and musical ear. For Mjön the five most important abilities appeared to be: to compose, to possess absolute pitch, to play by ear, to improvise a second voice, and to sing a second voice.[31]

Haecker and Ziehen obtained the bulk of their data on musical abilities by sending out 11,000 questionnaires.[32] Exceptional tonal memory seemed to them best to distinguish their more from their less musical respondents. An excellent prognostic sign for later musicality turned out to be precocity in things musical. They found vocal skill, a motor ability, to be little related to the several sensory skills, e.g., pitch discrimination.

Lowery has devised three tests, one of musical memory, another in which it must be decided which of two cadences is more complete, and a phrase test in which the problem is to tell whether or not a phrase has been repeated.[33] Ortmann has a battery of seven tests which has enjoyed use at the Peabody Conservatory of Music.[34] The members are: pitch memory, rhythm memory, melodic memory, harmonic memory, fusion, pitch discrimination, and time discrimination. Schoen, too, has offered a battery of tests.[35] These are for the measurement of relative pitch, where one must judge the difference in distance between two successive pitch intervals; tonal sequence, in which four two-phrase melodies are given with alternative endings; and rhythm discrimination, where a rhythm may either be repeated or reappear in somewhat altered form. A tonal

233

movement test of considerable promise is Franklin's *TMT*. Twenty-five unfinished melodies are presented to the testees with requests for the best final tone for each. Retest and split-half reliabilities in the ·80's are reported for an adult music student population. By the use of the *TMT* it is apparently possible to select the better from the poorer students at a level considerably better than chance.[36]

Among those who have used achievement tests as measures of aptitude is Madison, who has made an extensive study of the ability to discriminate intervals.[37] Since interval discrimination is basic to all musical perception, it would seem that Madison has specialized on a most important musical ability. Scores on Madison's measure have been found to correlate from ·46 to ·72 with grades in theory at the Juilliard School and from ·39 to ·71 with indices of musical ability at the secondary-school level. Lamp and Keys[38] have also studied aptitude by way of achievement. They trained pupils for several weeks on brass instruments, then on woodwinds, and later on strings (the order varied). After these weeks of training, ratings were made for achievement on each family of instruments. The authors hoped through such ratings to learn which of the three sorts of instruments was best suited to the aptitudes of each of their pupils. They appeared to enjoy mild success in their prognostications. These teachers also attempted, without success, to forecast later achievement through analyses of tooth evenness, lip thickness, and length and slenderness of fingers (p. 188).

No well standardized tests have so far been developed to measure control of pitch intonation, loudness, time, or rhythm. But a record of pitch control can be obtained through the use of instruments such as the tonoscope[39] and other standard stroboscopic devices[40] now on the market which show visually the accuracy of a person's vocal or instrumental attempts. Intensity meters and instruments to study dynamic control are available.[41] Ability to control time and rhythm can be studied through the Meyer "rhythmometer," mentioned above, or by means of R. H. Seashore's "rhythm meter," which is a phonograph with contacts imbedded in the turn-table at various points.[42] A number of different rhythms can be provided for the subject, who must make his taps on a telegraph key coincide with the clicks he hears.

C. E. Seashore and his students have felt that the ability to imagine tonal material is an important aspect of musical aptitude.[43] Their way of testing imagery is to present lists of questions which, it is hoped, will elicit images in the eight most important sensory areas. Naturally, their list for children differs from that appropriate to adults. The subjects, whatever their age, must introspectively evaluate the strengths of their images on a seven-point scale.

The Original Seashore Battery

The first really standardized aptitude tests were those devised by C. E. Seashore.[44] Seashore argued that since music was a phenomenon of tones, times, and rhythms, discrimination tests in these areas should make it possible to pick out the potentially musical, with those having the best acuities being expected to give the greatest musical promise. Seashore believed that his tests tapped basic physiological capacities which were inborn and could not be influenced by training. He admitted that his test battery was limited, that there were other capacities he was not measuring.

Seashore's test philosophy has been criticized on a number of counts.[45] Many psychologists and musicians have condemned its atomistic and unmusical orientation.[46] They have emphasized that the Seashore tests get at psychophysiological, and not necessarily at musical, differences. What is the good, they say, of a performer's being able to discriminate pitches which differ by as little as one cycle if his listeners can only discriminate pitches which are five or more cycles apart? If the performer is a pianist, why need he bother

235

with differences smaller than a half-tone? Other psychologists have been made unhappy by the Seashore claim that test scores reflect pure native capacity and cannot be improved by practice.[47] It has not proved possible to entice all music testers away from Seashore's hereditarian camp. But there has been amassed an impressive array of data which demonstrate beyond the possibility of doubt that the Seashore scores can be enormously improved if proper training procedures are employed (p. 186).

The original *Seashore Measures of Musical Talent* offered scores for sense of pitch, sense of intensity, sense of time, sense of consonance, and auditory memory span (tonal memory).[48] Six years later a sense of rhythm measure was added. Because of the many criticisms of it, the sense of consonance test was later dropped (p. 49). Norms for each member of the battery were made available for adults, for eighth-graders, and for fifth-graders, who were thought to be the youngest age group which could properly attend to the tonal stimuli of the tests.

There have been a number of attempts to improve the battery. Several have found that the norms, at least for the intensity test, vary somewhat with the type of phonograph employed. Others have advocated simplifying the directions, which are quite difficult for fifth-graders to comprehend.[49] Salisbury and Smith have modified the pitch test so that all of the items are scaled from less to more difficult, instead of from less to more and then more to less as in the original measure.[50] Hattwick has also modified the pitch test with the aim of adapting it to children of the first five grades.[51] Gaw, deciding that the time and tonal memory tests were too difficult for fifth-graders, dropped the most difficult items of these tests.[52] These changes did improve the tests somewhat, although the Gaw-modified tests are now a little too easy.[53] California adult norms for the rhythm test have been developed, since it has been found that West Coasters make better scores on this measure than do Iowans.[54] O'Connor would modify the tonal memory test by (1) better scaling of item difficulty, (2) greater temporal spacing between items, and (3) the use of the whole-tone as the minimal interval.[55]

Tilson-Gretsch Test for Musical Aptitude

Created to replace or at least to serve as a second form of the original Seashore battery, the Tilson-Gretsch tests played into bad luck in appearing shortly after the revised (1939) Seashore battery.[56] The Tilson-Gretsch presents tests in the areas of pitch, intensity and time sensitivities, and tonal memory. It is recorded on two phonograph records whereas its older rival was spread over six. Its directions are considerably more communicable than Seashore's but its items are too easy. Its reliabilities are approximately the same as Seashore's at the fifth- and eighth-grade levels but are considerably poorer in the adult range. This battery now has little excuse for continued existence.[57]

1939 Edition of the Seashore Measures of Musical Talents

Only minor changes in the Seashore test philosophy are reflected in this newer battery.[58] Musical "talent" has become musical "talents." As was mentioned above, there is no longer an attempt to measure consonance. The term "intensity" is replaced by the more appropriate "loudness." Sensitivity to timbre is recognized as of sufficient importance to justify the construction of a test to measure it. But the bulk of the objections raised in connection with the earlier edition still pertain. Two forms of the battery, A and B, were constructed, one an easier and the other a more difficult series, but Form B was later withdrawn from sale. Three sets of centile norms are now available for Form A—for the fourth and fifth grades, for the sixth, seventh, and eighth, and for grades nine through sixteen.

The basic tones of the pitch test are set at 500 cycles.[59] Each of the 50 items in the test consist of two tones which differ only in pitch. The subject's task is to state whether the second of each pair is higher or lower than the first. The test opens with differences of 17 cycles, moves to differences of 12 cycles, then to 8, 5, 4, 3, and finally to 2 cycles. The reliability (odd-even, raised by Spearman-Brown) ranges from ·79 in the lower grades to ·88 for adults.

The 50 items of the loudness test are also arranged in pairs. Here the subject must decide whether the second tone of each pair is weaker or stronger than the first. The range of loudness differences is from four decibels to a half-decibel. The reliabilities run from ·79 in the lower grades to ·88 at the adult level.

Similarly, in the time test the subject judges whether the second tone of each pair is held a longer or shorter time period than the first. Starting with differences of ·3 second, the test becomes progressively more difficult: ·2, ·15, ·125, ·10, ·075, and finally ·05 second. The time test is about equally reliable at all ages (·76).

Each item of the rhythm test consists in two patterns which may have either identical or different rhythms. With only 30 true-false items, the reliability of this test is the poorest of all at the adult and junior-high-school levels (·62 and ·69) and is second lowest at the grade-school level (·73).

The measure of timbre also uses the same-different scheme but has more items than the rhythm test. To change the timbre, the intensity of the tone's fourth partial was increased and that of the third partial was decreased by an amount necessary to keep the total intensity constant. In the first fifth of the 50 items this change is of 10 decibels. The changes in the more difficult items are first of 8·5, then of 7·0, 5·5, and finally of 4·0 decibels. The reliability ranges from ·69 to ·77.

The measure of tonal memory has 30 items and follows a multiple-choice plan. Hence, its reliability is high (from ·84 to ·88). Short series of tones are given and then repeated with one of the tones of each series changed in pitch. One-third of the series are three-tone sequences, another third are four-tone, and the remaining third are five-tone. While the Seashore tests are, in the main, relatively independent of one another, the tonal memory test correlates appreciably with the others.

VALIDITY OF SEASHORE BATTERIES. The majority of the many validity studies on these widely used tests have been concerned with the set of records Seashore brought out in 1919. The criteria against which the Seashore tests have been measured are several, with teacher ratings and grades in music appearing in perhaps most of the studies. Where correlations of any size have been found—and occasionally values in the ·60's and ·70's have been reported—they tend to be the highest for the tonal memory and pitch tests[60] and for the battery considered as a single measuring instrument.[61] In one of the few studies of the 1939 tests, Manor found that fourth-grade work in instrumental music could be forecast by the pitch test with a coefficient of correlation of ·49 and by the measure of tonal memory with a correlation value of ·32.[62]

Intelligence tests have been found to be of more worth than the Seashore tests in forecasting music grades in academic classes, e.g., history and appreciation of music, while the Seashore are of more value the more the classes are tonally conducted, e.g., classes in harmony.[63] Members of musical organizations make, in the main, higher than average Seashore scores.[64] High scorers show a greater preference for "classical" music than do the lower scorers says one study,[65] while, according to another, their preferences lean more toward the "romantic classical" (as opposed to "light classical").[66] Persons who regard themselves as more musical than average tend to achieve significantly higher music test scores, particularly in tonal memory, than those who think of themselves as below the musical average.[67]

From the discussion so far, it is apparent that the Seashore tests have at least some validity. Further support comes from data gathered at the Eastman Conservatory of Music,[68] where the music tests (1919 edition) were added to a measure of academic intelligence, a case history, and a test of tonal imagery, and the combined scores were used for selection purposes. Five levels of scores were studied. It was found that 60 per cent of the persons in the top fifth succeeded in graduating, but only 17 per cent of the bottom fifth were as successful. In a slightly later study at Eastman, it was shown that course grades in musical theory correlated ·59 with Seashore scores.[69] Less success was achieved with these music tests at the College of Music of Cincinnati, which concluded that although music tests are of some use, they should always be employed in conjunction with academic intelligence tests.[70] McLeish, a British psychologist, suggests that appreciation tests should also be used along with the Seashore battery.[71]

Kwalwasser-Dykema Music Tests

The Kwalwasser-Dykema battery, for a long time the Seashore's only serious rival, attempts to do all its competitor does and more.[72] It has measures for the Seashore-tested areas of pitch, intensity, time, quality (timbre), rhythm, and tonal memory. There are two tests of appreciation—melodic taste and tonal movement (described in Chap. 7). In addition, there are tests of pitch and rhythm imagery, which are measures of achievement rather than of aptitude. The tests are much briefer than the Seashore, the test items seem more musical, and the directions are easier to follow. But, except for the measures of tonal memory and tonal movement, the reliabilities are very low.[73] This poor reliability accounts in part for the fact that only the tonal memory test correlates at all well with its Seashore counterpart.

The structural arrangement of the individual tests is as follows.

The measure of tonal memory consists of 25 pairs of patterns which range in length from four to nine tones. The patterns are repeated either in original or in altered form, and the subject responds with the words "same" or "different." The test of quality discrimination presents 30 items, each composed of two tones played on some particular instrument and then repeated on that or a different instrument. Like the previous test, it calls for the responses "same" or "different." The stimuli of the time-discrimination test were recorded from a player-piano roll. Twenty-five tones lasting from ·03 to ·30 second are repeated unchanged or with a different duration. Twenty-five rhythmic patterns repeated in the same or in an altered form make up the rhythm-discrimination test. The K-D intensity-discrimination test offers 30 tones and chords and then repeats them at different intensities. The subjects judge the relative strengths of the second members of the pairs. In the pitch-discrimination test there are 40 items. Each tone, held for approximately 3 seconds, rises or falls in pitch and then returns to its original pitch position. The pitch changes range from ·6 to 50 d.v. In the pitch-imagery and rhythm-imagery tests, the subjects compare what they hear with what is on the printed blanks supplied them. Each of the 25 items is to be described as "same" or "different."[74]

Several persons have been disturbed by the fact that only one set of norms is offered for this battery.[75] Apparently the test designers feel that all persons, eight or eighty, trained or untrained, score similarly. But that several sets of norms are needed should not surprise anyone who is at all familiar with the area of aptitude testing.

The reliabilities of approximately half of the members of the K-D battery have been materially improved by Holmes, who has changed the plan of the tests from true-false to multiple-choice.[76] This he did solely by altering the directions for administering the several measures. Thus, the subject taking the Holmes-modified tonal-memory test must not only decide whether there has been a change

241

in pattern but, in addition, must check whether the second pattern of each item is, if changed, higher or lower than the first. The possible responses for the quality-discrimination test are now "equal," "different," "different and heavier," and "different and lighter." For the measure of intensity discrimination they are "equal," "different," "different and weaker," and "different and stronger;" for the tonal-movement measure, "up," "down," and "same as last note actually heard;" for the measure of time discrimination, "equal," "different," "different and longer," and "different and shorter;" for the test of rhythm discrimination, "equal," "different," "different because the time values have been changed," and "different because the accent has been changed;" for the pitch-discrimination measure, "equal," "different," "different and higher," and "different and lower;" and for the melodic-taste test, "A better," "B better," and "equally good." With these changes, the reliability of the battery now reaches ·91 (high-school level).

There are a number of studies in which the K-D battery has been employed to forecast teacher ratings and grades in sight-singing, ear-training, and in "all fine arts" courses. In some instances there has been little or no success reported, but in one study the astonishingly high correlation value of ·83 has been claimed.[77] Perhaps the modal forecast value for the battery as a whole would lie in the neighborhood of ·40, with that for the individual tests being considerably lower.

Kwalwasser Music Talent Tests

In 1953 there appeared a new Kwalwasser aptitude test which requires only ten minutes to take.[78] Accompanying Form A, the more difficult of the test's two phonograph records, is one set of norms for junior-high-school students and another set for senior-high and college groups. Form B is for grades 4, 5, and 6. Form A "consists of 50 three-tone patterns which are repeated with variation in one of the following respects: (*a*) pitch, (*b*) time, (*c*) rhythm, (*d*) loudness." The pitch differences range from 5 to 70 cents, the tempo changes from 40 to 5 per cent of the standard metronomic marking of 90 to the quarter-note, and loudness varies from 10 to 2 decibels from the standard. The rhythmic changes become more difficult as the test progresses. The corresponding values for the 40-item Form B are: pitch, 15–70 cents; time, 15–40 per cent; and loudness, 3–10 decibels. The rhythms proceed from more to less difficult changes in pattern. Kwalwasser, a staunch hereditarian and student of C. E. Seashore, closes his eyes to the research literature and maintains that training can have little or no effect on the scores made on his test. Kwalwasser has violated approved test practice by publishing a commercial test without reliability data of any kind.

The Drake Tests

In 1932 Drake offered the musical world four partially standardized aptitude tests.[79] These covered the areas of musical memory (melody memory), interval discrimination, retentivity (memory for isolated tones), and intuition (key center, phrase and time balance). In 1954 he replaced these with two well standardized tests, one in the area of musical memory and the other to forecast rhythmic ability.[80] The musical memory test has two equivalent forms, A and B, and the rhythm test has an easier Form A and a more difficult Form B. The musically naïve are tested on all four forms, but subjects with five or more years of musical training need take only Form B of the rhythm test and either form of the measure of musical memory. The two new Drake tests intercorrelate only slightly. With reliabilities in the high ·80's or low ·90's, they yield stable scores. Norms for them are available for music and non-music students, and for ages 11, 12, and 13; 14, 15, and 16; 17, 18, and 19; 20, 21, and 22; and 23 and

243

over. Sex differences in scores and those associated with racial and cultural background are said to be negligible.

The musical memory test is made up of especially composed melodies, which are either repeated or changed with respect to time, key, or note. The rhythm test presents the sound of a metronome beating at a certain rate and a voice which counts "one," "two," "three," and "four." The voice then either stops counting or proceeds at a different rate while the subject continues to count silently at the original rate until told to stop. His score is the difference between the metronome beat number and his own silent count.

Drake reports a coefficient of correlation of only ·17 between scores on his measure of rhythm and on the Seashore test of rhythm discrimination. The two memory tests, however, are tapping more similar variables and intercorrelate at ·55 (from unpublished data gathered at Stanford University). Drake's recent studies suggest that his new tests have considerable validity. He draws his support from the fact that when correlations are run against teacher estimates of musical talent, the values are generally above ·58 and have run as high as ·91.

Whistler-Thorpe Musical Aptitude Test

The developers of the *Whistler-Thorpe Musical Aptitude Test* pride themselves on presenting musical, not just tonal, stimuli (piano music).[81] The test has two "same-different" sections dealing with rhythm recognition, one fairly easy, and the other considerably more difficult. The "same-different" pattern is also followed in the melody-recognition portion. In the pitch-discrimination section, chords are given and then are repeated either with precisely the same structure or at a higher or lower pitch level. The section of the test devoted to pitch recognition is the most novel. Here a particular pitch is strongly emphasized. Then there follows a melody of four measures of 13 quarter-notes. The subject's task is to count the number of times the previously emphasized pitch has appeared. The *Whistler-Thorpe* has a reported reliability of ·93. It claims to correlate at ·78 with teacher estimates of vocal talent.

Lundin Tests

In an effort to measure musical behaviors not considered by the earlier testers, Lundin devised five rather different tests.[82] The first of these measures is in the area of interval discrimination. Fifty ascending and descending intervals make up the stimuli, which are either repeated without change or are modified in the second rendition. The responses of this and the other members of the Lundin battery are in terms of "same" or "different." The reliability is reported to be in the ·70's.

The melodic-transposition test offers 30 simple melodies. If on the second rendition the key alone is changed, the subject responds by "same." But if both the key and the melody are altered, the proper response is "different." The reliability is said to be ·65 for musicians and ·72 for unselected college students.

Mode discrimination is tested through the presentation of 30 pairs of chords. If the pair members are in the same mode, the response is "same." But if the mode is changed, the subject responds with "different." When employed on unselected students, this test has the poorest reliability of any member of the battery (one of ·10). For musicians the reliability value is in the middle ·60's.

Each of the 30 items of the melodic-sequences test contains three melodic groups which follow the same melodic order. A fourth group may or may not follow this pattern. The reliability of this measure falls in the ·70's. This test sets the pattern for the last member of the battery, the measure of rhythmic sequences, except, of course, that in the latter test rhythms and not melodies are involved. For musicians the rhythm test has a reliability of ·60; for unselected college students the value is ·72. The corresponding reliability coefficients for the battery as a whole are ·89 and ·85.

In one study by Lundin, when total battery scores were employed for forecasting pooled ratings made by six professors, the following correlation values emerged: melodic dictation, ·70; harmonic dictation, ·70; written harmonization, ·43; general ability in theory, ·63; performance, ·51; and sum of ratings, ·69. Lundin found the Seashore pitch, rhythm, and tonal memory tests and Drake's musical memory measure (original form) to forecast these criteria less well.

Wing Standardized Tests of Musical Intelligence

A British flavor can be seen in the Wing tests, although the measures are not so different from the much condemned American tests as one might guess from a perusal of the Wing monograph.[83] Recorded on ten records are seven tests. Although their reliabilities range as low as ·65, the battery reliability is a satisfactory ·93 or so. Five-step norms are available for each year from age eight through seventeen. The selection of the tests was based on factor analyses. That the battery has considerable validity was shown in a study of 333 adolescent boys who had at one time studied or were still studying some musical instrument. Wing gave his tests to these lads and classified their scores into three classes. He found that 40 per cent of the below-average group had already given up studying. The comparable values for the average and above-average groups were 27 and 2 per cent, respectively.

Wing's chord-analysis test requires the subject to count the number of notes in a series of single chords. In the measure of pitch change, chords are played and repeated either with exactly similar structure or with some one note pitched higher or lower. The memory measure presents tunes which are either repeated or altered. If they are modified, the subject must tell which are the altered notes. In the test of rhythmic accent, melodies are either repeated in identical form or with the accents rearranged. The subject notes the changes, if any, and states which versions better fit the tune. The intensity and phrasing tests are similarly arranged except that it is now the intensity or the phrasing which is altered. The harmony test presents tunes which are either repeated exactly or altered. Each item must be assessed for identity or else a decision must be made as to the better of the two versions.

Strong Vocational Interest Test

A rather different sort of test and one which is only in part an aptitude measure is the Strong musician scale.[84] Strong's well-known set of questions on interests has for some time had a scale for men whose criterion group was composed of 250 musicians, largely symphony performers. Their average age was 32·6 and their years of schooling 12·4. The scale's reliability is ·87. The test score indicates the degree of resemblance between the answer profile of the person tested and that of the criterion group. Judged by the high validity that the Strong scales achieve in other areas where validity is relatively easy to ascertain, e.g., life insurance, Strong's musician scale merits respectful attention.

During 1952, the *Music Journal* gathered data for four other Strong musician scales. It tested 500 men (average age, 41·4; years of schooling, 17·0) to form one of its two "music teacher" scales and another 450 men (average age, 36·4; education, 13·6) for a "music performer" scale. In an attempt to build parallel scales for women, the *Journal* tested 450 women music teachers (average age, 43·8; years of schooling, 16·5) and 290 performers (average age, 34·2; years of schooling, 15·5). Although the project is not as yet completed, the scales are available to anyone interested.

247

The Future of Music Aptitude Tests

It would be foolish to attempt too precise a forecast of the course music tests will take in the next few years. But it seems clear that the testers will make increasing use of musical materials and that their tests will not be as atomistic as are the Seashore measures. More than a half-century ago, the intelligence testers tried to forecast achievement by the use of simple items at the sensory level. They then moved to an omnibus or buckshot approach with their I.Q. tests, and still later worked out a sort of compromise of these extremes with their measures of primary mental abilities. The music testers, too, began their labors with the aid of simple sensory materials. The progressive educators, in particular, condemned this approach and argued for the omnibus stand; yet they did little to make tests in this model. The philosophy of the more recent testers, however, would seem to allow as test items at least a modicum of sensory material as well as bits of real musical behavior.

Musical memory has come to be the one area which all testers agree merits the most careful attention. Other ability areas may or may not be important to the potential performer. As was mentioned earlier, the violinist needs far better pitch discrimination than does the pianist, yet neither instrumentalist should necessarily score near the top of the Seashore range. Music testers must get away from the philosophy of "better score, better musical potential." They should follow the course blazed by the college aptitude testers and study more intensively the minimum levels necessary for later success in the several kinds of musical skills. More and more they can be expected to add to their batteries measures of academic aptitude, interest, personality, and perhaps even taste, to give a broader base to their forecasting efforts. It is likely that they will pay less and less attention to the nature-nurture problem. Instead, the emphasis will be turned toward the practical issue of deciding which persons will profit most, given a minimum of practice opportunities.

Notes

1] A number of paper-and-pencil tests in music give no publication dates. Hence, in the interest of uniformity, no dates will be given here even when available.

2] F. A. Beach and H. E. Schrammel, *Beach Standardized Music Tests*, Emporia, Kans., Bureau of Ed. Meas., Kansas State Normal School.

3] G. Gildersleeve and W. Soper, *Music Achievement Tests*, N.Y., Bureau of Publications, Teachers College, Columbia U.

4] T. L. Torgerson and E. Fahnestock, *Torgerson-Fahnestock Music Test*, Bloomington, Ill., Public School Publ.

5] J. Kwalwasser and G. Ruch, *Kwalwasser-Ruch Tests of Musical Accomplishment*, Iowa City, Iowa, Bureau of Ed. Res. and Serv., State U., Iowa.

6] C. E. Strouse and H. E. Schrammel, *Strouse Music Test*, Emporia, Kans., Bureau Ed. Meas., Kansas State Teach. Coll.

7] H. E. Hutchinson, *Hutchinson Music Tests*, Bloomington, Ill., Public School Publ.

8] W. E. Knuth, *Knuth Achievement Tests in Music*, Philadelphia, Ed. Test Bureau.

9] C. J. McCauley, *McCauley Experiment in Public School Music*, Knoxville, Tenn., J. E. Avent.

10] R. D. Allen, W. H. Butterfield, and M. Tully, *Providence Inventory Test in Music*, Yonkers, N.Y., World Book.

11] L. C. Pressey, *The Specialized Vocabularies of the Public School Subjects*, Bloomington, Ill., Public School Publ.

12] C. P. Wood, *Ear Tests in Harmony*, N.Y., American Book.

13] M. L. Kotick and T. L. Torgerson, *Diagnostic Tests of Achievement in Music*, Los Angeles, Calif. Test Bureau.

14] S. E. Farnum, *Farnum Music Notation Test*, N.Y., Psychological Corp.

15] J. Aliferis, *Aliferis Music Achievement Test*, Minneapolis, U. of Minnesota Press.

16] *Graduate Record Examinations, Advanced Music Test*, Princeton, N.J., Ed. Test. Service.

17] E. K. Hillbrand, *Hillbrand Sight-Singing Test*, Yonkers, N.Y., World Book.

18] R. M. Mosher, *Mosher Test of Individual Singing*, Teach. Coll. Contrib. Educ., No. 194, N.Y., Bureau of Publications, Teachers Coll., Columbia U.

19] A. W. Otterstein and R. M. Mosher, *O-M Sight-Singing Test*, Stanford, Calif., Stanford U. Press.

20] J. G. Watkins, *Objective Measurement of Instrumental Performance,* Teach. Coll. Contrib. Educ., No. 860, N.Y., Bureau of Publications, Teachers Coll., Columbia U.

21] J. G. Watkins and S. E. Farnum, *The Watkins-Farnum Performance Scale*, Winona, Minn., Leonard Music.

22] See, for example, *Plymouth Educational Tests*, Chicago, Plymouth Press; *Music Achievement Test,* Baltimore, Dept. Ed.; *Krone Recognition, Tonal and Rhythmic Dictation Tests*, Indianapolis, M. T. Krone, Butler U.; *Mosher Group Tests*, Teach. Coll. Contrib. Educ. No. 194, N.Y., Columbia U. See also A. Roe, "A Study of the Accuracy of Perception of Visual Musical Stimuli," *Arch. Psychol., 158* (1933); F. S. Salisbury and H. D. Smith, "Prognosis of Sight Singing Ability of Normal School Students," *J. Appl. Psychol., 13* (1929): 425–439; T. G. Stelzer, "Construction, Interpretation, and Use of Sight Reading Scale in Organ Music, with an Analysis of Organ Playing into Fundamental Abilities," *J. Exp. Ed., 7* (1938): 35–43; S. T. Burns, "The Value of Prognostic Tests for Instrumental Pupils," *Sch. Mus., 31* (1931): 6–9.

23] C. Stumpf, "Akustische Versuche mit Pepito Areola," *Zsch. f. Ang. Psychol., 21* (1909): 1–11.

24] T. H. Pear, "The Classification of Observers as 'Musical' and 'Unmusical'," *Brit. J. Psychol., 4* (1911): 89–94.

25] M. F. Meyer, "Special Ability Tests as Used in Missouri; Including a Demonstration of a Typical Test," *Psychol. Bull., 21* (1924): 114–116.

26] G. Révész, *The Psychology of a Musical Prodigy*, N.Y., Harcourt, Brace, 1925.

27] G. Révész, *Introduction to the Psychology of Music*, Norman, U. of Oklahoma Press, 1954.

28] H. Rupp, "Über die Prüfung musikalischer Fähigkeiten," *Zsch. f. Ang. Psychol., 9* (1919): 1–76.

29] T. Billroth, *Wer ist musikalisch?* Gebrüder Paetel, 1898.

30] J. von Kries, *Wer ist musikalisch?* Berlin, Springer, 1926.

31] J. A. Mjön, "Zur psychologischen Bestimmung der Musikalität," *Zsch. f. Ang. Psychol., 27* (1926): 217–273.

32] V. Haecker and T. Ziehen, *Zur Vererbung und Entwicklung der musikalischen Begabung,* Leipzig, Barth, 1923.

33] H. Lowery, "Cadence and Phrase Tests in Music," *Brit. J. Psychol., 17* (1926–27): 111–118.

34] O. Ortmann, *Tests of Musical Talent*, Baltimore, Peabody Conservatory of Music, unpublished.

35] M. Schoen, "Tests of Musical Feeling and Musical Understanding," *J. Comp. Psychol., 5* (1925): 31–52.

36] E. Franklin, *Tonality as a Basis for the Study of Musical Talent*, Göteborg, Sweden, Gumperts Förlag, 1956.

37] T. H. Madison, "Interval Discrimination as a Measure of Musical Aptitude," *Arch. Psychol.*, No. 268 (1942).

38] C. J. Lamp and N. Keys, "Can Aptitude for Specific Musical Instruments Be Predicted?" *J. Educ. Psychol., 26* (1935): 587–596.

39] C. E. Seashore, "The Tonoscope and Its Use in the Training of the Voice," *The Musician, 11* (1906): 331–332; E. W. Scripture, "Das Strobilion," *Zsch. f. Psychol., 59* (1928): 166–170; P. R. Farnsworth, "Two Independent Developments of the Strobilion," *J. Gen. Psychol., 2* (1929): 556–558.

40] J. Kwalwasser, *Exploring the Musical Mind*, N.Y., Coleman-Ross, 1955, Chap. 10.

41] O. I. Jacobsen, "Dynamic and Temporal Control in Music," *J. Gen. Psychol., 15* (1936): 171–190.

42] R. H. Seashore, "Studies in Motor Rhythm," *Ia. Stud. Psychol., 9* (1926): 142–199; J. T. Nielsen, "A Study in the Seashore Motor Rhythm Test," *Psychol. Monog., 40* (1930): 74–84. For a note on the Sievers rhythm test see H. M. Williams, "A Study in the Prediction of Motor Rhythmic Performance of School Children," *J. Genet. Psychol., 43* (1933): 377–388.

43] C. E. Seashore, *The Psychology of Musical Talent*, Boston, Silver, Burdett, 1919, Chap. 11. See also G. H. Smith, "Auditory Imagery in Music Reading," Thesis, Stanford U., 1947.

44] C. E. Seashore, *Manual of Instructions and Interpretations for Measures of Musical Talent*, N.Y., Columbia Graphophone, 1919.

45] H. Lowery, "On the Integrative Theory of Musical Talent," *J. Musicol., 2* (1940): 1–14; J. Mainwaring, "The Assessment of Musical Ability," *Brit. J. Educ. Psychol., 17* (1947): 83–96.

46] The leader of this group was J. L. Mursell. See his *The Psychology of Music*, N.Y., Norton, 1937.

47] R. Wyatt, "A Note on the Use of 'Omnibus' Training to Validate Seashore's Capacity Hypothesis," *Amer. J. Psychol., 52* (1939): 638–640.

48] C. E. Seashore, *Manual of Instructions and Interpretations for Measures of Musical Talent*, N.Y., Columbia Graphophone, 1919. For a survey through 1930 of the research articles on this first set of Seashore measures see P. R. Farnsworth, "An Historical, Critical, and Experimental Study of the Seashore-Kwalwasser Test Battery," *Genet. Psychol. Monog., 9* (1931): 291–393.

49] E. M. McGinnis, "Seashore's Measures of Musical Ability Applied to Children of the Pre-school Age," *Amer. J. Psychol., 40* (1928): 620–623.

50] F. S. Salisbury and H. B. Smith, "Prognosis of Sight Singing Ability," *J. Appl. Psychol., 13* (1929): 425–439.

51] M. S. Hattwick, "Manual of Instructions and Interpretations for a Pitch Discrimination Test for Young Children," *U. of Ia. Stud. Child. Welf., 11* (1935): 69–74.

52] E. A. Gaw, "Five Studies of the Music Tests," *Psychol. Monog., 39* (1928): 145–156.

53] P. R. Farnsworth, "Studies in the Psychology of Tone and Music," *Genet. Psychol. Monog., 15* (1934): 45–49; "Further Notes on the Seashore Music Tests," *J. Gen. Psychol., 18* (1938): 429–431.

54] M. E. Brown, "A Note Concerning the Seashore Measures of Musical Talent," *Sch. and Soc., 30* (1929): 274–275.

55] J. O'Connor, "Steps toward the Isolation of Tonal Memory as a Mental Element," *Hum. Engng. Lab. Tech. Rep., 21* (1938).

56] L. M. Tilson, *The Tilson-Gretsch Musical Aptitude Test*, Chicago, Publ. Sch. Music Dept., Fred Gretsch Mfg., 1941.

57] P. R. Farnsworth, "Data on the Tilson-Gretsch Test for Musical Aptitude," *J. Musicol., 4* (1945): 99–102.

58] C. E. Seashore, D. Lewis, and J. G. Saetveit, *Manual, Seashore Measures of Musical Talents*, N.Y., Psychol. Corp., 1956.

59] J. G. Saetveit, D. Lewis, and C. E. Seashore, *Revision of the Seashore Measures of Musical Talent*, Iowa City, U. of Iowa Press, 1940. Several researchers have adapted portions of the Seashore battery for their own, nonmusical purposes. See A. Ford, "The UCDWR Pitch-Memory Selection Test," *OSRD Report*, March, 1944; J. D. Harris and D. Charney, "A Revision of the Navy Pitch-Memory Test," *Med. Res. Lab.*, U.S. Naval Submarine Base, New London, Conn., *9* (1950): 1–10.

60] F. S. Salisbury and H. R. Smith, "Prognosis of Sight-Singing Ability of Normal School Students," *J. Appl. Psychol., 13* (1929): 425–439.

61] F. A. Wright, "The Correlation between Achievement and Capacity in Music," *J. Educ. Res., 17* (1928): 50–56.

62] H. C. Manor, "A Study in Prognosis," *J. Educ. Psychol., 41* (1950): 31–50.

63] P. R. Farnsworth, "Are Music Capacity Tests More Important than Intelligence Tests in the Prediction of Several Types of Music Grades?" *J. Appl. Psychol., 19* (1935): 347–350.

64] C. H. Lawshe, Jr., and W. F. Wood, "Membership in Musical Organizations as a Criterion of Talent," *Amer. J. Psychol., 60* (1947): 250–253.

65] P. J. Fay and W. C. Middleton, "Relationship between Musical Talent and Preferences for Different Types of Music," *J. Educ. Psychol., 32* (1941): 573–583.

66] E. C. Dunlevy, "Musical Training and Measured Musical Aptitude," *J. Musicol., 4* (1944): 1–5.

67] P. R. Farnsworth, "The Relation of the Auditory Capacities to the Feeling of Being Musical," *J. Musicol., 2* (1941): 119–122.

68] H. M. Stanton, "Measurement of Musical Talent: The Eastman Experiment," *U. of Ia. Stud. Psychol. Music., 2* (1935): 1–140.

69] W. S. Larson, "Practical Experience with Music Tests," *Mus. Ed. J., 24* (1938): 31. See also R. C. Larson, "Finding and Guiding Musical Talent," *Mus. Ed. J., 42* (1955): 22–25.

70] E. M. Taylor, "A Study in the Prognosis of Musical Talent," *J. Exp. Ed.*, 10 (1941): 1–28.

71] J. McLeish, "The Validation of Seashore's Measures of Musical Talent by Factorial Methods," *Brit. J. Psychol., Stat. Sect.*, 3 (1950): 129–140.

72] J. Kwalwasser and P. W. Dykema, *Kwalwasser-Dykema Music Tests*, N.Y., Fischer, 1930.

73] P. R. Farnsworth, "Studies in the Psychology of Tone and Music," *Genet. Psychol. Monog.*, 15 (1934): Sect. 9.

74] For descriptions of the K-D measures of melodic taste and tonal movement see Chapter 7.

75] G. M. Gilbert, "'Aptitude' and Training: A Suggested Restandardization of the K-D Music Test Norms," *J. Appl. Psychol.*, 25 (1941): 326–330; P. R. Farnsworth, *op. cit.*

76] J. A. Holmes, "Increased Reliabilities, New Keys, and Norms for a Modified Kwalwasser-Dykema Test of Musical Aptitudes," *J. Genet. Psychol.*, 85 (1954): 65–73.

77] M. T. Whitley, "A Comparison of the Seashore and Kwalwasser-Dykema Music Tests," *Teach. Coll. Rec.*, 33 (1932): 731–751.

78] J. Kwalwasser, *Kwalwasser Music Talent Test*, N.Y., Mills Music, 1953.

79] R. M. Drake, "Four New Tests of Musical Talent," *J. Appl. Psychol.*, 17 (1933): 136–147.

80] R. M. Drake, *Drake Musical Aptitude Tests*, Chicago, Science Research Associates, 1954.

81] H. S. Whistler and L. P. Thorpe, *Whistler-Thorpe Musical Aptitude Test*, Los Angeles, Calif. Test Bureau, 1950.

82] R. W. Lundin, "The Development and Validation of a Set of Musical Ability Tests," *Psychol. Monog.*, 63, No. 10 (1949).

83] H. Wing, "Tests of Musical Ability and Appreciation," *Brit. J. Psychol. Monog. Suppl.*, No. 27 (1948); "Some Applications of Test Results to Education in Music," *Brit. J. Educ. Psychol.*, 24 (1954): 161–170.

84] E. K. Strong, Jr., *Vocational Interest Blank for Men, Revised Form M*, Stanford, Calif., Stanford U. Press, 1938. For a further attempt to construct Strong scales for music teachers, see M. Kleist, C. H. Rittenhouse, and P. R. Farnsworth, "Strong Vocational Interest Scales for Music Teachers," *Occupations*, 28 (1949): 100–101.

CHAPTER TEN

Applications of Music to Therapy and Industry

INCREASINGLY over the years, music is being employed both as a therapy for the emotionally ill and as a goad to increase industrial output. Indeed, the job of furnishing music to shops and stores has already become a sizable and lucrative business. Yet the student who asks for proof of the medical and industrial worth of music is offered little that he will recognize as having scientific validity. More than likely he will be fed anecdotes and legends, e.g., the Bible story of the mentally disturbed King Saul listening to young David's harp playing. He may be shown data which demonstrate unmistakable improvement in work output or emotional adjustment. But then he learns that the music was given along with a host of other therapies or changes in industrial atmosphere and he is left puzzling over the part music may have played in the process, wondering if it was really the music that induced the changes.

Physiological Changes

As a preliminary step toward getting a clearer picture of the potential role of music in therapy and industry it may be well to examine what is known of its power to affect human physiology. The thesis that music can elicit and modify moods needs no further defense (p. 94). But can tone and rhythm affect blood pressure, pulse, respiration rate, and other physiological manifestations of man's life processes?

It may be categorically stated that music can markedly affect the bodily processes. Yet the effects are not so striking as was once thought. It was believed at one time, for instance, that the heart would, within limitations, accommodate its beat to the pulse of the music being heard. By the use of better apparatus and controls, however, it has been possible to re-examine the problem and collect additional data.[1] Of the subjects so far studied, only one showed any tendency for synchrony of heartbeat and musical pulse, and even here the correspondence was so slight that it may have been a matter of chance.

Diserens and Fine, after having carefully combed the experimental literature up through the middle 1930's for studies of musical effects on physiological processes, offer the following conclusions:

> Music...increases bodily metabolism...increases or decreases muscular energy...accelerates respiration and decreases its regularity...produces marked but variable effect on volume, pulse and blood pressure...lowers the threshold for sensory stimuli of different modes...influences the internal secretions.[2]

With some rephrasing the conclusions of Diserens and Fine can still be accepted. It is reasonably clear that music has on occasion increased the bodily metabolism of a certain few people and has affected their muscular energy, respiration, and/or circulation. But generalization in this area is dangerous since humans are not automatons reacting in a pushbutton fashion to music. Nor is all music the same, and the effect of one composition does not necessarily resemble that of another. The idea that music can lower thresholds (raise acuities) in other sensory areas is held by contemporary Soviet experimenters.[3] However, this notion has been questioned by Dannenbaum, who found the visual acuity of each of his subjects significantly impaired, not improved, by the presence of music.[4] But whether or not music can improve visual acuity as such, it is able, according to Lowenstein,[5] to restore the size of eye-pupils which have been experimentally fatigued by many exposures to light and thus reduced in size. It should be added, however, that Lowenstein obtained this effect with "very musical people" only. He is, therefore, inclined to think that this "restitution phenomenon," as he calls it, is not a function of tonal stimuli per se but rather of psychological stimuli, i.e., of stimuli which have real musical significance to the listener. At any rate, here is an example of the fatigue-reducing capacity of music.

An unpublished study by Dreher[6] showed that the unmusical as well as the more musical exhibit galvanic changes[7] while listening to music. But these electrical changes were found to be much weaker in the unmusical subjects. There was a direct correspondence between the degree of galvanic change and the importance of music in the life of the listener.

Thirty-six students, randomly selected by Ellis and Brighouse from volunteers in undergraduate psychology,[8] listened to three recordings—Hall's *Blue Interval*, Debussy's *Prelude to the Afternoon of a Faun*, and Liszt's *Hungarian Rhapsody No. 2*—while records were made of their heart and respiration rates. Physiological records were also kept for several minutes before, and for as long as five minutes after, the playing of the music. These experimenters report that no statistically significant changes in heartbeat were found at any time. But increases in respiration rate were apparent in almost all subjects, particularly during the playing of the Liszt and Hall numbers. It is of interest that no respiration change lasted for longer than five minutes after the cessation of the listening session, a finding which offers little encouragement to the music therapists.

It goes almost without saying that the findings of the Ellis-Brighouse experiments might have been greatly different if either the extremely musical or monotones had been tested, or if quite dissimilar compositions had been presented. From what is known of psychology we should expect enormous individual differences to exist in physiological responses to music. And contemporary experiments bear out this expectation. In fact there are persons so readily affected by music that listening to certain compositions leads to epileptic attacks.[9] And at the other extreme there are the pitch-deaf, who can get little or nothing from music except through the kinesthetic and tactual senses. The physiological effects of music on the listener will be large or small, depending on the nature of the composition which is being heard. A number of variables are of importance here, including, among others, the presence or absence of abrupt tempo changes, the acceptability or unacceptability of the composition, and the personal associations the music has for the listener. As Miles and Tilly have demonstrated, change in tempo is the chief cause of respiratory changes.[10] While tempo change is also a factor in altering circulation, the attitude of the listener toward the composition seems to be a far more important variable. These principles hold both while the listener is alert and while he is hypnotized. As the music becomes more familiar, more "understood" and appreciated, the physiological changes tend to become more marked.

How extensive, then, is music's power to affect body processes? The answer is not an easy one to make. For the physiological changes music elicits, while substantial and varied in certain musical persons, are relatively insignificant in the unmusical and appear to be short-lasting at best. By and large, the effects are greater the more the music has "meaning" for the listener. That is, a given composition may call forth one set of effects in a musical person and quite different changes in one not musically inclined. Or the effects may differ from one time to another in the same person depending on the training the individual has received in the meantime, on the associations he has picked up, and on his changes in mood. It would follow from these facts that no composition will be found which can be guaranteed to produce identical or even nearly identical physiological

257

changes among the members of any sizable population. One is not likely to find any considerable degree of generality of body change except perhaps where the effects are elicited through the hearing of national and church hymns, music most of us have known well since early childhood. With music which is less a part of the common heritage, the chances of securing identical effects are slighter.

The Present Status of Music Therapy

Since music can undeniably alter both moods and some basic physiological processes of many persons, it may have some potential for therapy.[11] It has, we know, long been used to treat the mentally and the physically ill in both preliterate and civilized cultures.[12] Why, then, are its medical qualities not more easily demonstrated? A partial answer can be found in the way therapy is employed in mental hospitals. It is natural that the psychiatrists should want to improve mental health to the point where their patients can be safely and speedily returned to their homes. Most mental hospitals are dreadfully crowded, and many more emotionally disturbed persons are usually waiting to enter than can be accepted.

Under such pressures, a research program on musical or any other kind of therapy can be only incidental, at best. On the curative side, a "buckshot" policy must be followed. That is, a variety of therapies must be tried on each patient in the hope that some one of them or a combination of treatments will effect a cure. But this multiplicity of therapies makes it impossible to tell which one is mainly responsible when the patient improves, if he does improve. As a matter of fact, it may sometimes be that no one therapy by itself contributes very much to the subsequent "cure." The active agent may be the friendly attention the patient has been receiving, or there may perhaps be some dynamic personality change which would have occurred even though no therapy at all had been attempted.

With the situation so beclouded, the one clear fact is that definitive statements about the medical value of music must await the establishment of research-oriented hospitals where first one therapy and then another can be put through its paces. But this research-heaven is still some years away. And until it comes, there is little one can do but examine the anecdotes which abound and the beliefs the specialists accept and from them try to winnow at least a few grains of fact.[13]

Music in Physical Therapy

Boring indeed are the exercises that the muscle- and joint-injured must practice day after day. But if set to music, the exercises become, if not actually enjoyable, at least considerably more endurable. It is relatively easy to find music with tempos and rhythms to fit the needs of each patient. For leg injuries dancing is often encouraged. Finger exercise needs may call for the playing of the piano. If facial and throat muscles need to be strengthened, the playing of brass or wood-wind instruments may be appropriate. For the leg-injured patient who possesses no musical or dancing skill, the foot pumping of a small organ may be prescribed. Time seems to pass more quickly when music accompanies the therapeutic exercises, and patient morale tends to be better maintained. This type of musical therapy is usually administered in hospitals but it will be reasonably beneficial in the home, although here the additional benefit derived from seeing others also exercising is missing.

Music in Mental Therapy

ESTABLISHING CONTACT WITH THE PATIENT. When the patient has withdrawn into a world of daydreams, an early step in therapy is to re-establish the patient's contact with the world of reality. Often the psychotic will not talk or take much interest in his surroundings. Yet the patient who earlier had a deep love of music and no frustrations associated with it will sometimes respond to melody and rhythm when he will not react favorably to verbal stimulation. In such cases, Altshuler suggests the use of his "iso" principle.[14] The music is chosen so as to be isomoodic and isotempic, to match so far as possible the mood and "mental tempo" of the patient. Thus, quiet, unobtrusive music is selected for the withdrawn, lively music for the maniacal, "feminine" music for one of feminine mentality, etc. Later, after the attention has been aroused and held, a gradual shift in type of music is engineered in the hope that the patient's mental and physiological states will also change.

PLEASANTNESS AND THE FEELING OF BEING RESTED. Many of us feel more alert and rested after listening to our favorite compositions. A somewhat similar situation exists among those in mental hospitals. But among the hospitalized, listening to music has the additional advantage of helping to pass the time, which can drag frightfully. Research has shown that a fairly strong relationship exists between the feeling of restfulness and the pleasantness of music (or between tiredness and unpleasantness).[15] During the course of life, pleasantness and rest become associated. We should keep the fact of this association in mind and not listen to strange, and so potentially unpleasant, music at a time when we feel mentally fatigued. Striving to understand the unfamiliar is not a restful undertaking.

MUSIC AS A SOCIALIZING AGENT. The psychotic can be regarded as a person who is poor in his interpersonal adjustments. He badly needs music or some other resocializing agent. To supply such a need, unison group singing and dancing are encouraged in the more therapeutically oriented of our mental hospitals. These activities take a minimum of alertness. Yet they bring about vitally needed interpersonal contacts, they break the monotony of institutional life, and, for a short time at least, they may dissipate the personal worries which have beset the patient. While engaged in dancing or group singing, the patient is once again a member of a functioning group.

THE SENSE OF ACHIEVEMENT AND PRESTIGE. Music lessons are often given in mental hospitals so that the patient can feel that he is achieving a real skill, one that he can continue to enjoy after he leaves the institution. With skill in playing a musical instrument comes the opportunity to perform in the hospital's orchestra or band, or with vocal skill a place in the chorus. Such ensemble work brings a sense of achievement, bestowes prestige on the performers, and aids in the process of socialization.

OTHER ATTEMPTS TO USE MUSIC. With so many physicians and musicians convinced of the existence of large physiological effects from music, it was inevitable that music should have been used in hospitals and clinics to quiet the apprehensive, to calm the hyper-active, to stimulate the depressed, to reduce accidents,[16] and to distract those about to undergo dental work or surgery. The reported successes of such uses of music vary with the enthusiasms of the therapists. Sad to relate, therapy data are rarely recorded in terms which mean much to the scientist. To what extent the perceived benefit is more properly attributable to the attention the patient gets than to the music cannot at present be figured. But it may be an appreciable fraction of the therapeutic effect. The fact still remains, however, that there are patients who are visibly less apprehensive, less maniacal, or less depressed after sessions with musical therapy.

THE "MUSICOPOEIA." Although normal persons and psychotics of like subculture react in a fairly similar fashion to music, there seems to be enough dissimilarity to justify the rule that all music to be employed with psychotics should be pretested on psychotics.[17] This rule appears to be followed rather religiously in some quarters while in others the therapist's own feelings or those of his friends furnish the guide for his selection of the compositions he will use. If he is psychoanalytically oriented, he may start his convalescing patients on simple folk tunes, following the theory that these "seem to resupply or reactivate the mother-child complex."[18]

Each musical therapist seems to have his favored list of musical compositions. Thus, for relieving serious headaches Brown offers some 40 pieces including such old "classics" as Liszt's *Hungarian Rhapsody No. 1*, Mendelssohn's *Elijah*, Mozart's *Don Giovanni*, Offenbach's *Tales of Hoffmann*, Beethoven's *Fidelio*, and Borodin's *Prince Igor*; "popular" ones like Grofé's *Mississippi* and Gershwin's *American in Paris*; and "moderns" like Khachaturian's *Masquerade Suite* and Copland's *Lincoln Portrait*.[19]

Arrington suggests the following "reassuring" compositions for use just before electroshock treatment: Largo from Bach's *Concerto in A*, Beethoven's *Moonlight Sonata*, Brahms's *Intermezzo in E Flat*, Chopin's *First Piano Concerto* (Second Movement), Mendelssohn's *Italian Symphony* (Second Movement), and Rachmaninov's *Second Concerto* (Second Movement). During the awakening period Arrington considers these as appropriate: Kern's *Show Tunes*, Fields's *The Way You Look Tonight*, Chopin's *Waltzes in A and C*, Berlin's *Eddie Duchin Album*, and Adamson's *Time on My Hands*. To Arrington these eight are musical tonics: Tchaikovsky's *Sixth Symphony* (Third Movement), Beethoven's *Egmont Overture*, Chopin's *Prelude, Opus 28 No. 1*, Liszt's *Hungarian Rhapsody No. 2*, Bizet's *Toreador's Song*, Sousa's Military Marches, Offenbach's *Gaieté Parisienne*, and Bach's *Prelude and Fugue in E Minor*; and these nine are musical sedatives: Mascagni's *Cavalleria Rusticana* (Intermezzo), Schubert's *Ave Maria*, Saint-Saëns's *The Swan*, Brahms's *Lullaby*, Beethoven's *Sixth Symphony* (Second Movement), Chopin's *Nocturne in G Minor*, Debussy's *Clair de Lune*, Schubert's

Quartet in B Flat Minor (Andante), and Beethoven's *Moonlight Sonata*.[20]

Sugarman attempts to lower "emotional high blood pressure" through renditions of a variety of compositions which include: Bach's *Concerto in D Minor for Violin*, Bartók's *Sonata for Piano*, Bruckner's *Mass in E Minor*, Ives's *Symphony No. 3*, Rachmaninov's *Isle of the Dead*, and Tchaikovsky's *Swan Lake Ballet Suite*. To accompany eating he suggests 20 pieces, among which are Bartók's *Sonata for Violin*, Ravel's *La Valse*, Debussy's *Children's Corner Suite*, Liszt's *Concerto No. 2 in A*, and Ives's *Sonata No. 2 for Violin and Piano*.[21]

To replace jealousy and suspicion with contentment, Hillard offers Anthiel's *Piano Sonata No. 4*, Bach's *Cantata No. 21*, Bartók's *Quartet No. 5*, Chopin's *Nocturne in D Flat*, Milhaud's *Suite Française*, and Ravel's *Quartet in F*. To relieve chronic hatred this same author mentions Bach's *Italian Concerto*, Haydn's *Clock Symphony*, and Sibelius's *Finlandia*.[22]

Girard claims to reduce anger with Bach's *Cantata No. 2*, Beethoven's *Moonlight Sonata*, Grofé's *Aviation Suite*, Prokofiev's *Sonata in D*, and Franck's *Symphony in D Minor*. To overcome anxiety, Girard would play Chopin's *Mazurkas* and *Preludes*, the Strauss *Waltzes*, Nevin's *Narcissus*, and Rubinstein's *Melody in F*.[23]

The lists above are typical of what one finds in the current literature.[24] Quite clearly they are the resultants of "rule of thumb" rather than scientific procedures. It is very probable, of course, that changes both in mood and in overt activity have sometimes occurred following the playing of these and other musical compositions, but the causal connections between the music and the behavioral changes are obscure. Moreover, at this stage in the history of the institutional use of music, little or no generalization from one therapeutic venture to another is warranted. The reader should not conclude, however, that music has no future in therapy. Indeed, later research may demonstrate large benefits attributable to the music alone. At the very least, it would seem that the morale lift many patients receive from this kind of treatment amply justifies the effort involved. And surely no great harm is likely to come from the use of music.

The Effects of Music on Achievement

MUSIC AND ACTIVITY.   Although many of the phenomena of the laboratory cannot be replicated in "real" life, many others will carry over or at least can be made to yield cues and principles which may facilitate later work outside the laboratory. Thus, Husband's finding, that several rather different sorts of music all increased the sway of people who were attempting to stand still, would seem to be applicable to life generally.[25] As might have been guessed, jazz caused greater sway than music of other styles. Work at the Stanford University laboratories has carried the Husband study farther to show that even thinking of jazz music can increase sway. That is, subjects told to stand as quietly as possible swayed more while they imagined hearing strongly rhythmical music than when they imagined themselves studying in an easy chair. It would seem, then, that the activation of either the ear or the "mind's ear" can lead to slight body movements which are of measurable size.[26]

Diserens and Fine report a series of laboratory experiments on the influence of music on behavior. As pioneer work their research should be commended. However, viewed from the vantage-point of the present day it must be said that the study generalizes too freely and concerns too few subjects. Its conclusions are given here only to show the variety of areas it encompassed.

Music tends to reduce or delay fatigue and consequently increases muscular endurance. Music has no definite effect on precision or accuracy of movement, if the rhythm is not adapted to the rhythm of the work. It reduced accuracy in typewriting and handwriting, the result being shown in an increased number of errors. Music speeds up such voluntary activities as type-writing and handwriting. It also accelerates respiration. Music increases the extent of muscular reflexes employed in writing, drawing, etc. Music reduces normal suggestibility, except in the case of direct suggestion involving color, in which case suggestibility is increased. Music seems to have a tendency to produce a shift in normal preference for chromatic and achromatic impressions, the change being toward the blue end of the spectrum and the white end of the achromatic series. Music has a tendency to reduce the extent of illusion by acting as a distracting factor. Music influences the electrical conductivity of the human body as manifested by increased fluctuations in the psychogalvanic reflex.[27]

TYPING, MEMORY, AND READING. Jensen has studied the effects of jazz and dirges on typing.[28] Although jazz seemed to have no effect on the speed of his subjects' typing, it did increase their errors. Dirges, on the other hand, decreased the typing speed but had no effect on errors. Jensen's findings appear reasonable. Dirge time is obviously not in synchrony with good typing speed. And work accuracy would very likely be affected by factors of the environment which, like jazz, compete for attention. Music was found by Whitely to have a very small detrimental influence on the learning and retention of verbal material.[29] The effects were so insignificant, however, that with slightly changed conditions they might not have appeared at all.

It might be fitting to describe here some experiments at Stanford University in which subjects were engaged in pursuit and code-learning tasks while in the presence of attention-getting noise at approximately the 70-decibel level.[30] After a number of trials, one-half of the subjects continued their tasks with the noise still booming in their ears while the other group proceeded in relative quiet. It is of interest that no consistent or significant differences appeared between the performances of these two groups during any of the trials. Here is an example of the fact that man is a rather adaptable organism who will learn and retain under extremely trying circumstances.

Although learning can proceed reasonably well in the face of what one might think would be a considerable distraction, there are limits beyond which the disturbance becomes a real detriment to learning. Thus, Fendrick showed that music could be a serious distraction to persons reading very difficult material.[31]

It may be that psychologists are minimizing the distracting effects of music through their almost exclusive use of college students as subjects. If persons fifty years of age or more were to be tested, the data might look quite different, for these older persons learned to read and study without the blaring of radio or phonograph. For them music is not an integral part of the reading process. When Henderson and his colleagues demonstrated that popular music lessened only slightly the paragraph comprehension of their college subjects and did not harm vocabulary learning at all, and that "classical" music had no effect on either of these aspects of reading skill, they were presenting data which perhaps relate solely to college populations.[32] The fact that some of these latter claimed to study without the "aid" of music and still were not bothered by the music of the experiment is of interest but cannot be taken at face value. For even these atypical students are far more likely than are their elders to have come from homes noisy with music from phonograph or radio. To read in the sanctuary of a quiet study is not characteristic of the modern youth.

So far the discussion has centered on music as a distraction. It might be expected, however, that readers can sometimes benefit from background music, particularly if they are young and accustomed to the simultaneity of such auditory and visual stimulation. True to expectation, examples of actual gain in reading speed can be seen in the data of Freeburne and Fleischer who played jazz compositions to college subjects as they studied.[33] No other sort of music had a facilitating effect. Hall, too, found music beneficial to the reading of some persons.[34] Almost 60 per cent of his junior-high-school group made higher scores on the *Nelson Silent Reading Test* while hearing background music. Mikol and Denny demonstrate that music may have a facilitating effect on rotary pursuit performances.[35]

The data so far considered indicate that for many persons the forced hearing of music during study hours has little or no effect on reading and study habits. For others there may be adverse consequences and for still others there may be measurable benefit. The type of music that is heard, the difficulty of the material to be read, and the study and reading habits of the person being tested appear to be the pertinent variables which account for the diversity of effects so far reported.

REPETITIVE WORK. The proof of music's usefulness for industry has been best demonstrated for repetitive work. This is not surprising when it is recalled that Negro stevedores and laborers the world over have typically synchronized their work speeds to the tempos of music and have derived much benefit therefrom. Their morale has been lifted and their work movements have been made smoother and more efficient by the directing force of group singing. Modern shops, too, have work which is highly repetitive, and it is for these factory workers that most music in industry is played. For them music has a number of possible benefits: It may relieve fatigue and make for smoother motor performance.[36] It may supply food for the daydreams which occupy much of the mental life of those engaged in this class of labor. Moreover, the fact that the worker is allowed to hear music while laboring may signify to him that the management has his interests at heart and is attempting to improve his working conditions. There may be, then, a considerable raising of morale.

267

NONREPETITIVE WORK. With nonrepetitive factory work requiring little intellectual effort the introduction of several periods of music each day may prove quite worth while. But where considerable intellectual effort is involved music is less often beneficial and may have a harmful effect on output. It should be noted that the feeling the worker has for the music may have little to do with its value to his work.[37] He may desire it and be quite certain that it is aiding his work when in reality it is not. In those fewer instances, usually in offices, where music is found to be of benefit to the worker who uses his brain more than his hands, the type of music found to be appropriate resembles but little the kind used for workrooms where the labor is more manual. As might be guessed, office music must be far softer, less regularly rhythmic, with fewer dynamic changes, and without words.

OTHER CLAIMS FOR MUSIC. Proponents of industrial music have at one time or another maintained that, by the proper use of music, absenteeism and personnel turnover can be reduced; and physical health, punctuality and plant safety can be improved. There are other students of plant music, however, who have not found these effects. So far, these alleged benefits have not been reported in the better controlled studies. Yet it is conceivable that they could occur on occasion. For might not a worker be so filled with good will toward a company which brought music to its workers that he would become more punctual and less prone to "play" sick or to quit his job?

THE FORMULAE FOLLOWED. The authorities are by no means in complete agreement in their musical prescriptions. They do agree, however, that care should be taken lest music be conditioned to the beginning of recess periods. That is, if music were played each day just before time to stop work, its presentation would give the workers a "going home" cue which obviously would not lead to enthusiasm for work.

Some students of industrial music take great pains to give the workers exactly what they want to hear while others feel that the preference aspect has been much overemphasized. These latter assert that research attention should rather be focused on output changes. But where preference is emphasized, folk music and operas are often played to the foreign-born workers. The female voice is broadcast much less often than the male, since its higher register is not so appreciated. The British, as a matter of fact, rule out all vocal music because they have noticed a tendency for the laborer to stop work and write down the lyrics he particularly enjoys. Sex differences for the sort of music most preferred seem few in number. Generation differences loom larger, with the older workers preferring, on the whole, quieter and more serious music.

In one extensive study of factory music, the optimum effect on output was found to occur when music was played 12 per cent of the time for the day shift and 50 per cent for the night crew.[38] The Muzak Corporation, the leading firm devoted to supplying music to industry, has a rule of not more than three hours of music for each eight-hour workday. A common formula is to have ten to fifteen minutes of music each half-hour in factories and ten to twenty minutes each hour in those offices where music seems to be favorably received.

LIMITATIONS OF CONCLUSIONS. We have seen that the claims made on behalf of industrial music largely await validation. Perhaps the most promising area is that of worker morale, for with factory workers playing an ever growing role in plant management, worker morale is becoming of increasing importance to all concerned. But even here definitive experiments have yet to be made. With so many workers calling for music in their factories, it is probable that management will continue to provide for this desire, thus giving further opportunities for the gathering of sound data. Eventually, then, a more adequate assessment of industrial music may be forthcoming.[39]

Notes

1] D. M. Johnson and M. Trawick, "Influence of Rhythmic Sensory Stimuli upon the Heart-Rate," *J. Psychol., 6* (1938): 303–310.

2] C. M. Diserens and H. Fine, *A Psychology of Music*, Cincinnati, published by the authors, 1939, p. 253.

3] I. D. London, "Research on Sensory Interaction in the Soviet Union," *Psychol. Bull., 51* (1954): 531–568.

4] A. Dannenbaum, "The Effect of Music on Visual Acuity," *Sarah Lawrence Stud., 4* (1945): 18–26.

5] O. Lowenstein, *Der psychische Restitutionseffekt*, Basel, Schwabe, 1937. See also M. Grunewald in *Music Therapy*, E. Podolsky, ed., N.Y., Philosophical Library, 1954, 241–251.

6] R. E. Dreher, "The Relationship between Verbal Reports and Galvanic Skin Responses to Music," Thesis, Indiana U., 1947.

7] The galvanic skin response refers to the fact that the electrical resistance of the skin is measurably decreased whenever, during emotional states, perspiration is produced on the skin surfaces; R. I. Henkin, "The Prediction of Behavior Response Patterns to Music," *J. Psychol., 44* (1957): 111–127.

8] D. S. Ellis and G. Brighouse, "Effects of Music on Respiration and Heart-Rate," *Amer. J. Psychol., 65* (1952): 39–47; also published in *Music Therapy*, E. Podolsky, ed., N.Y., Philosophical Library, 1954, 158–169.

9] M. Critchley, "Two Cases of Musicogenic Epilepsy," *J. Royal Naval Med. Serv., 28* (1942): 182–184; S. Taylor, "Musicogenic Epilepsy: Case," *J. Royal Naval Med. Serv., 28* (1942): 394–395.

10] J. R. Miles and C. R. Tilly, "Some Physiological Reactions to Music," *Guy's Hospital Gazette, 49* (1935): 319–322.

11] Music therapy now denotes a very young but growing profession. The house-organ of the therapists is the *Bulletin of the National Association for Music Therapy*.

12] F. Densmore, "Importance of Rhythm in Songs for the Treatment of the Sick by American Indians," *Sci. Month., 79* (1954): 109–112.

13] That music therapy is in its infancy can also be seen in the fact that the first four-year course designed to create specialists in this field was not introduced until 1944. The institution which started the curriculum was Michigan State University.

14] I. M. Altshuler, "Rational Music-Therapy of the Mentally Ill," *Mus. Teach. Nat. Assoc. Proc.,* 1939, 153–157.

15] W. C. Middleton, *et al.,* "The Effect of Music on Feelings of Restfulness-Tiredness, and Pleasantness-Unpleasantness," *J. Psychol., 17* (1944): 299–318.

16] H. S. Whiting, in "Effect of Music on Hospital Accident Rate," *Amer. J. Ment. Def., 51* (1947): 397–400, maintains that music played over the radio in a hospital for mental defectives can produce a drastic reduction in the number of accidents on the wards. For further material on music in hospitals for mental defectives see A. Wendelin and T. L. Engle, "A Survey of Musical Activities in Institutions for the Mentally Deficient," *Amer. J. Ment. Defic., 59* (1954): 206–209.

17] B. Simon, *et al.,* "The Recognition and Acceptance of Mood in Music by Psychotic Patients," *J. Nerv. Ment. Dis., 114* (1951): 66–78.

18] G. W. Ainlay, "The Place of Music in Military Hospitals," *Etude, 63* (1945): 433, 468, 480.

19] L. M. Brown in *Music Therapy,* E. Podolsky, ed., N.Y., Philosophical Library, 1954, 135–138.

20] G. E. Arrington, Jr., in *Music Therapy,* E. Podolsky, ed., N.Y., Philosophical Library, 1954, 252–287. See also the longer lists from the chapter by H. G. Price, *et al.,* in the same book, pp. 95–100.

21] P. Sugarman in *Music Therapy,* E. Podolsky, ed., N.Y., Philosophical Library, 1954, 151–154.

22] B. Hillard in *Music Therapy,* E. Podolsky, ed., N.Y., Philosophical Library, 1954, 121–129.

23] J. Girard in *Music Therapy,* E. Podolsky, ed., N.Y., Philosophical Library, 1954, 101–106.

24] For further references on music therapy, see L. Gilman and F. Paperte, *Music and Your Emotions,* N.Y., Liveright, 1952, 24–55; S. H. Licht, *Music in Medicine,* Boston, New England Conservatory of Music, 1946; D. M. Schullian and M. Schoen, eds., *Music and Medicine,* N.Y., Schuman, 1948; D. Soibelman, *Therapeutic and Industrial Uses of Music,* N.Y., Columbia U. Press, 1948; W. Van de Wall, "Functional Use of Music in Industry and Therapy," *Mus. Teach. Nat. Ass. Proc.,* 1944, 147–153.

25] R. W. Husband, "The Effects of Musical Rhythms and Pure Rhythms on Bodily Sway," *J. Gen. Psychol., 11* (1934): 328–336.

26] That music can stimulate compensatory movements which can aid one's sense of balance has been demonstrated by W. Lavere in "The Influence of Musical Training and Musical Accompaniment on the Sense of Equilibrium," Master's Thesis, Syracuse U., 1950.

27] C. M. Diserens and H. Fine, *A Psychology of Music,* Cincinnati, published by the authors, 1939, pp. 273–274.

28] M. B. Jensen, "The Influence of Jazz and Dirge Music upon Speed and Accuracy of Typing," *J. Educ. Psychol., 22* (1931): 458–462.

29] P. L. Whitely, "The Influence of Music on Memory," *J. Gen. Psychol., 10* (1934): 137–151.

30] P. R. Farnsworth, "Continued Training with the Omission of Certain Nebenreize," *J. Genet. Psychol., 50* (1937): 277–282.

31] P. Fendrick, "The Influence of Music Distraction upon Reading Efficiency," *J. Educ. Res., 31* (1937): 264–271.

32] M. T. Henderson, A. Crews, and J. Barlow, "A Study of the Effect of Music Distraction on Reading Efficiency," *J. Appl. Psychol., 29* (1945): 313–317.

33] C. M. Freeburne and M. Fleischer, "The Effect of Music Distraction upon Reading Rate and Comprehension," *J. Educ. Psychol., 43* (1952): 101–109.

34] J. C. Hall, "The Effect of Background Music on the Reading Comprehension of 278 8th and 9th Grade Students," *J. Educ. Res., 45* (1952): 451–458.

35] B. Mikol and M. R. Denny, "The Effect of Music and Rhythm on Rotary Pursuit Performance," *Percep. Mot. Skills, 5* (1955): 3–6.

36] According to E. Podolsky as reported in *Music for Your Health*, N.Y., Ackerman, 1945, almost any musical rhythm can be employed in factories since the rhythm of the worker's task is little affected by the rhythm of the music he hears. This is an astonishing claim which needs verification. See also "Soap Wrappers' Jig," *J. Amer. Med. Assoc., 157* (1955): 1329–1330.

37] W. McGehee and J. E. Gardner, "Music in a Complex Industrial Job," *Personnel Psychol., 2* (1949): 405–417.

38] H. C. Smith, "Music in Relation to Employee Attitudes, Piecework Production, and Industrial Accidents," *Appl. Psychol. Monog.*, No. 14 (1947).

39] For a most optimistic report of British industrial music see L. Kaplan and R. Nettel, "Music in Industry," *Biol. Hum. Affairs, London, 13* (1948): 129–135. For a discussion of the part played by Muzak in getting music to industry see E. M. Werner, *Work Music by Muzak*, N.Y., Muzak Corp., 1948. See also R. L. Cardinell, "Music in Industry," in *Music and Medicine*, D. M. Schullian and M. Schoen, eds., N.Y., Schuman, 1948, 352–366.

Epilogue

Music has been variously called the most mathematical of the arts, the purest, and the least universal. That it is highly mathematical we have already seen, particularly in the data of Chapter 2. In no place in the book, however, has there been the suggestion that a satisfactory mathematical formula for forecasting musical taste or beauty has been or is likely to be discovered. Since there is no invariant relationship between musical stimuli and human responses, since attitudes toward the same stimuli change with the years, such a formula would be unthinkable. The mathematics of the Lydian mode has not been altered over the years since Plato banned this arrangement of tones as harmful to man's character. But to many people of the contemporary Western world this sequence has become the only "proper" scale.

Music is pure in the sense that it only rarely copies the sounds of nature. Music tells no clear-cut story with universal meaning. Yet each listener is trained to read local meanings into what he hears. He recognizes a Wagnerian motive, a needed resolution, or a church hymn and thus shares in the enjoyment of his associates. It is, however, the very paucity of these local meanings which gives him the opportunity to implant in the music his own personal images and associations. Thus this art medium serves as an important aid to his fantasy life.

The acceptability of any musical form grows, but later diminishes. Listener satiations gradually build up and eventually lead to change. Sometimes the changes are in the direction of innovations, while at other times they point back toward what was acceptable at an earlier time. If the new forms differ too markedly from the old they do not achieve general acceptance. But every change is a violation of some rule and is apt at first to seem undesirable to the conservative.

A major thesis developed in this book is the notion that music must look for its explanations far more often to social science than to physical science. It is granted that the very beginnings of music are tied to man's physical surroundings, to the presence of instrument-building materials, and to the physics of simple ratios. Man's psychophysiological potentialities also affect music's development. But the fact that the music of one culture has gone through certain phases that are not duplicated in another culture must be explained largely on the basis of sociopsychological and historical factors, not physical or physiological factors. Music's changes, like style changes generally, are lawful, not in an absolutistic or metaphysical sense, but in the way that other social phenomena are lawful.

This book has attempted to uncover a number of the sociopsychological variables behind music change. No doubt in the years to come many other factors will be isolated. Research of the sort described here should lead to greater, not less, musical enjoyment, for it seems to be a fairly general principle that the more man understands the complexities of a phenomenon the more delight he takes in it.

1. The Musical Taste of an American Élite[1]

I n Chapter 6 it was noted that in 1938 the members of the American Musicological Society had been sent questionnaires through which it was hoped a measure of their musical taste might be obtained. Again in 1944 and still later in 1951 the members of this elite organization were interrogated. At the time of the last data-gathering, the 375 who cooperated were given two questionnaires, one containing 225 names of composers born before 1870 and the other listing 249 born since 1870. There were two tasks. The first was for the musicologist-respondent to check in each of the two questionnaires the ten musicians he felt had composed music most worthy to be called to the attention of his children and his lay contemporaries. As a second task he was to consider all 474 names and, with the same criterion in mind, was to choose the top 25.

The first of the tables below gives the 50 who were the most frequently chosen among the composers born since 1870. The second table gives the 101 selected most often from the combined lists. Note that 24 of the first table appear also in the second. Such a finding gives no support to the notion so commonly held that the musically élite honor neither their contemporaries nor those recently deceased.

1] See P. R. Farnsworth, "The Musical Taste of an American Élite," *Hinrichsen's Musical Year Book*, 7 (1952): 112–116.

COMPOSERS BORN SINCE 1870

Rank Order		Rank Order	
29·5	Barber, S.	45·5	Malipiero, G.
2	Bartók, B.	36	Martinu, B.
49	Bax, A.	20	Menotti, G.
12	Berg, A.	13	Milhaud, D.
43	Berlin, I.	23	Piston, W.
11	Bloch, E.	27	Poulenc, F.
9	Britten, B.	6	Prokofiev, S.
40	Chávez, C.	10	Rachmaninov, S.
8	Copland, A.	4	Ravel, M.
32	Dohnányi, E.	24	Reger, M.
16	Falla, M. de	25·5	Respighi, O.
14	Gershwin, G.	45·5	Romberg, S.
45·5	Grainger, P.	5	Schönberg, A.
29·5	Griffes, C.	49	Schuman, W.
29·5	Hanson, H.	21	Scriabin, A.
25·5	Harris, R.	29·5	Sessions, R.
3	Hindemith, P.	15	Shostakovich, D.
33·5	Holst, G.	49	Sowerby, L.
18	Honegger, A.	1	Stravinsky, I.
40	Ibert, J.	45·5	Thompson, R.
17	Ives, C.	42	Varèse, E.
37	Khachaturian, A.	7	Vaughan Williams, R.
33·5	Kodály, Z.	19	Villa-Lobos, H.
40	Kreisler, F.	22	Walton, W.
35	Krenek, E.	38	Webern, A.

EMINENT COMPOSERS OF ALL TIME

Rank Order		Rank Order	
88·5	Bach, J. C.	59·5	Britten, B.
2	Bach, J. S.	41	Bruckner, A.
71	Bach, K. P. E.	52	Buxtehude, D.
16	Bartók, B.	27	Byrd, W.
1	Beethoven, L.	100	Chausson, E.
72	Berg, A.	11	Chopin, F.
21	Berlioz, H.	47	Copland, A.
55·5	Bizet, G.	43	Corelli, A.
66	Bloch, E.	40	Couperin the Great
3	Brahms, J.	6·5	Debussy, C.

Rank Order		Rank Order	
92	Donizetti, G.	10	Palestrina, G.
82·5	Dowland, J.	80	Pergolesi, G.
36	Dufay, G.	74	Perotinus
78	Dunstable, J.	88·5	Piston, W.
38	Dvořák, A.	34	Prokofiev, S.
100	Elgar, E.	45·5	Puccini, G.
76	Falla, M. de	20	Purcell, H.
61·5	Fauré, G.	55·5	Rachmaninov, S.
97	Foster, S.	49	Rameau, J.
28·5	Franck, C.	26	Ravel, M.
53·5	Frescobaldi, G.	85·5	Respighi, O.
45·5	Gabrieli, G.	44	Rimsky-Korsakov, N.
58	Gershwin, G.	59·5	Rossini, G.
85·5	Gesualdo, D.	74	Saint-Saëns, C.
66	Gibbons, O.	69	Scarlatti, A.
28·5	Gluck, C.	35	Scarlatti, D.
84	Gounod, C.	22	Schönberg, A.
66	Gregory the Great	6·5	Schubert, F.
48	Grieg, E.	12	Schumann, R.
8	Handel, G.	31	Schütz, H.
100	Hanson, H.	94·5	Scriabin, A.
4	Haydn, F. J.	57	Shostakovich, D.
23	Hindemith, P.	30	Sibelius, J.
80	Honegger, A.	82·5	Smetana, B.
77	Ives, C.	97	Sousa, J
33	Josquin des Prés	51	Strauss, J. Jr.
88·5	Landino, F.	18	Strauss, R.
25	Lasso, O.	13	Stravinsky, I.
32	Liszt, F.	92	Sullivan, A.
74	Lully, J.	94·5	Sweelinck, J.
66	MacDowell, E.	19	Tchaikovsky, P.
42	Machaut, G.	92	Telemann, G.
38	Mahler, G.	50	Vaughan Williams, R.
97	Massenet, J.	14	Verdi, G.
17	Mendelssohn, F.	61·5	Victoria, T.
80	Menotti, G.	88·5	Villa-Lobos, H.
70	Milhaud, D.	38	Vivaldi, A.
15	Monteverdi, C.	9	Wagner, R.
24	Moussorgsky, M.	53·5	Weber, C. M. von
5	Mozart, W.	63	Wolf, H.
66	Ockeghem, J.		

2. Glossary*

ability. Skill of any sort; relative importance of inheritance and environment not considered (cf. *capacity, talent*).

absolute or *positive pitch*. Ability to locate a pitch without the need of a reference tone; the allowable error is very slight, perhaps less than 10 cents.

accidental signs. Signs indicating sharps, flats, double sharps, double flats, naturals.

arpeggio. Tones of a chord played in rapid succession.

atonality. Absence of key in music.

beats. Throbbing effect elicited when two tones very close together in pitch are simultaneously sounded.

beta learning. Negative practice, that is, the errors are deliberately practiced.

cadence. Melodic or harmonic figure which has come to have an association with the ending of a phrase, a section, or composition.

capacity. Basic potentiality; importance of heredity is stressed.

cent. Tonal span of 1/1200 of an octave.

---

* This glossary attempts to define psychological terms for the musician and musical terms for the psychologist. It is to be expected that the psychologist will prefer to see the terms of his craft described in more exact language, as will the musician his.

chromesthesia. Visual image of hallucinatory intensity aroused by some auditory stimulus (cf. *synesthesia*).

coefficient of correlation. Measure of correspondence between two sets of measurements; values vary from 1·00 (perfect correspondence) through zero to − 1·00 (completely inverse relationship).

decibel. Logarithmic unit of intensity so chosen as to be equal, under certain conditions, to one just-noticeable difference in loudness.

difference tone. Tone sometimes elicited when two tones separated in pitch are simultaneously sounded; its frequency is the difference of the frequencies of the other two.

double stopping. Fingering two strings of a bowed instrument at once.

double vibration (d.v.). Frequency (number of cycles) with which a sound-giving body is vibrating.

drone. A tone held for the duration of a melody or at least for a considerable period of time.

eidetic imagery. Imagery so intense that the person behaves as though he were directly perceiving the music.

extrovert. A person who attends more to external events and objects than to his own attitudes and mental processes.

factor analysis. Method of resolving a set of interrelated variables or tests into a few "factors" which are regarded as being the fundamental variables underlying the original complex of variables.

fifth. Span of 7 semitones.

fourth. Span of 5 semitones.

fugal form. A round; each new voice chases the preceding one.

galvanic skin response. Change in the electrical resistance of the skin whenever, during emotional states, perspiration is produced on the skin surfaces.

goal gradient.   Change in degree of motivation with distance to a goal.

harmonics.   Cf. *overtones*.

homophony.   Music in which the voices move in step, e.g., hymn.

idiot savant.   Person of very low I.Q. who has above average achievement in some specialized area.

interval.   Pitch span between two notes played simultaneously or successively.

    augmented.   Perfect or major increased by a semitone.

    diminished.   Perfect or minor decreased by a semitone.

    major.   Spans of 2, 4, 9, or 11 semitones (second, third, sixth, or seventh).

    minor.   Spans of 1, 3, 8, or 10 semitones (second, third, sixth, or seventh).

    parallel.   Span separating two melodies which are identical but in different registers.

    perfect.   Spans of 5, 7, or 12 semitones (fourth, fifth, or octave).

introvert.   Person preoccupied with his own attitudes and mental processes.

iso principle.   Notion that a patient's mood and "mental tempo" should match the mood and tempo of the music.

key.   Family of tones held together by their relation to a tonic from which the key is named.

key-note.   Lowest and principal note of a scale; the tonic.

leading tone.   Major seventh or subtonic, so-called because it leads up to the tonic.

leger lines.   Additional short lines added above or below the staff for notes than cannot be accommodated on the staff.

major.

    chord.   Three simultaneously or successively played notes comprising intervals of a major third plus a minor third.

interval. Cf. *interval*.

mode. Cf. *mode*.

second. Span of 2 semitones.

sixth. Span of 9 semitones.

seventh. Span of 11 semitones.

third. Span of 4 semitones.

massed practice. Concentration of time devoted to learning with little interval between successive practice sessions.

melody. Series of successively sounded tones felt to possess internal organization.

microtone. Scale step smaller than a semitone.

minor.

chord. Three simultaneously or successively played notes comprising intervals of a minor third plus a major third.

interval. Cf. *interval*.

mode. Cf. *mode*.

second. Span of 1 semitone.

sixth. Span of 8 semitones.

seventh. Span of 10 semitones.

third. Span of 3 semitones.

mode. Forerunner of the key; differs in that the mode has several possible arrangements of scale steps, e.g., 2, 2, 1, 2, 2, 2, 1 semitone steps, or 2, 1, 2, 2, 2, 1, 2 steps, etc.; now only two: major and minor.

modulation. Transition of a melody from one key up or down to another key.

monotone. Person so weak in pitch sensitivity that he cannot recognize or carry a tune.

noise. Complex of sounds in which no definite pitch can be detected.

octave. Span of 12 semitones.

organum. Theme with other voices a fourth below or a fifth above moving parallel to it.

overlearning. Continuing practice beyond the trial where the material can for the first time be reproduced correctly.

overtone. Tone elicited by the vibration of some fraction of the major vibrating body, e.g., 1/2, 1/3, 1/4, etc.

partial. Cf. *overtone.*

phon. Unit of loudness in which the value is equal to the number of decibels a tone of 1000 d.v. is above the reference intensity when judged equal in loudness to the tone in question.

polyphony. Applied to music in which several melodies are played simultaneously.

polytonality. Presence of several simultaneous keys in a musical composition.

portamento. The carrying on of the tone from note to note without gaps (voice and bowed instruments); half-staccato (piano).

Prägnanz, law of. Persons tend to perceive objects in the simplest arrangement possible.

register. Pitch level.

reliability. Degree of self-consistency; extent to which the measure is uninfluenced by factors intrinsic to or associated with it.

retroactive inhibition. Impairment of learning by the later learning of something very similar.

rho. Type of correlation coefficient obtained through the handling of rank differences.

rhythm.
   objective. Periodicity with one element regularly emphasized.
   polyrhythm. Complex of several simultaneously played rhythms.
   subjective. Rhythm read into sheer periodicity or into weak objective rhythm.

scale. Series of tones arranged in order of pitch and employed as the accepted notes of some system.

    chromatic. The twelve-semitone scale of white and black notes.

    diatonic. Seven-note scale in the major or minor mode.

    equally tempered. Where chromatic steps are all equal in ratio.

    just-intoned. Where the ratios use only the primes 1, 3 and 5.

    mean-tone. Compromise scale with some tempering which allowed for a degree of modulation.

    Pythagorean. Where the ratios use only the primes 1 and 3.

    whole-tone. Where each step is a whole tone from its nearest neighbor.

score.

    mean. Sum of all the scores divided by the number of cases.

    median. Middle value.

    modal. Most frequently occurring score.

sensations.

    kinesthetic. Those arising from the stimulation of receptors in muscles, tendons, and joints.

    organic. Those arising from the stimulation of receptors in the internal organs.

sensitivity. Degree to which one can distinguish stimuli which differ very slightly.

sonance. Qualitative effects due to progressive ("horizontal") changes and fusions, e.g., vibrato.

sostenuto pedal. Pedal found mainly on American and Canadian pianos which maintains raised dampers.

stroboscope. Instrument for observing the successive phases of a periodic motion by means of a light periodically interrupted. Cf. *tonoscope.*

syncopation. Placing an accent where there would normally be no accent.

synesthesia. Image of hallucinatory intensity in one sensory area aroused by a stimulus from some other sense modality. Cf. *chromesthesia.*

takt. Cf. *true beat.*

talent. Usually taken to mean high capability; heredity is emphasized.

tempo. Rate of speed at which a musical passage moves.
  allegro. Lively tempo.
  andante. Slow tempo.
  presto. Quick tempo.

tests.
  achievement. Tests taken to measure what has been learned.
  aptitude. Tests used to forecast whether or not training in a particular area will be profitable.

threshold. Inverse of sensitivity (as used in this book).

timbre. Effect due to the constellation of partial tones present; "vertical" quality.

tone clusters. Tones elicited by depressing the piano keys with the fist, flat of the hand, or with the forearm.

tone symbol. Tonal ratio with powers of 2 extracted.

tonic. Cf. *key-note.*

tonoscope. Stroboscope which gives a visual picture of a vocal or instrumental tone.

tremolo. Vibrato with abnormally wide pitch span; also used to describe a rhythmic unit with three unaccented elements.

trill. Rapid oscillation of two tones which are perceived as two tones.

tritone. Span of six semitones.

true beat. Pulsations which underlie phrase rhythms irrespective of time signatures or number of notes in the phrase.

validity.   Extent to which a test is measuring what it claims to be measuring.

vibrato.   Periodic oscillations of the vocal or instrumental tone in pitch, intensity, and sometimes in quality; rate is approximately 6·5 per second.

whole learning.   Material to be learned is gone through from beginning to end, i.e., is not broken down into parts which are to be learned separately.

3. Key to Reference Abbreviations

Acta Oto-laryngologica, Stockholm	*Acta Oto-laryng.*
Acta Psychologica	*Acta Psychol.*
American Imago	*Amer. Imago*
American Journal of Mental Deficiency	*Amer. J. Ment. Defic.*
American Journal of Psychiatry	*Amer. J. Psychiat.*
American Journal of Psychology	*Amer. J. Psychol.*
American Journal of Sociology	*Amer. J. Sociol.*
American Psychologist	*Amer. Psychol.*
American Sociological Review	*Amer. Sociol. Rev.*
Annals of the New York Academy of Sciences	*Annals, N.Y. Acad. Sc.*
Applied Psychology Monographs	*Appl. Psychol. Monog.*
Archiv für die Gesamte Phonetik	*Arch. Ges. Phonet.*
Archiv für die Gesamte Psychologie	*Arch. Ges. Psychol.*
Archiv für Musikforschung	*Arch. Musikforsch.*
Archiv für Rassen- und Gesellschafts-Biologie, Einschliesslich Rassen- und Gesellschafts-Hygiene	*Arch. Rass.- u. Ges.-Biol.*
Archives of Neurology and Psychiatry	*Arch. Neur. and Psychiat.*
Archives of Otolaryngology, Chicago	*Arch. Otolaryngol.*
Archives of Psychology	*Arch. Psychol.*
Australian Journal of Psychology	*Austral. J. Psychol.*
Beihefte zur Zeitschrift für Experimentelle und Angewandte Psychologie	*Beihefte z. Zsch. f. Ang. Psychol.*

Bell Laboratories Record	Bell Lab. Rec.
Biology and Human Affairs, London	Biol. Hum. Affairs
British Journal of Educational Psychology	Brit. J. Educ. Psychol.
British Journal of Psychology	Brit. J. Psychol.
British Journal of Psychology, General Section	Brit. J. Psychol., Gen. Sec.
British Journal of Psychology, Monograph Supplement	Brit. J. Psychol., Monog. Suppl.
British Journal of Psychology, Statistical Section	Brit. J. Psychol., Stat. Sec.
Bulletin of Mathematical Biophysics	Bull. Math. Biophysics
Character and Personality	Char. and Person.
Child Development	Child Devel.
Child Development Monographs	Child Devel. Monog.
Deutsche Zeitschrift für Nervenheilkunde	Dtsch. Zsch. f. Nervenhk.
Dioptric Review and British Journal of Physiological Optics	Diopt. Rev. and Brit. J. Physiol. Opt.
Genetic Psychology Monographs	Genet. Psychol. Monog.
Harvard Psychological Studies	Harvard Psychol. Stud.
Human Biology	Human Biol.
Human Engineering Laboratory, Technical Report	Hum. Engng. Lab., Tech. Rep.
Indiana University Publications, Humanity Series	Indiana U. Publ., Humanity Ser.
Institute of Radio Engineers, Proceedings	Inst. Radio Eng., Proc.
International Congress of Musicology	Int. Congr. Musicol.
Internationale Zeitschrift für Individual-Psychologie	Int. Zsch. f. Indiv.-Psychol.
Journal of Abnormal and Social Psychology	J. Abn. Soc. Psychol.

Journal of the Acoustical Society of America	*J. Acoust. Soc. Amer.*
Journal of Aesthetics and Art Criticism	*J. Aesth.*
Journal of the American Medical Association	*J. Amer. Med. Assoc.*
Journal of Applied Psychology	*J. Appl. Psychol.*
Journal of Clinical Psychology	*J. Clin. Psychol.*
Journal of Comparative Psychology	*J. Comp. Psychol.*
Journal of Educational Psychology	*J. Educ. Psychol.*
Journal of Educational Research	*J. Educ. Res.*
Journal of Experimental Education	*J. Exp. Ed.*
Journal of Experimental Psychology	*J. Exp. Psychol.*
Journal of the Franklin Institute	*J. Franklin Inst.*
Journal of General Psychology	*J. Gen. Psychol.*
Journal of Genetic Psychology	*J. Genet. Psychol.*
Journal of Gerontology	*J. Gerontol.*
Journal of Heredity	*J. Hered.*
Journal of Musicology	*J. Musicol.*
Journal of Nervous and Mental Disease	*J. Nerv. Ment. Dis.*
Journal of Psychology	*J. Psychol.*
Journal de Psychologie Normale et Pathologique	*J. Psychol. Norm. Path.*
Journal of the Royal Naval Medical Service	*J. Royal Nav. Med. Serv.*
Journal of Social Psychology	*J. Soc. Psychol.*
Kwartalnik Psychologiczny	*Kwart. Psychol.*
Medical Research Laboratory, U.S. Naval Submarine Base, New London	*Med. Res. Lab.*
Monographs of the Society for Research in Child Development	*Monog. Soc. Res. Child Devel.*
Music Educators Journal	*Mus. Ed. J.*

Music Educators' National Conference, Yearbook	Mus. Educ. Nat. Conf. Yearb.
Music Supervisors Journal	Mus. Superv. J.
Music Supervisors National Conference, Yearbook	Mus. Superv. Nat. Conf. Yearb.
Music Teachers National Association, Proceedings	Mus. Teach. Nat. Assoc. Proc.
Musical Quarterly	Music. Quart.
Office of Scientific Research and Development, Report	OSRD Report
Peabody Bulletin	Peabody Bull.
Research Studies in Music, Peabody Conservatory of Music	Peabody Cons. Mus. Res. Stud.
Pedagogical Seminary	Ped. Sem.
Perceptual and Motor Skills	Percep. Mot. Skills
Personnel Psychology	Personnel Psychol.
Philologisch-historische Klasse, Sitzungsberichte	Phil.-hist. Klasse Sitzungs-berichte
Pillsbury Foundation Studies	Pillsbury Found. Stud.
Popular Science Monthly	Pop. Sci. Month.
Proceedings of the Iowa Academy of Science	Proc. Ia. Acad. Sci.
Psychiatrie, Neurologie, and Medizinische Psychologie, Leipzig	Psychiat. Neurol. Med. Psychol.
Psychiatry	Psychiat.
Psychoanalytic Quarterly	Psychoanal. Quart.
Psychoanalytic Review	Psychoanal. Rev.
Psychological Bulletin	Psychol. Bull.
Psychological Monographs	Psychol. Monog.
Psychological Record	Psychol. Rec.
Psychological Review	Psychol. Rev.
Psychologische Rundschau	Psychol. Rundschau
Public Health Reports, Washington	Publ. Hlth. Rep.

289

Public Opinion Quarterly	Publ. Opin. Quart.
Revue Internationale de Philosophie	Rev. Intern. Phil.
Sarah Lawrence Studies	Sarah Lawrence Stud.
School Musician	Sch. Mus.
School and Society	Sch. and Soc.
Schweizerische Zeitschrift für Psychologie und ihre Anwendungen	Schweiz. Z. Psychol. Anwende.
Scientific Monthly	Sci. Month.
Smith College Studies in Social Work	Smith Coll. Stud. Soc. Wk.
Social Forces	Soc. Forces
Teachers College Contributions to Education	Teach. Coll. Contrib. Educ.
Teachers College Record	Teach. Coll. Rec.
Tohoku Psychologica Folia	Tohoku Psychol. Folia
University of Iowa Studies, Studies in Child Welfare	U. of Ia. Stud. Child Welf.
University of Iowa Studies, Studies in the Psychology of Music	U. of Ia. Stud. Psychol. Mus.
University of Oregon Publication	U. of Oregon Publ.
Zeitschrift für Experimentelle und Angewandte Psychologie	Zsch. f. Ang. Psychol.
Zeitschrift für Laryngologie, Rhinologie, Otologie, und ihre Grenzgebiete	Zsch. f. Laryngol.
Zeitschrift für Pädagogische Psychologie	Zsch. Padg. Psychol.
Zeitschrift für Psychologie und Physiologie der Sinnesorgane	Zsch. f. Psychol.
Zeitschrift für Psychotherapie und Medizinische Psychologie	Zsch. f. Psychother. Med. Psychol.
Zentralblatt für die gesamte Neurologie und Psychiatrie	Zentralbl. ges. Neurol. u. Psychiat.
Zentralblatt für Physiologie	Zentralbl. f. Physiol.

Subject Index

(See also entries in Glossary beginning on page 280.)

ability, musical, *see* musical ability
absolute pitch, 59–61, 78, 87, 231
accidentals, 20, 29
achievement, effects of music on, 264–270
activity, music and, 264–265
adaptation, in consonance perception, 48
adjectives, mood, 96–99, 102
Adler Music Appreciation Tests, 162
Aeolian Corporation, The, 69
aesthetics, experimental, 7–13
African drums, rhythmic patterns in, 73, 119
age, and hearing ability, 65
Aliferis Music Achievement Test, 229
American Musicological Society, 121, 123, 127–128, 275
aptitude tests, unstandardized, 231–235
  see also musical aptitude tests
art, vs. psychoneuroses, 209, 213
atonal music, 29, 45–46
attention and learning, principles of, 57–58
Ave Maria, Schubert, 95

Bach family, 187
bagpipes, timbre of, 65
baroque organ, 65
basic abilities, 231–233
baton movements, 5
Beach Standardization Music Tests, 226
Beale Street Mamma, 90
beat, true, 4–5
beat-instants, and baton movements, 5–6
beauty, defined, 142
  Seashore's rule of, 67

beta learning, 202
biographies, musical, 210–211
"blues" singers, 89–90
bodily metabolism, music and, 255
body structures, and musical ability, 188–193
Boston Symphony Orchestra, 110, 130, 135, 141
  program choices of, 133, 167–168
Bower Musical Moods Test, 161

cadence test, 164
Caprice Viennois, Kreisler, 89
cent, in scale measurement, 25, 32
centitone, 25
child prodigies, 198
children, musical ability in, 197
Chinese melodies, finality in, 43
Chinese music, mistunings in, 120
chordal structure, 110
chord-analysis test, 246
chord recognition, 232
chromatic scale, 90
chromesthesia, 91–93
Cincinnati College of Music, 240
Clair de Lune, Debussy, 96
clarinet, timbre of, 64–65
"classical music," layman's reaction to, 11
climatic cycles, musical taste and, 146–147
college aptitudes, "critical levels" of, 11
color-tone linkage, 90–93
common sense, unreliability of, 3
communication, desire for, 84–85

Name Index

NAME INDEX